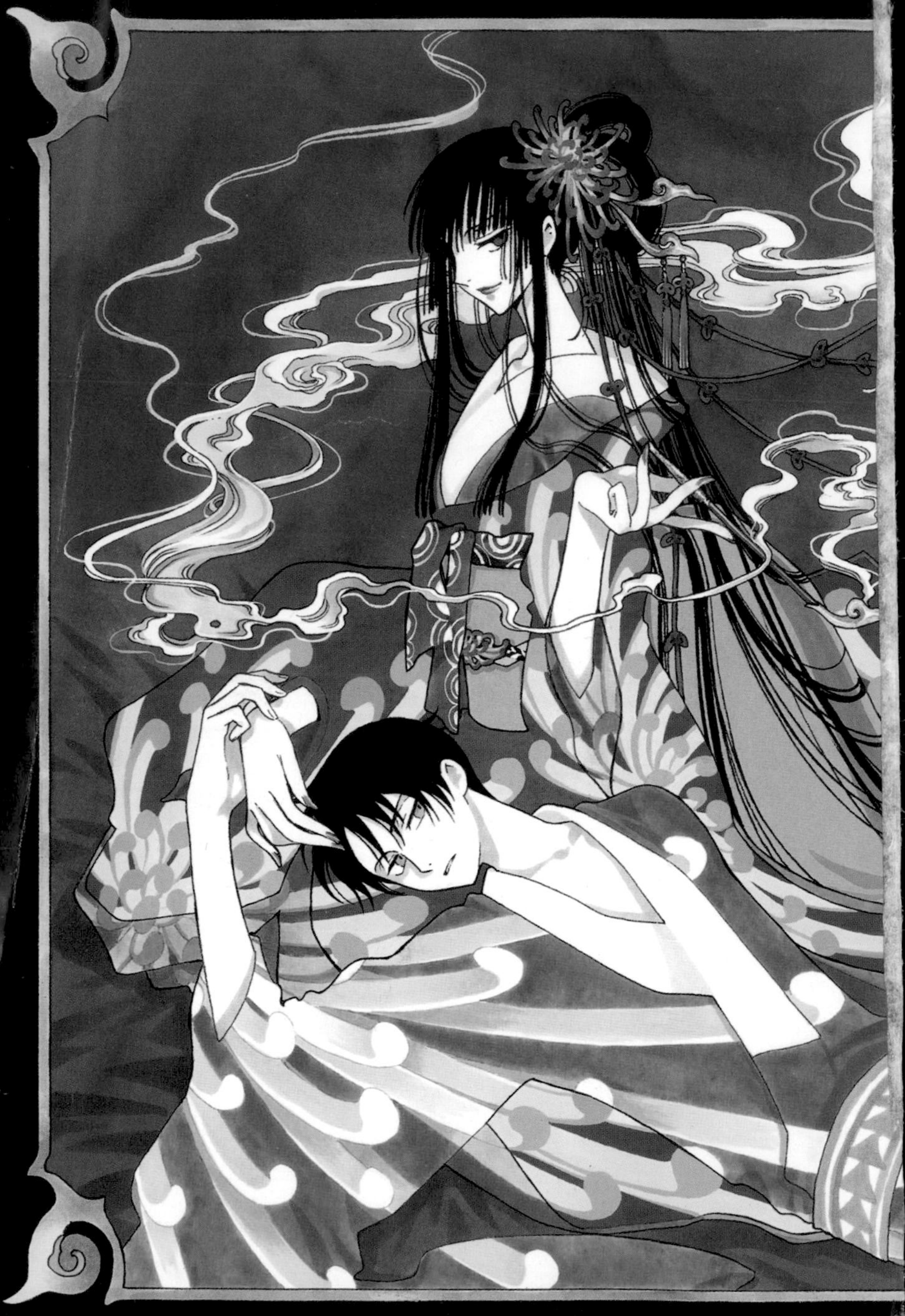

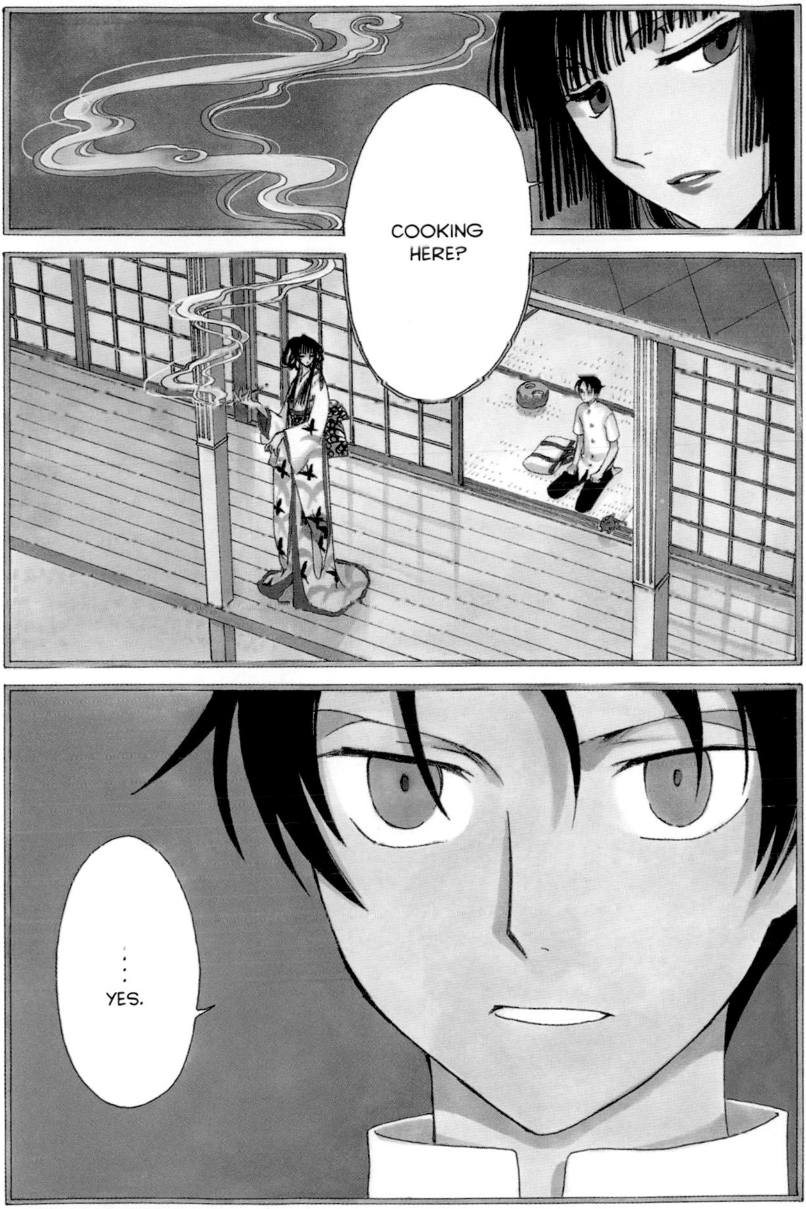
COOKING HERE?
....
YES.

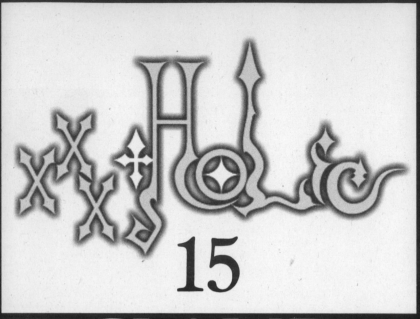

# 15

## CLAMP

TRANSLATED AND ADAPTED BY
William Flanagan

LETTERED BY
North Market Street Graphics

BALLANTINE BOOKS · NEW YORK

A Del Rey Manga/Kodansha Trade Paperback Original

*xxxHOLiC*, volume 15 copyright © 2009 CLAMP
English translation copyright © 2010 CLAMP

Published in the United States by Del Rey, an imprint of The Random House Publishing Group, a division of Random House, Inc., New York.

DEL REY is a registered trademark and the Del Rey colophon is a trademark of Random House, Inc.

Publication rights arranged through Kodansha Ltd.

First published in Japan in 2009 by Kodansha Ltd., Tokyo

ISBN 978-0-345-52112-5

Printed in the United States of America

www.delreymanga.com

9 8 7 6 5 4 3 2 1

Translator and Adapter—William Flanagan
Lettering—North Market Street Graphics

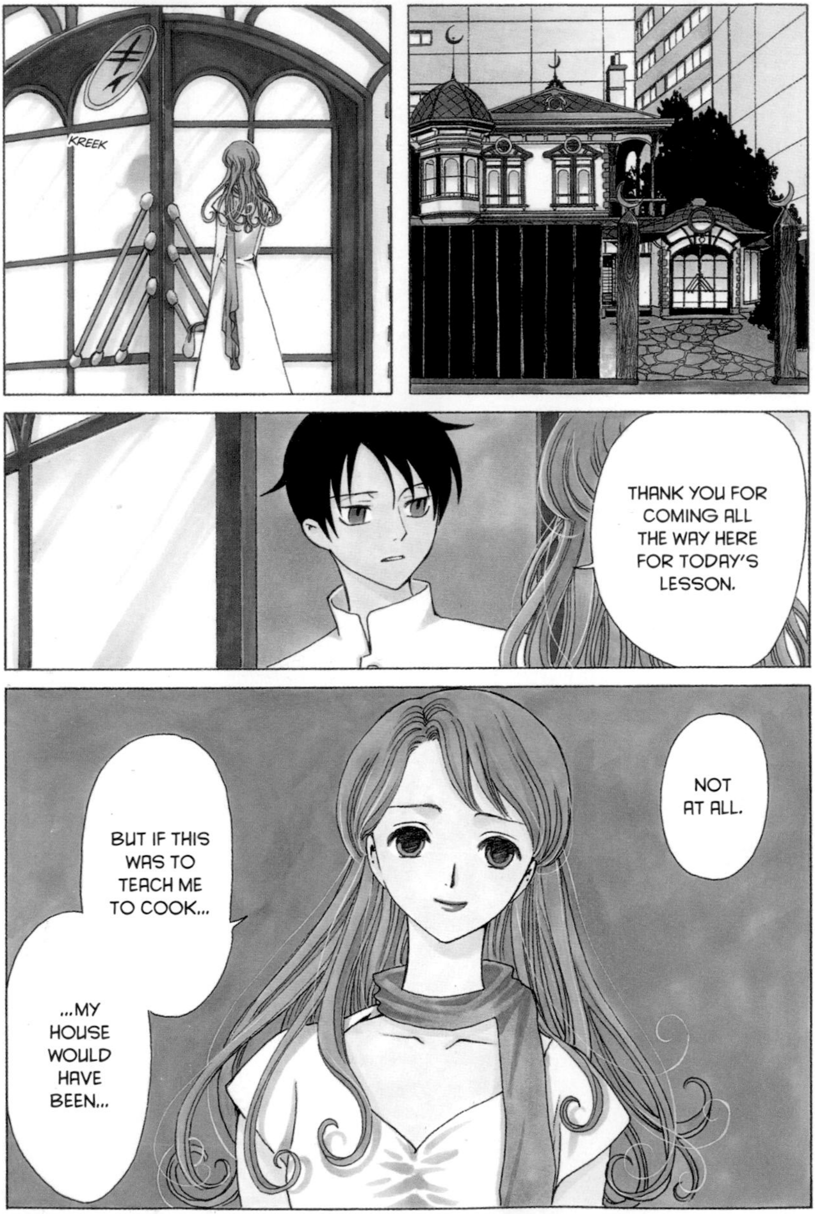
KREEK
THANK YOU FOR COMING ALL THE WAY HERE FOR TODAY'S LESSON.
NOT AT ALL.
BUT IF THIS WAS TO TEACH ME TO COOK...
...MY HOUSE WOULD HAVE BEEN...

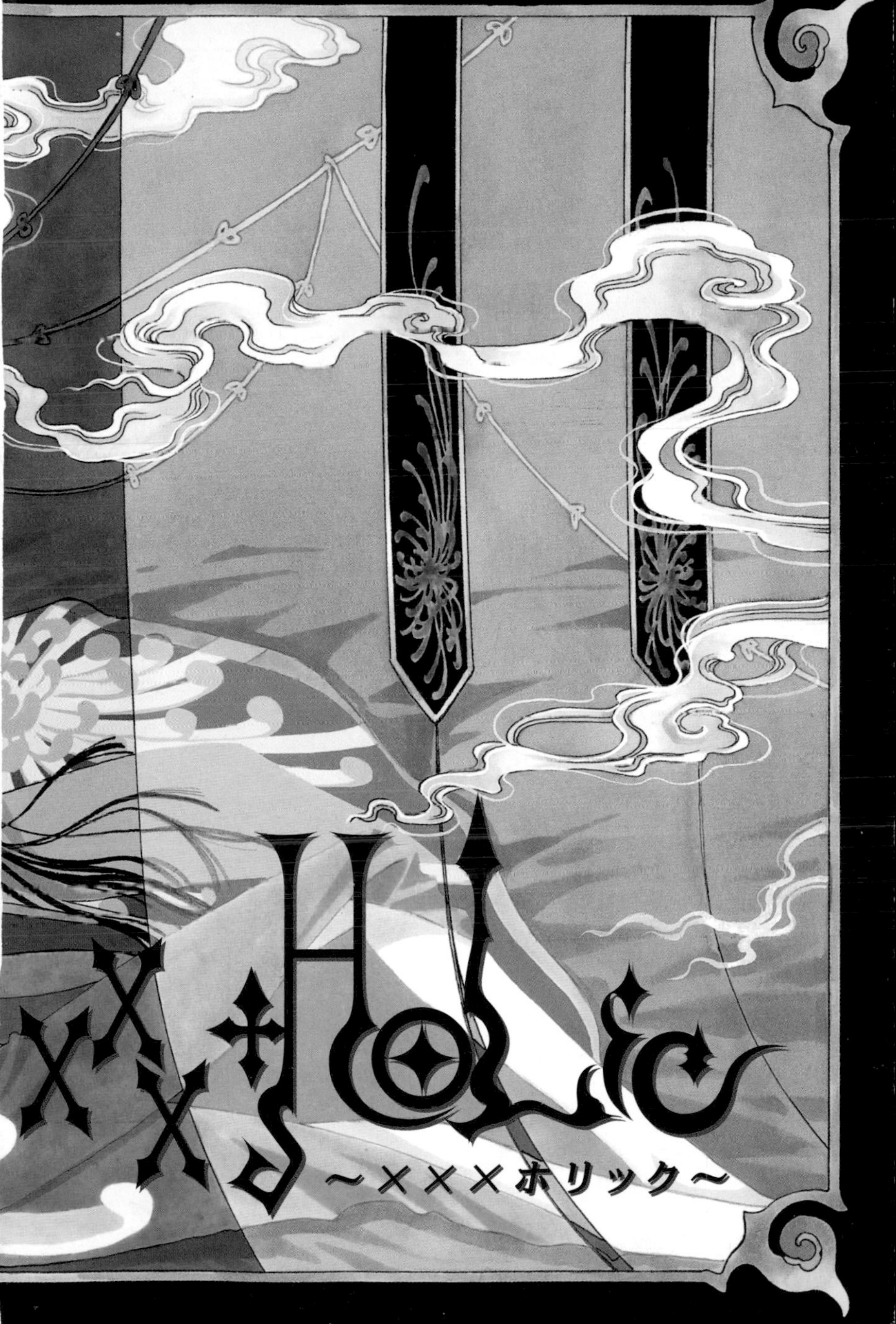
xxxHOLiC
~×××ホリック~

*xxxHOLiC* crosses over with *Tsubasa*. Although it isn't necessary to read *Tsubasa* to understand the events in *xxxHOLiC*, you'll get to see the same events from different perspectives if you read both series!

# Contents

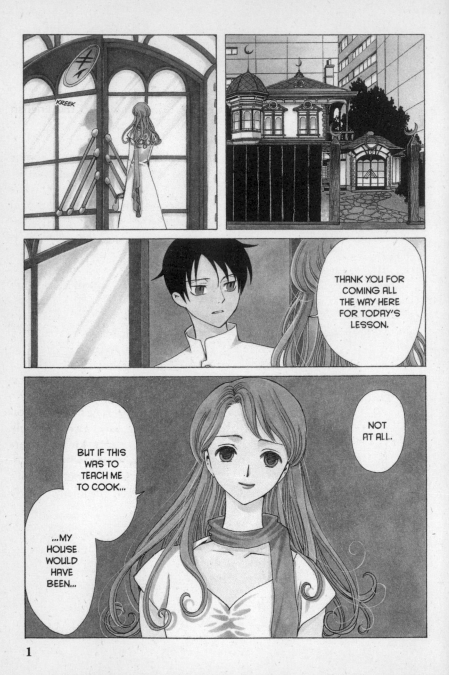

1

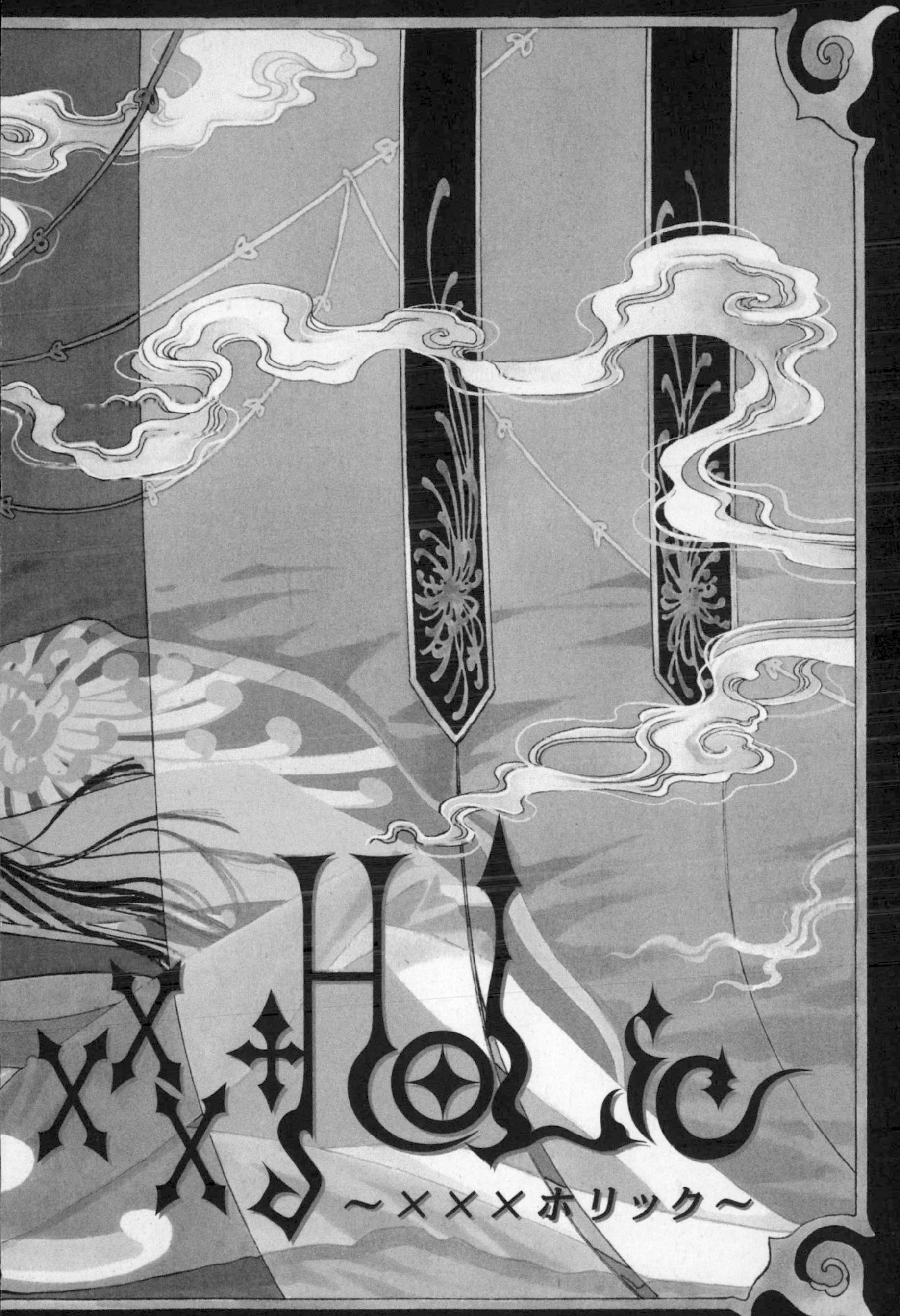
xxxHOLiC
〜×××ホリック〜

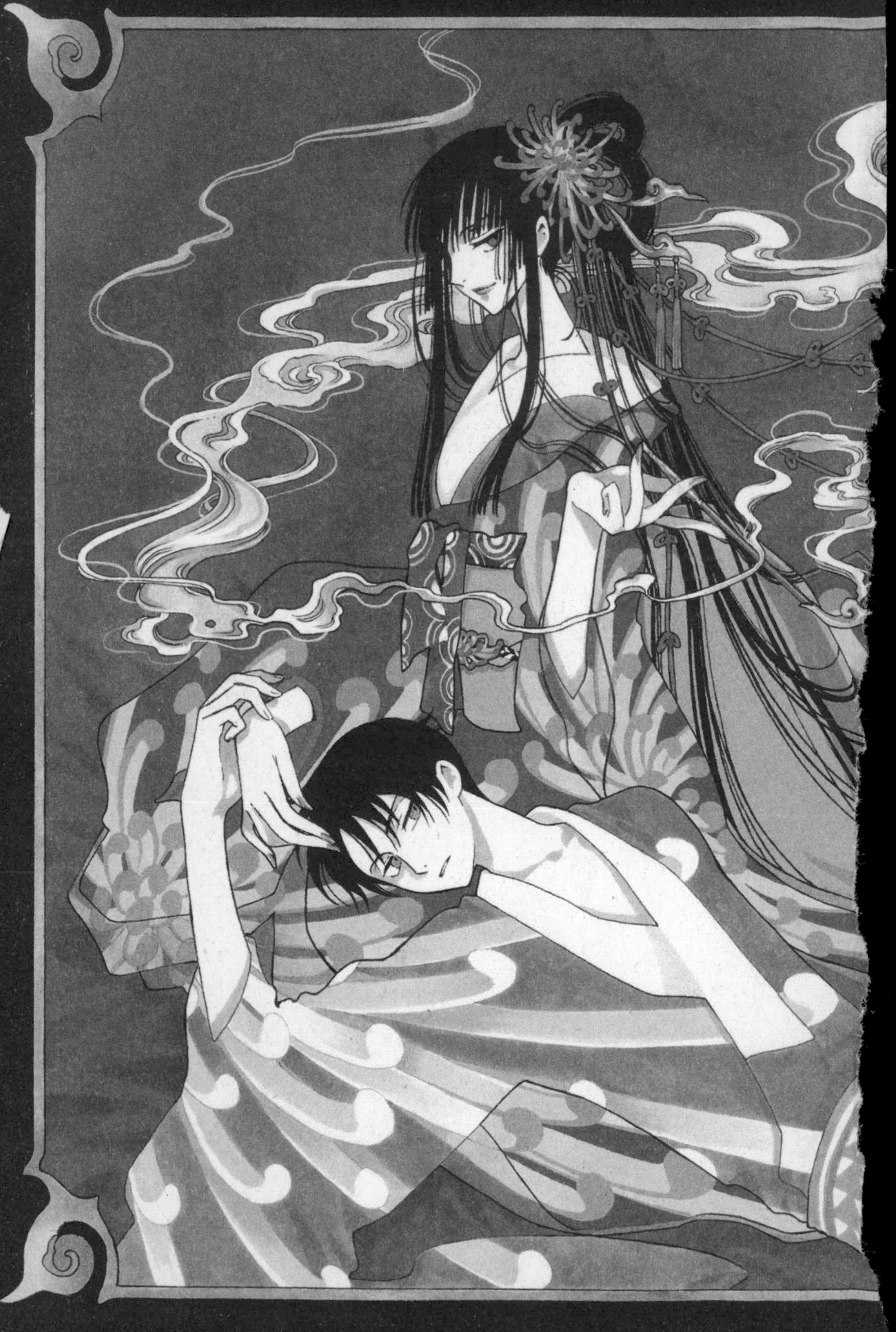

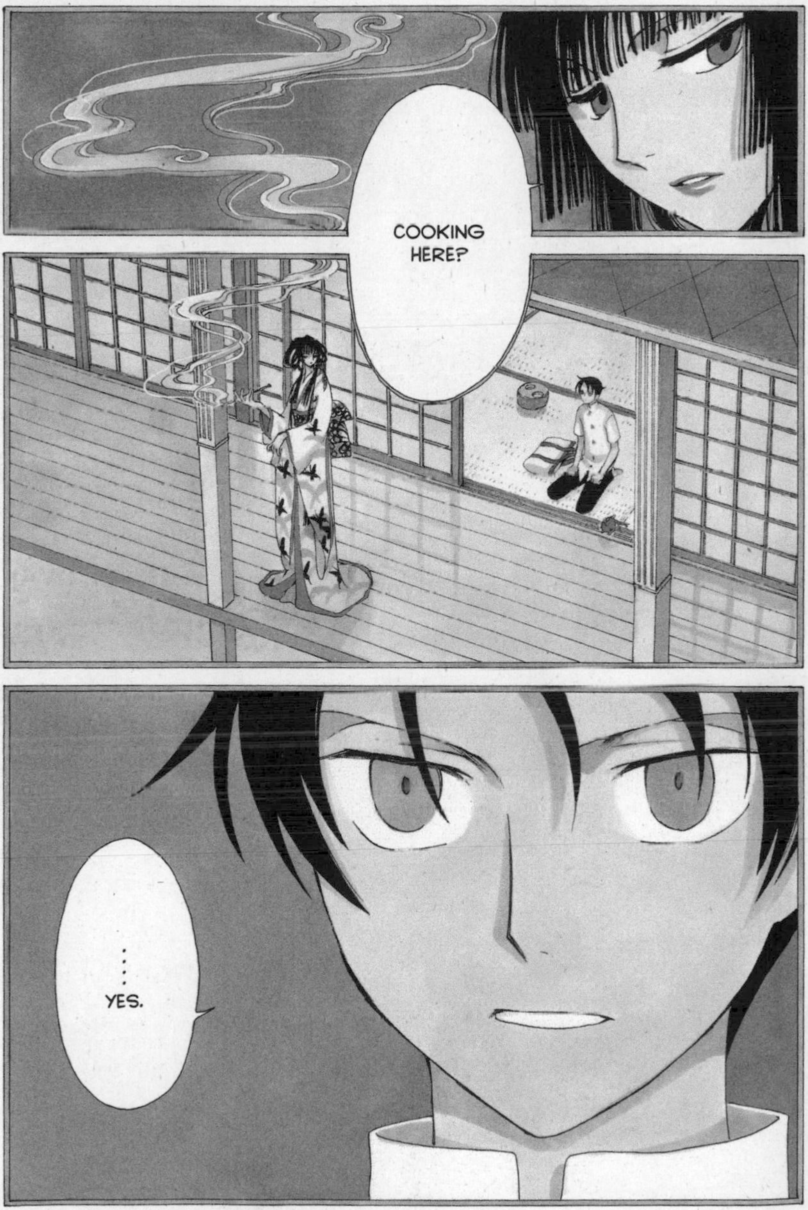
COOKING HERE?
....
YES.

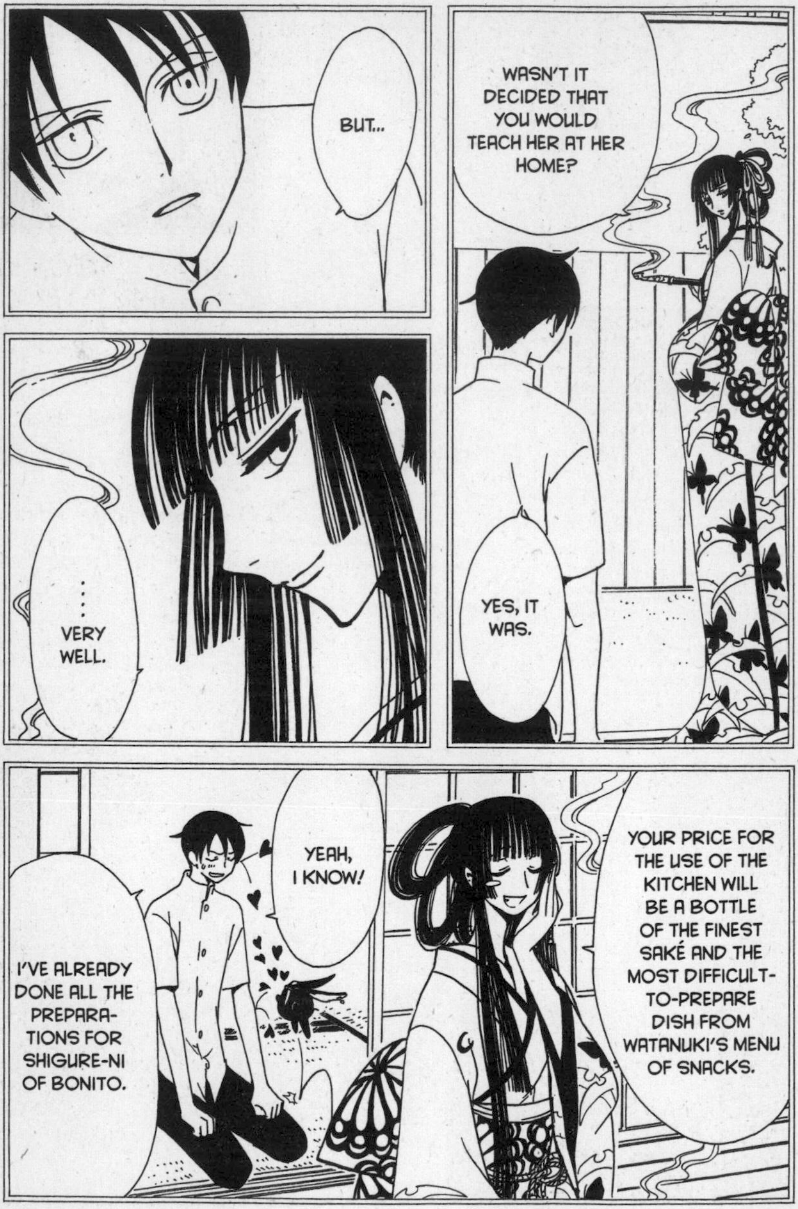
WASN'T IT DECIDED THAT YOU WOULD TEACH HER AT HER HOME?
YES, IT WAS.
BUT...
.... VERY WELL.
YOUR PRICE FOR THE USE OF THE KITCHEN WILL BE A BOTTLE OF THE FINEST SAKÉ AND THE MOST DIFFICULT-TO-PREPARE DISH FROM WATANUKI'S MENU OF SNACKS.
YEAH, I KNOW!
I'VE ALREADY DONE ALL THE PREPARATIONS FOR SHIGURE-NI OF BONITO.

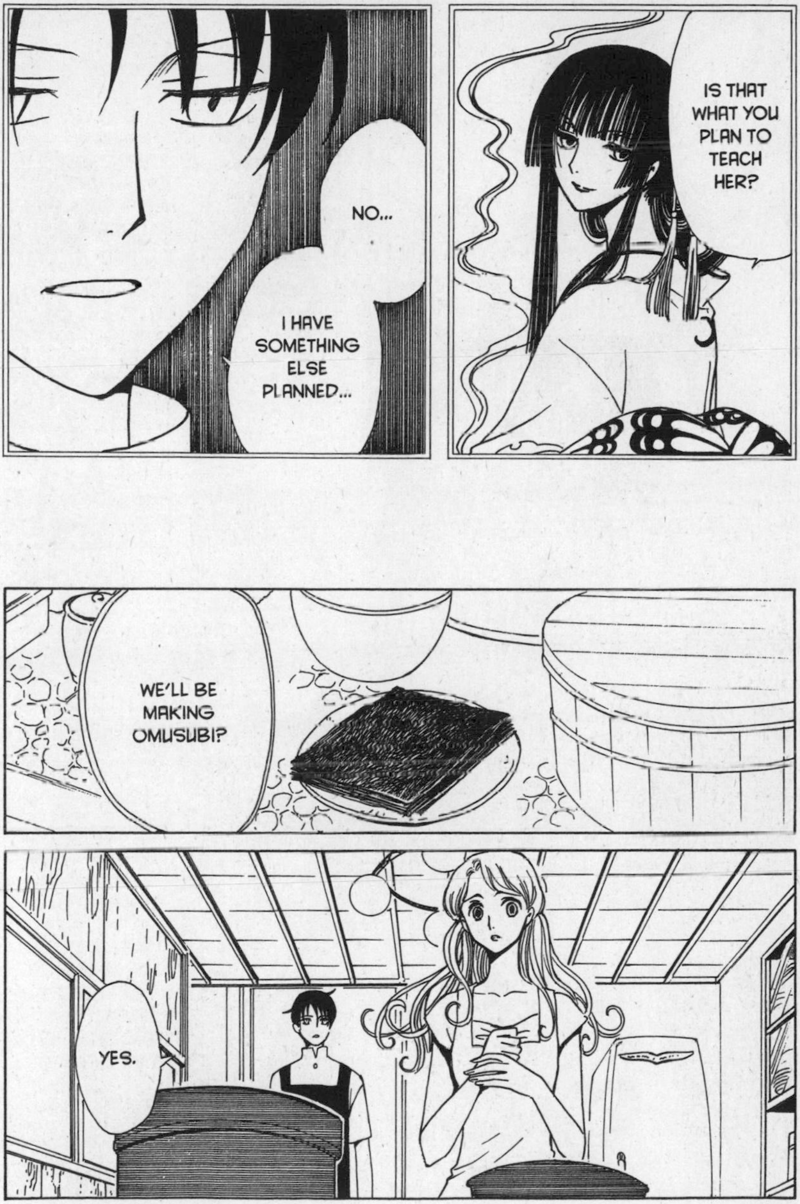
IS THAT WHAT YOU PLAN TO TEACH HER?
NO...
I HAVE SOMETHING ELSE PLANNED...
WE'LL BE MAKING OMUSUBI?
YES.

# Honorifics Explained

Throughout the Del Rey Manga books, you will find Japanese honorifics left intact in the translations. For those not familiar with how the Japanese use honorifics and, more important, how they differ from American honorifics, we present this brief overview.

Politeness has always been a critical facet of Japanese culture. Ever since the feudal era, when Japan was a highly stratified society, use of honorifics—which can be defined as polite speech that indicates relationship or status—has played an essential role in the Japanese language. When you address someone in Japanese, an honorific usually takes the form of a suffix attached to one's name (example: "Asuna-san"), is used as a title at the end of one's name, or appears in place of the name itself (example: "Negi-sensei," or simply "Sensei!").

Honorifics can be expressions of respect or endearment. In the context of manga and anime, honorifics give insight into the nature of the relationship between characters. Many English translations leave out these important honorifics and therefore distort the feel of the original Japanese. Because Japanese honorifics contain nuances that English honorifics lack, it is our policy at Del Rey not to translate them. Here, instead, is a guide to some of the honorifics you may encounter in Del Rey Manga.

**-san:** This is the most common honorific and is equivalent to Mr., Miss, Ms., or Mrs. It is the all-purpose honorific and can be used in any situation where politeness is required.

**-sama:** This is one level higher than "-san" and is used to confer great respect.

**-dono:** This comes from the word "tono," which means "lord." It is an even higher level than "-sama" and confers utmost respect.

**-kun:** This suffix is used at the end of boys' names to express familiarity or endearment. It is also sometimes used by men among friends, or when addressing someone younger or of a lower station.

**-chan:** This is used to express endearment, mostly toward girls. It is also used for little boys, pets, and even among lovers. It gives a sense of childish cuteness.

**Bozu:** This is an informal way to refer to a boy, similar to the English terms "kid" and "squirt."

**Sempai/Senpai:** This title suggests that the addressee is one's senior in a group or organization. It is most often used in a school setting, where underclassmen refer to their upperclassmen as "sempai." It can also be used in the workplace, such as when a newer employee addresses an employee who has seniority in the company.

**Kohai:** This is the opposite of "sempai" and is used toward under-classmen in school or newcomers in the workplace. It connotes that the addressee is of a lower station.

**Sensei:** Literally meaning "one who has come before," this title is used for teachers, doctors, or masters of any profession or art.

**-[blank]:** This is usually forgotten in these lists, but it is perhaps the most significant difference between Japanese and English. The lack of honorific means that the speaker has permission to address the person in a very intimate way. Usually, only family, spouses, or very close friends have this kind of permission. Known as *yobisute*, it can be gratifying when someone who has earned the intimacy starts to call one by one's name without an honorific. But when that intimacy hasn't been earned, it can be very insulting.

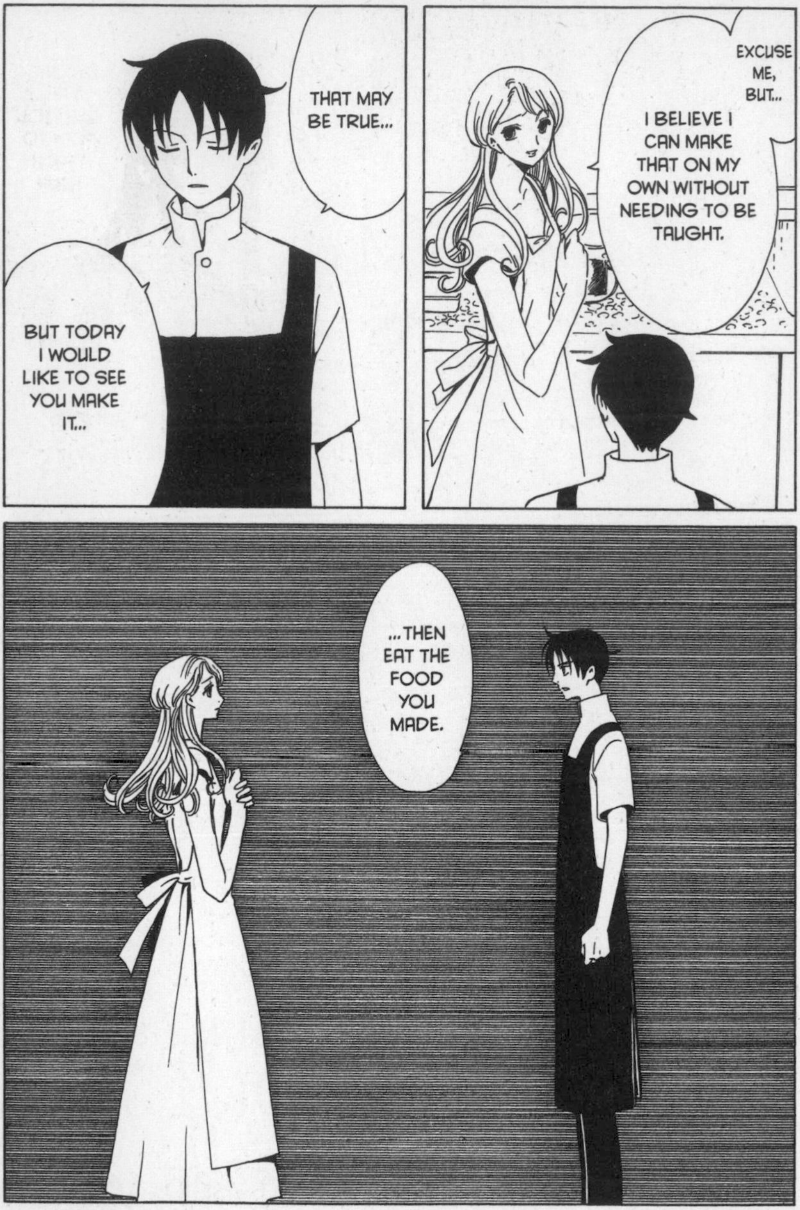
EXCUSE ME, BUT...
I BELIEVE I CAN MAKE THAT ON MY OWN WITHOUT NEEDING TO BE TAUGHT.
THAT MAY BE TRUE...
BUT TODAY I WOULD LIKE TO SEE YOU MAKE IT...
...THEN EAT THE FOOD YOU MADE.

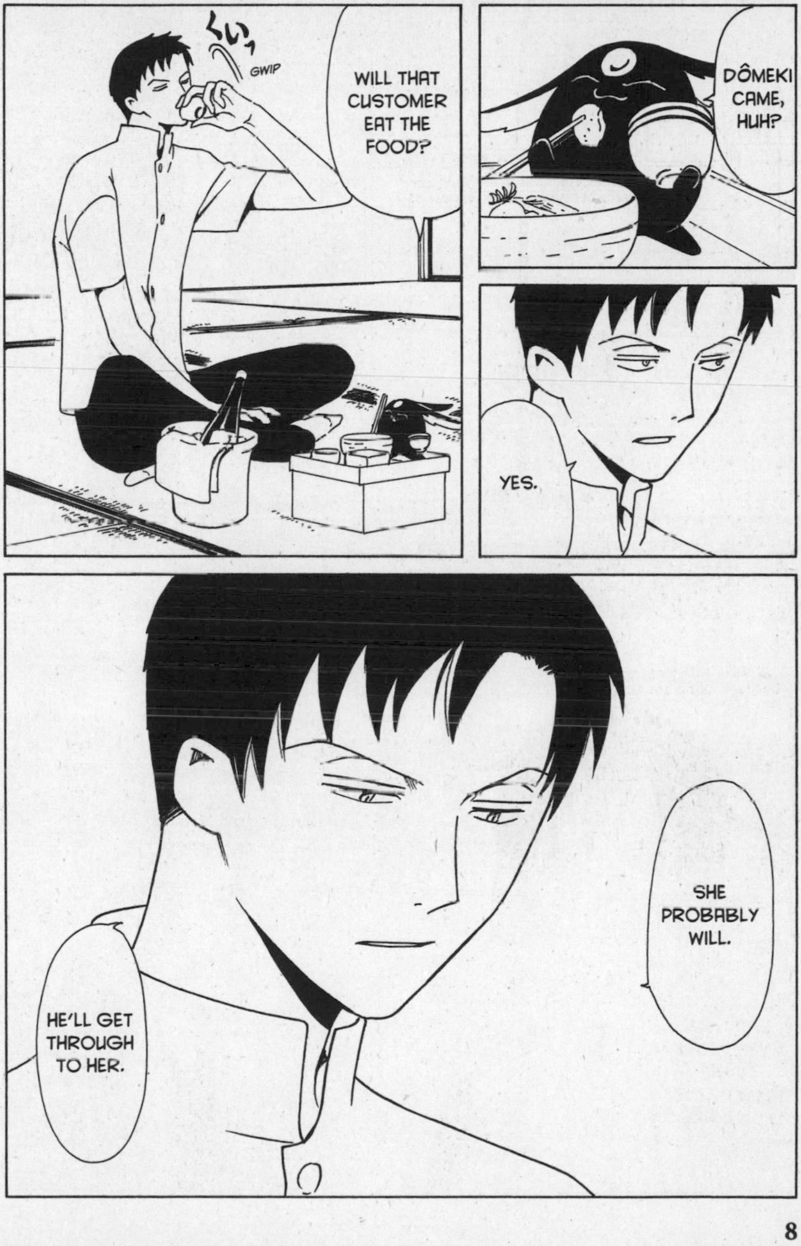
DÔMEKI CAME, HUH?
YES.
くいっ
GWIP
WILL THAT CUSTOMER EAT THE FOOD?
SHE PROBABLY WILL.
HE'LL GET THROUGH TO HER.

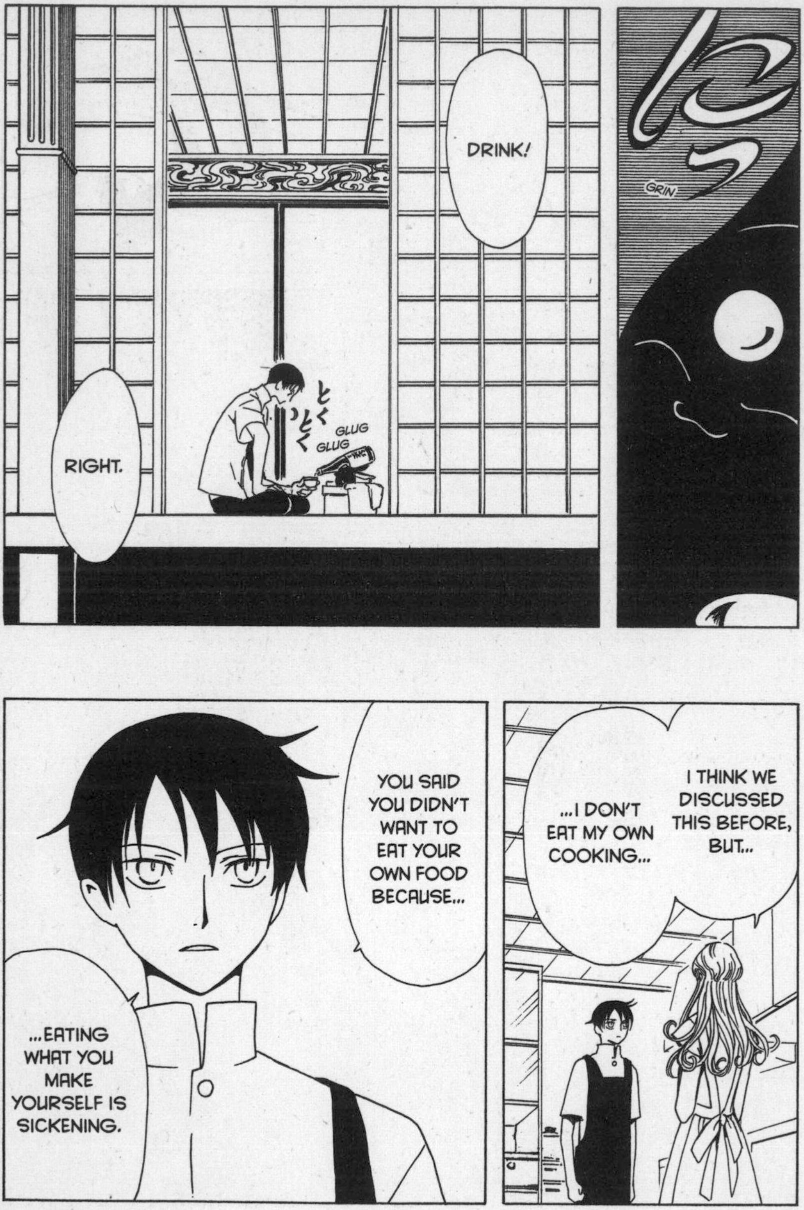
GRIN
DRINK!
とく
とく
GLUG
GLUG
RIGHT.
I THINK WE DISCUSSED THIS BEFORE, BUT...
...I DON'T EAT MY OWN COOKING...
YOU SAID YOU DIDN'T WANT TO EAT YOUR OWN FOOD BECAUSE...
...EATING WHAT YOU MAKE YOURSELF IS SICKENING.

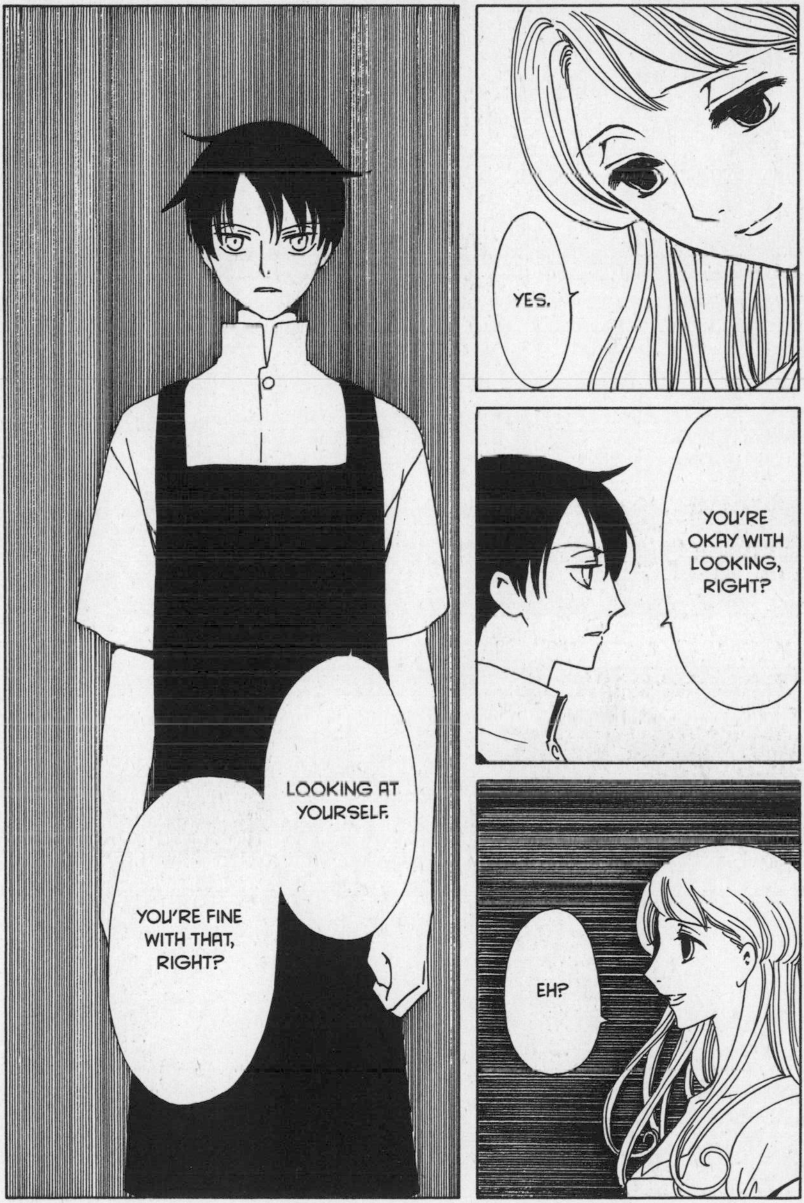
YES.
YOU'RE OKAY WITH LOOKING, RIGHT?
EH?
LOOKING AT YOURSELF.
YOU'RE FINE WITH THAT, RIGHT?

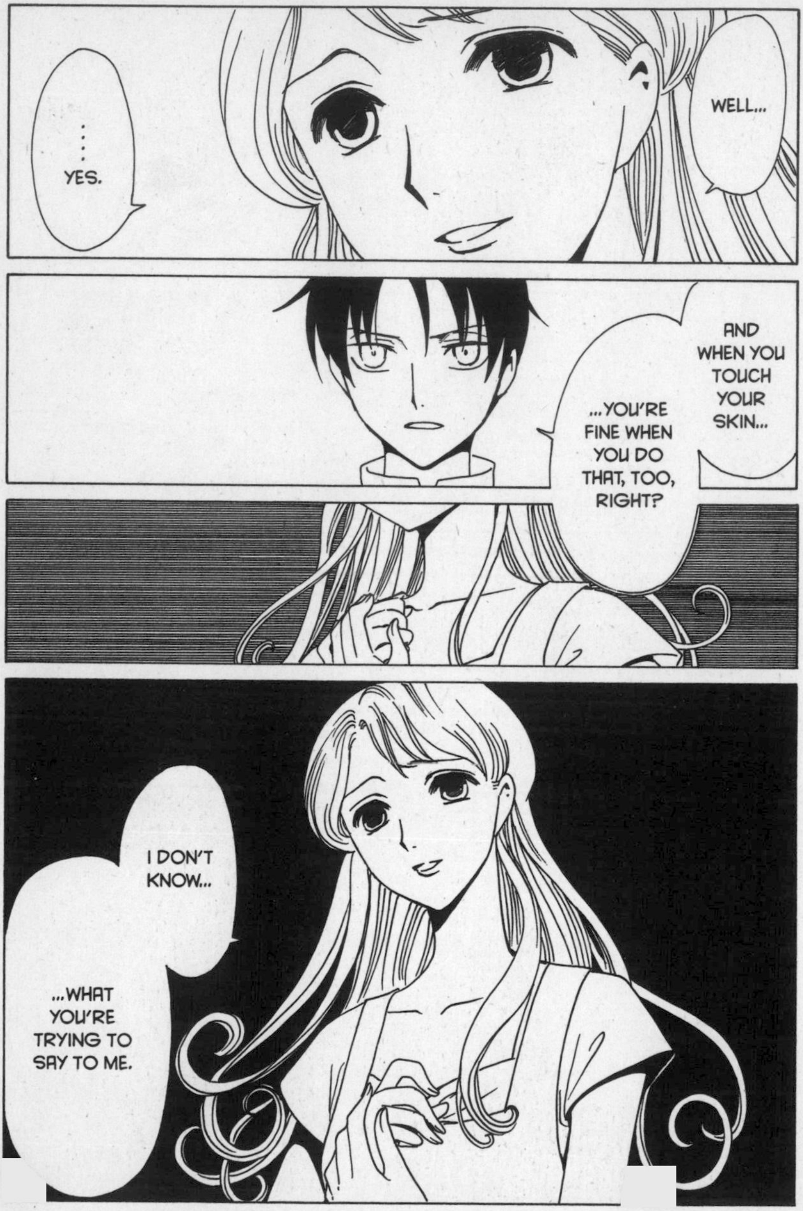
WELL...
......YES.
AND WHEN YOU TOUCH YOUR SKIN...
...YOU'RE FINE WHEN YOU DO THAT, TOO, RIGHT?
I DON'T KNOW...
...WHAT YOU'RE TRYING TO SAY TO ME.

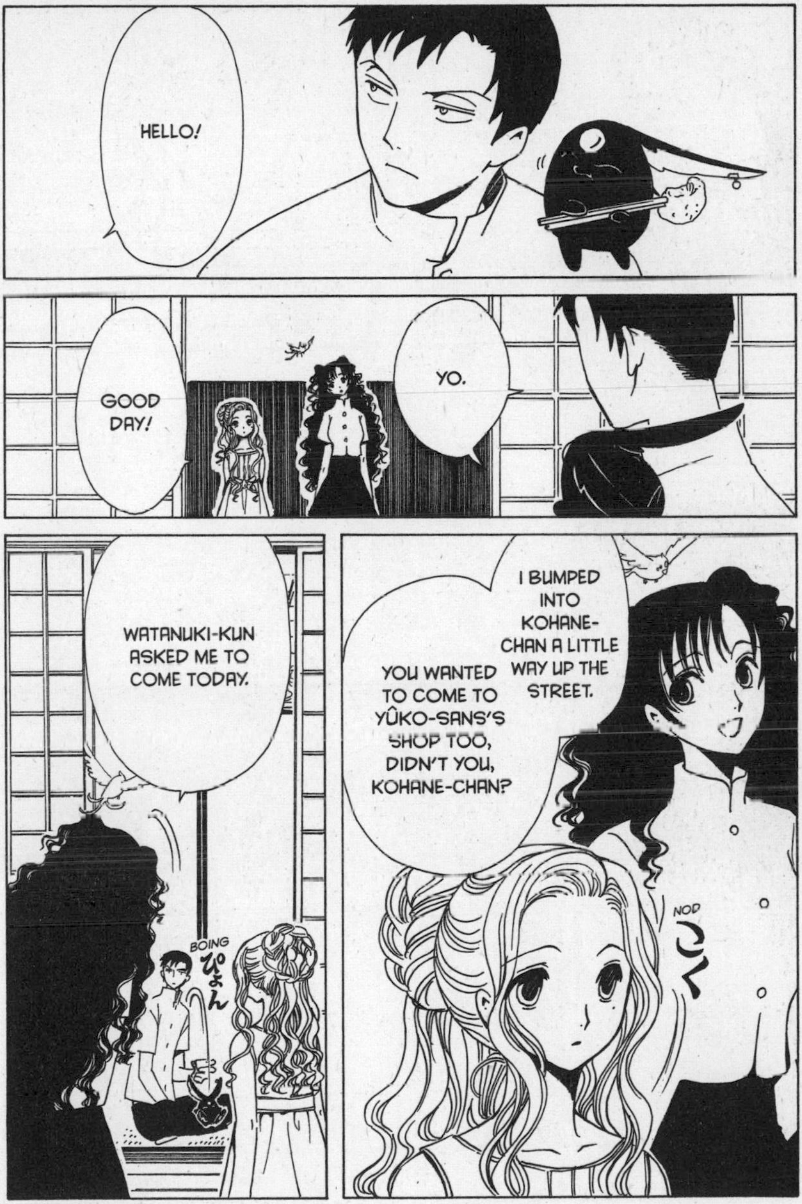
HELLO!
YO.
GOOD DAY!
I BUMPED INTO KOHANE-CHAN A LITTLE WAY UP THE STREET.
YOU WANTED TO COME TO YÛKO-SANS'S SHOP TOO, DIDN'T YOU, KOHANE-CHAN?
NOD こく
WATANUKI-KUN ASKED ME TO COME TODAY.
BOING ぴょん

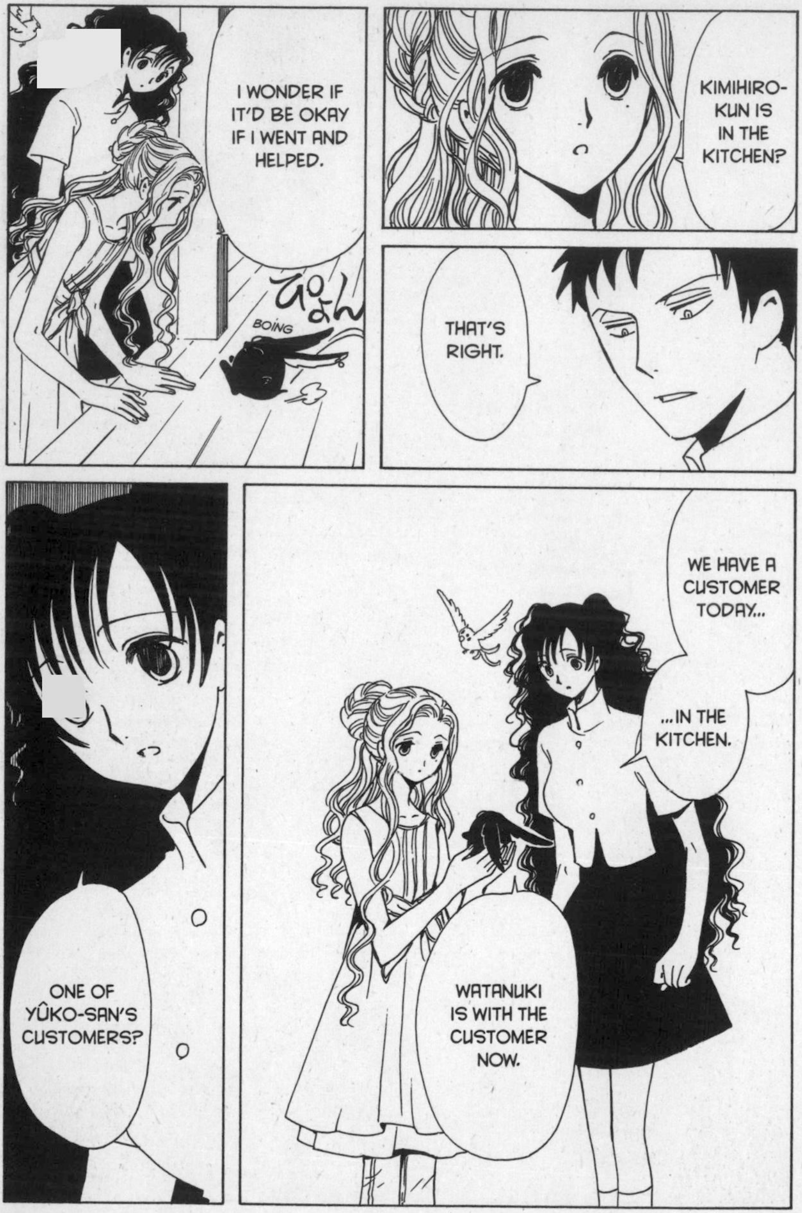
KIMIHIRO-KUN IS IN THE KITCHEN?
THAT'S RIGHT.
I WONDER IF IT'D BE OKAY IF I WENT AND HELPED.
ぴょん
BOING
WE HAVE A CUSTOMER TODAY...
...IN THE KITCHEN.
WATANUKI IS WITH THE CUSTOMER NOW.
ONE OF YÛKO-SAN'S CUSTOMERS?

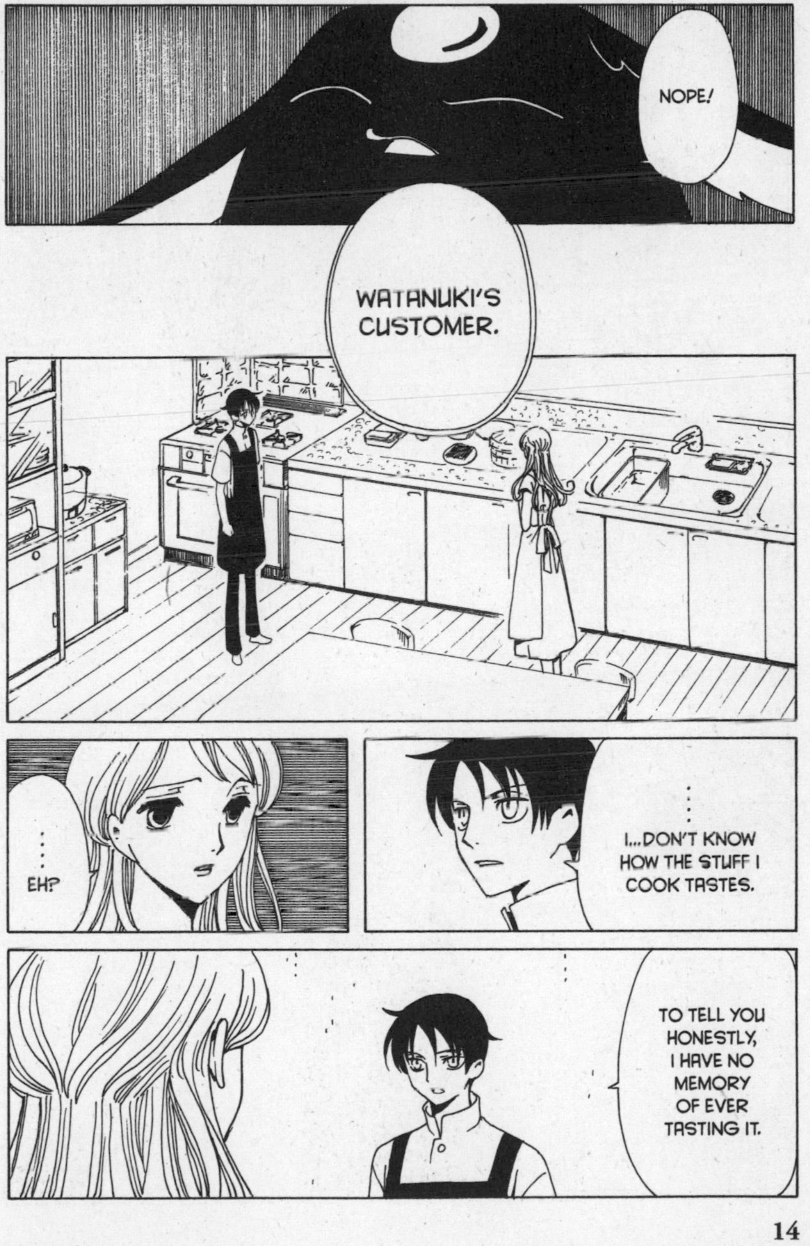
NOPE!
WATANUKI'S CUSTOMER.
I...DON'T KNOW HOW THE STUFF I COOK TASTES.
EH?
TO TELL YOU HONESTLY, I HAVE NO MEMORY OF EVER TASTING IT.

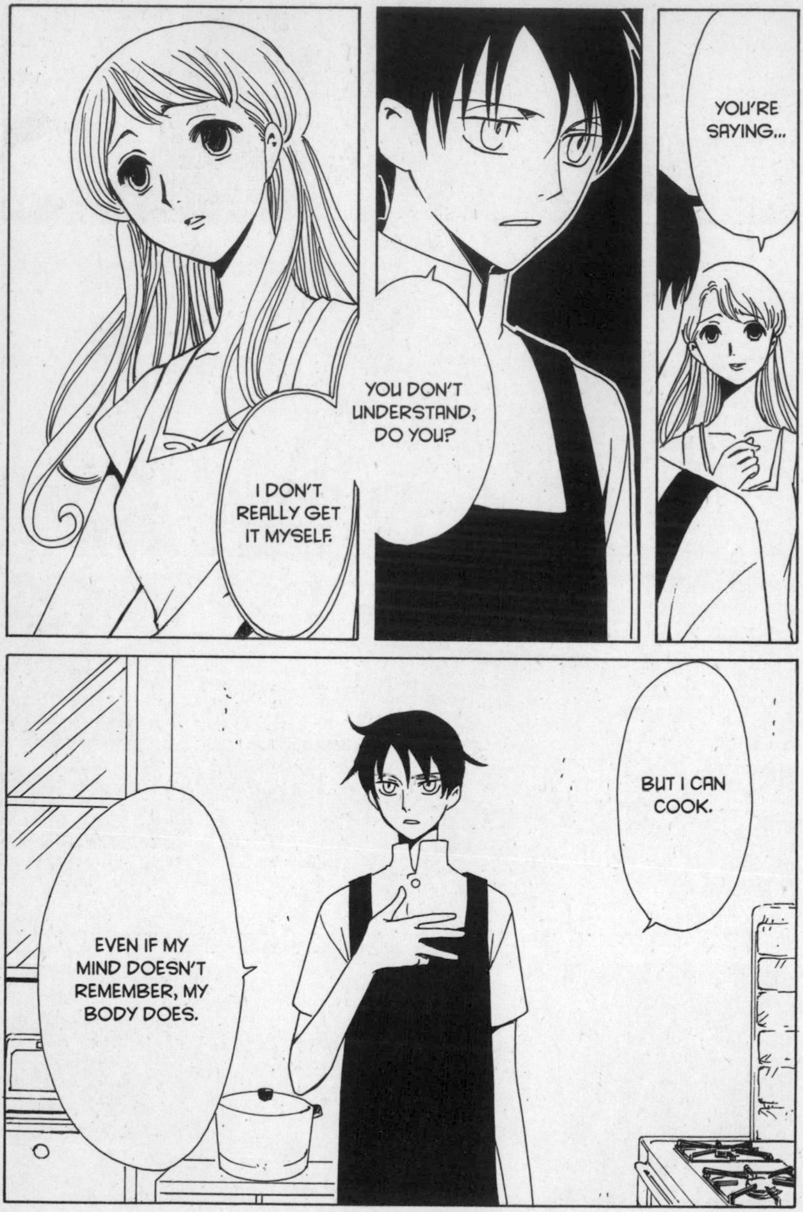
YOU'RE SAYING...
YOU DON'T UNDERSTAND, DO YOU?
I DON'T REALLY GET IT MYSELF.
BUT I CAN COOK.
EVEN IF MY MIND DOESN'T REMEMBER, MY BODY DOES.

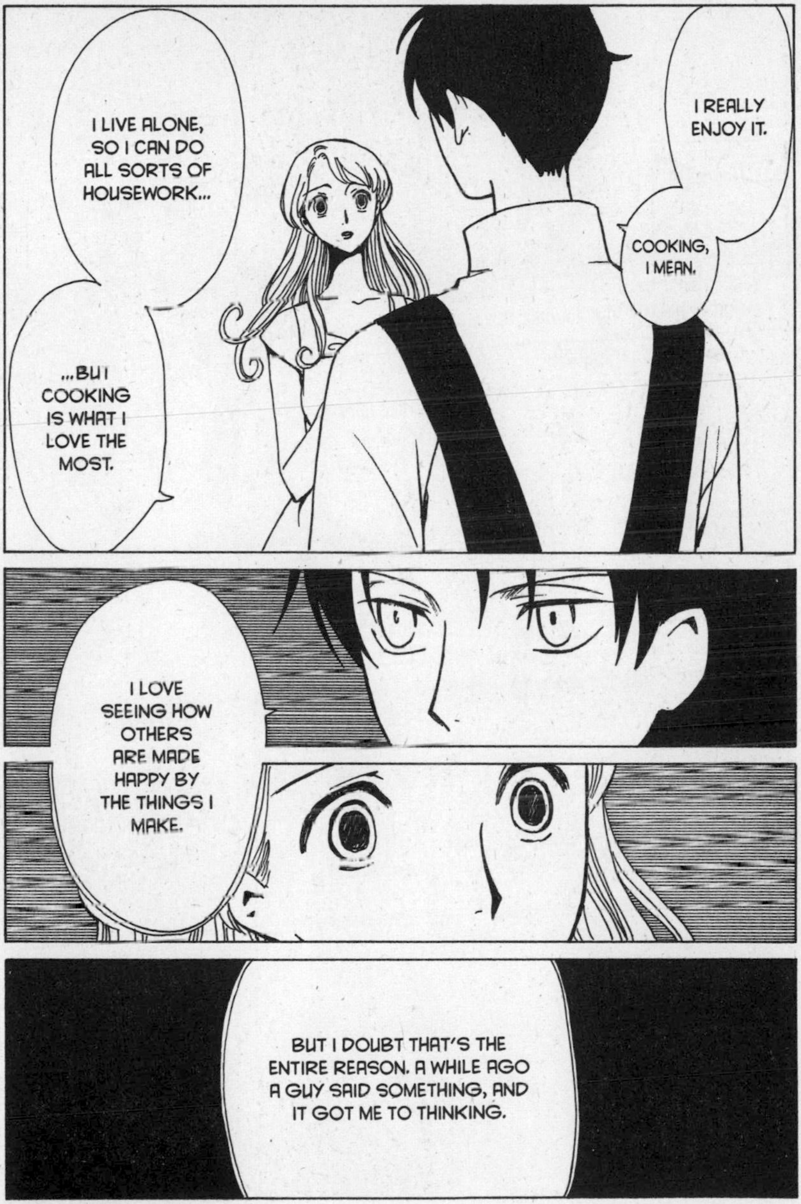
I REALLY ENJOY IT.
COOKING, I MEAN.
I LIVE ALONE, SO I CAN DO ALL SORTS OF HOUSEWORK...
...BUT COOKING IS WHAT I LOVE THE MOST.
I LOVE SEEING HOW OTHERS ARE MADE HAPPY BY THE THINGS I MAKE.
BUT I DOUBT THAT'S THE ENTIRE REASON. A WHILE AGO A GUY SAID SOMETHING, AND IT GOT ME TO THINKING.

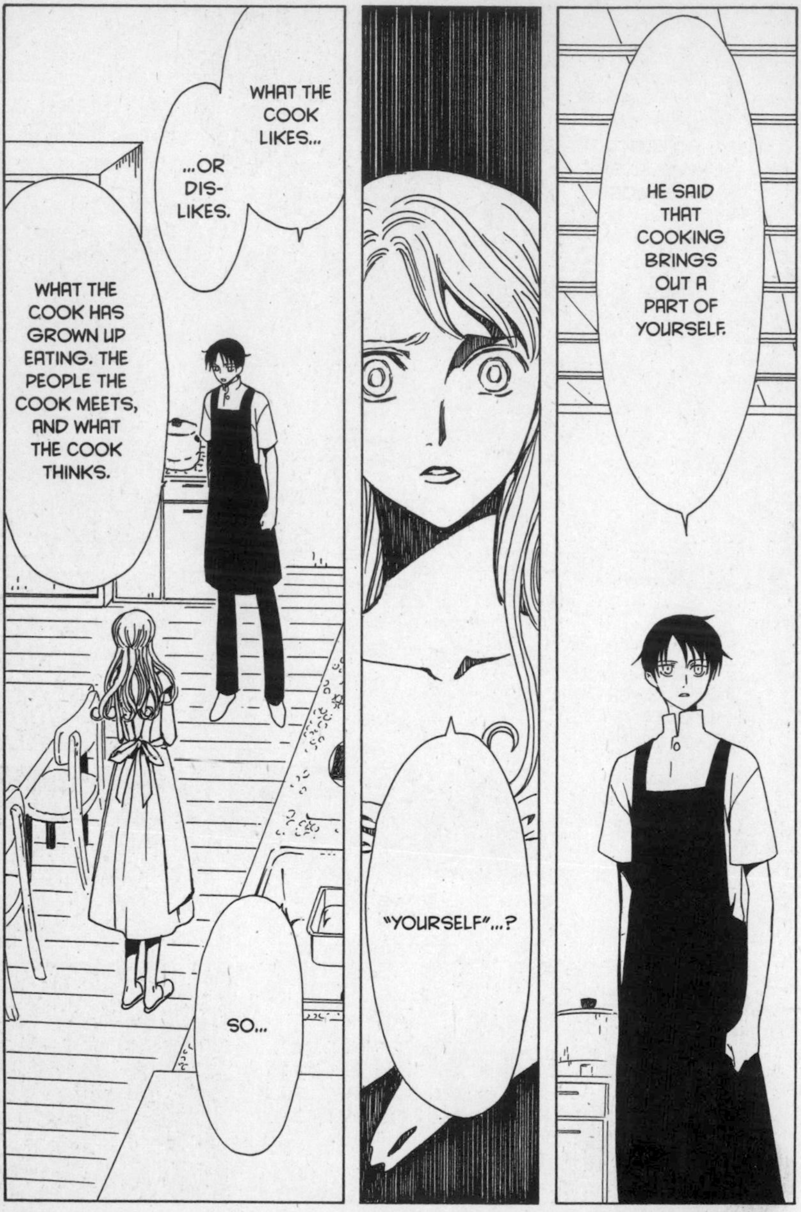
HE SAID THAT COOKING BRINGS OUT A PART OF YOURSELF.
"YOURSELF"...?
WHAT THE COOK LIKES...
...OR DIS-LIKES.
WHAT THE COOK HAS GROWN UP EATING. THE PEOPLE THE COOK MEETS, AND WHAT THE COOK THINKS.
SO...

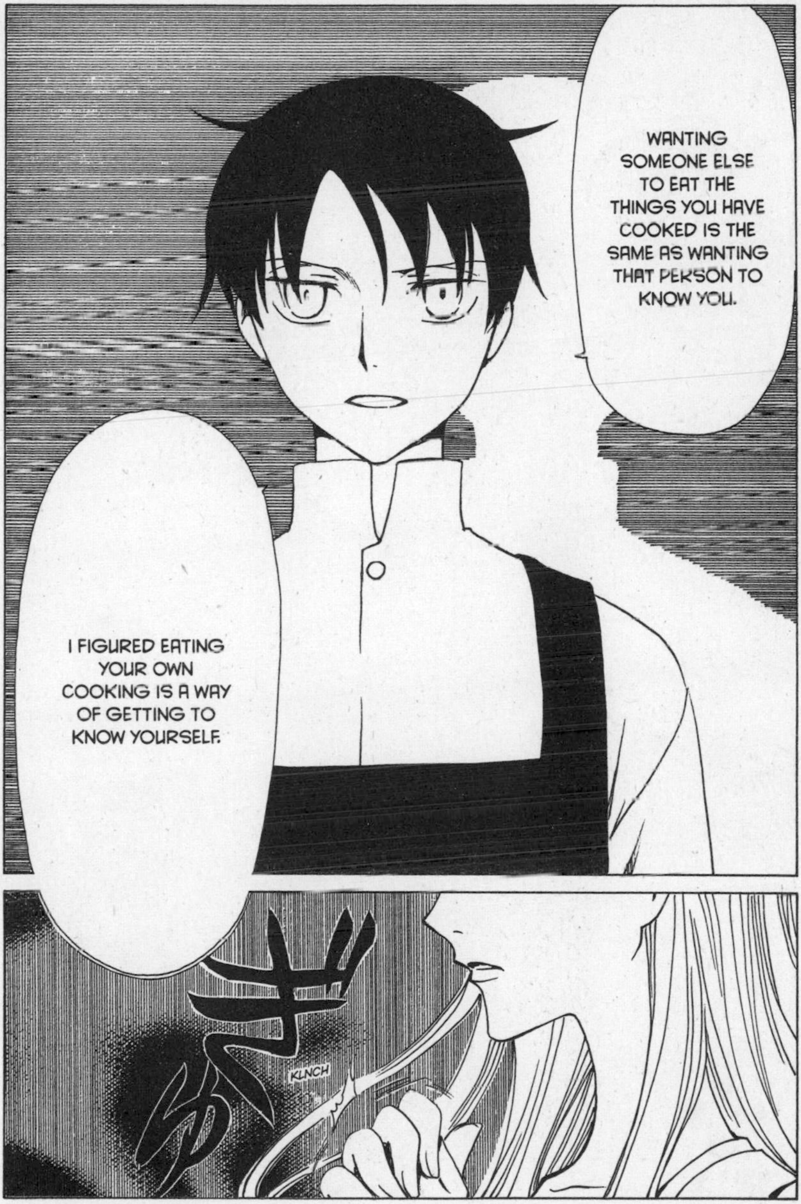
WANTING SOMEONE ELSE TO EAT THE THINGS YOU HAVE COOKED IS THE SAME AS WANTING THAT PERSON TO KNOW YOU.
I FIGURED EATING YOUR OWN COOKING IS A WAY OF GETTING TO KNOW YOURSELF.
KLNCH

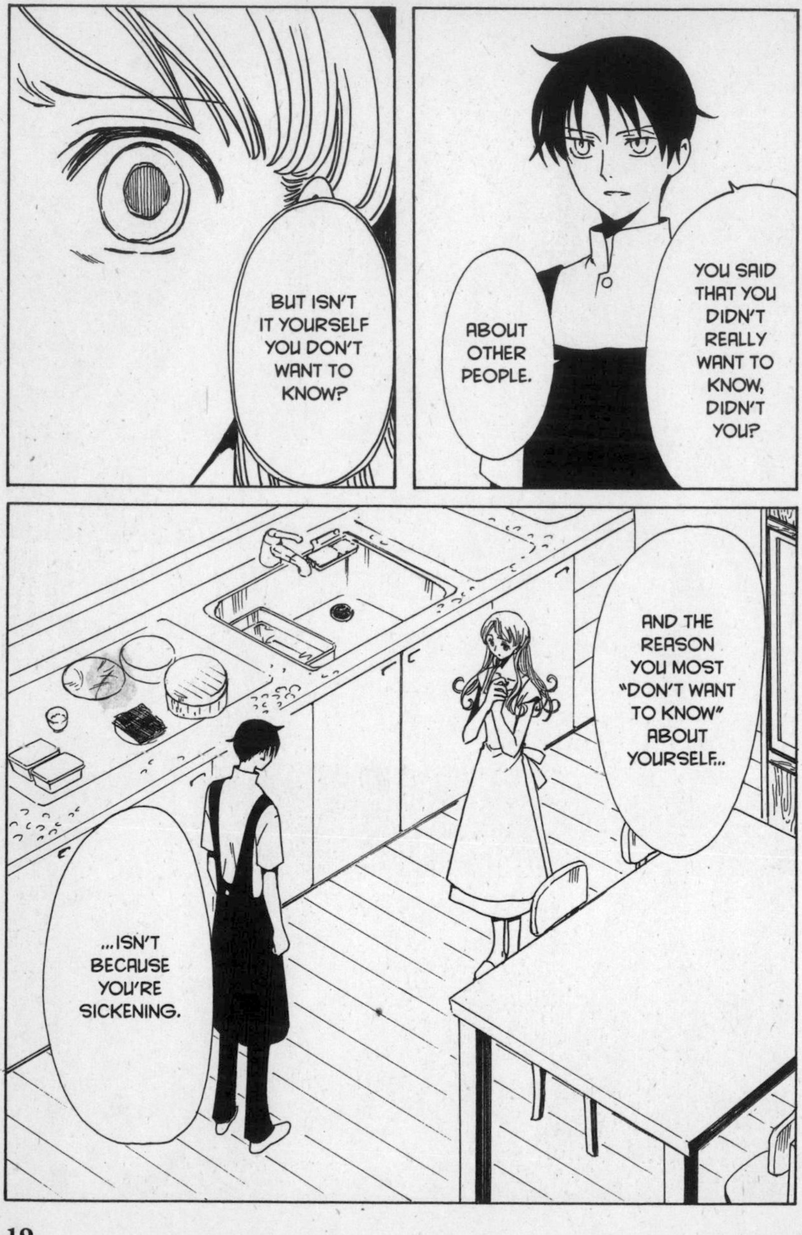
YOU SAID THAT YOU DIDN'T REALLY WANT TO KNOW, DIDN'T YOU?
ABOUT OTHER PEOPLE.
BUT ISN'T IT YOURSELF YOU DON'T WANT TO KNOW?
AND THE REASON YOU MOST "DON'T WANT TO KNOW" ABOUT YOURSELF...
...ISN'T BECAUSE YOU'RE SICKENING.

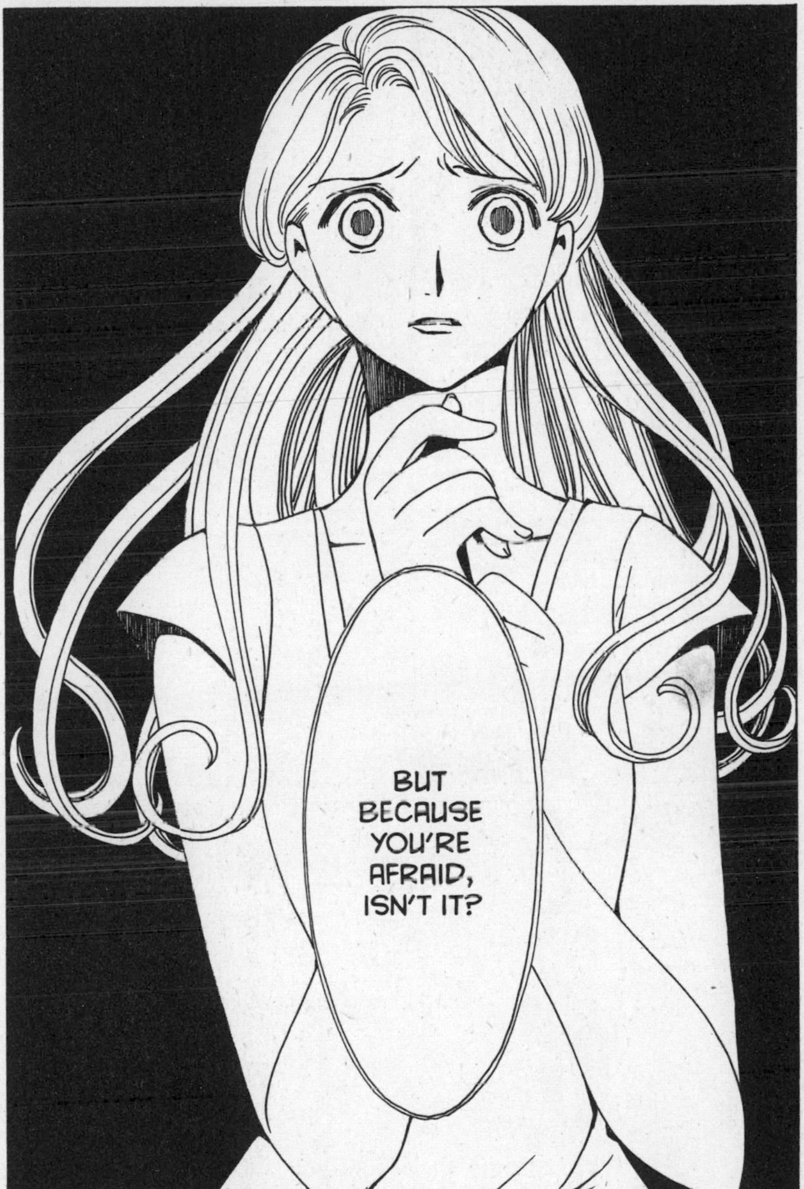
BUT BECAUSE YOU'RE AFRAID, ISN'T IT?

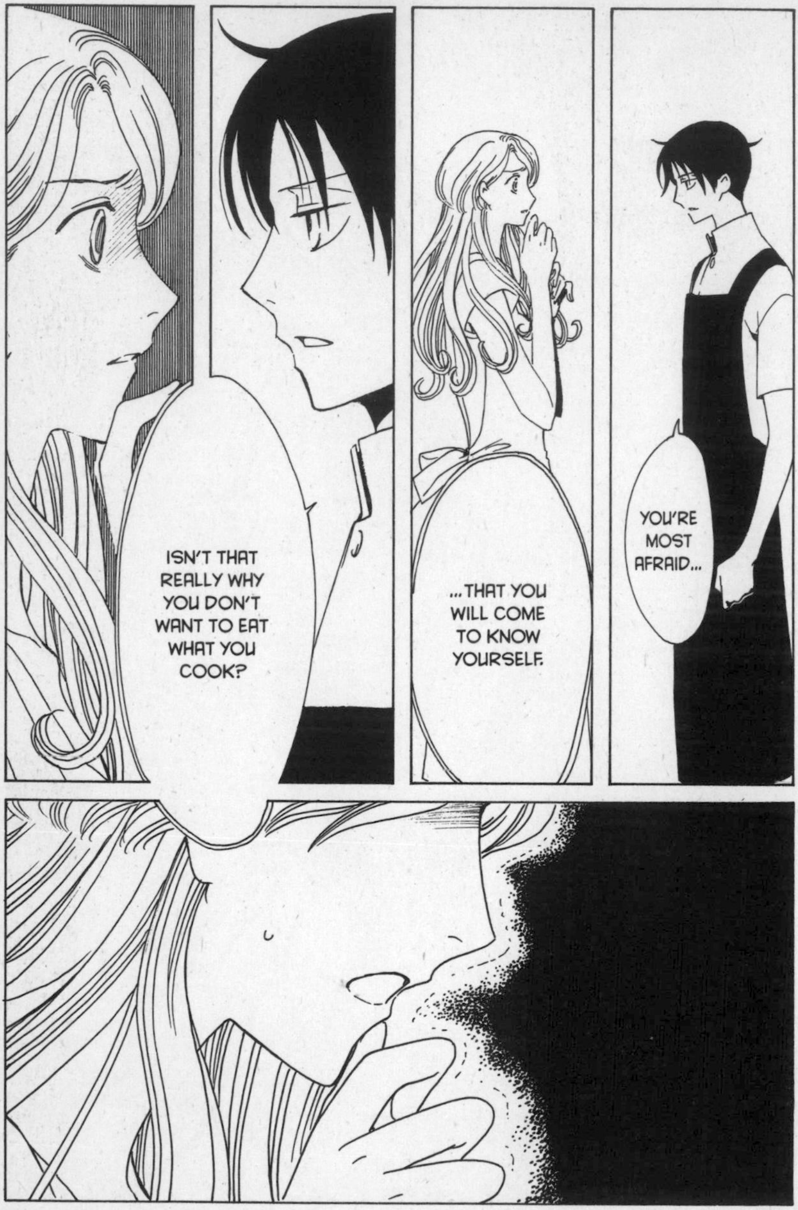
YOU'RE MOST AFRAID...
...THAT YOU WILL COME TO KNOW YOURSELF.
ISN'T THAT REALLY WHY YOU DON'T WANT TO EAT WHAT YOU COOK?

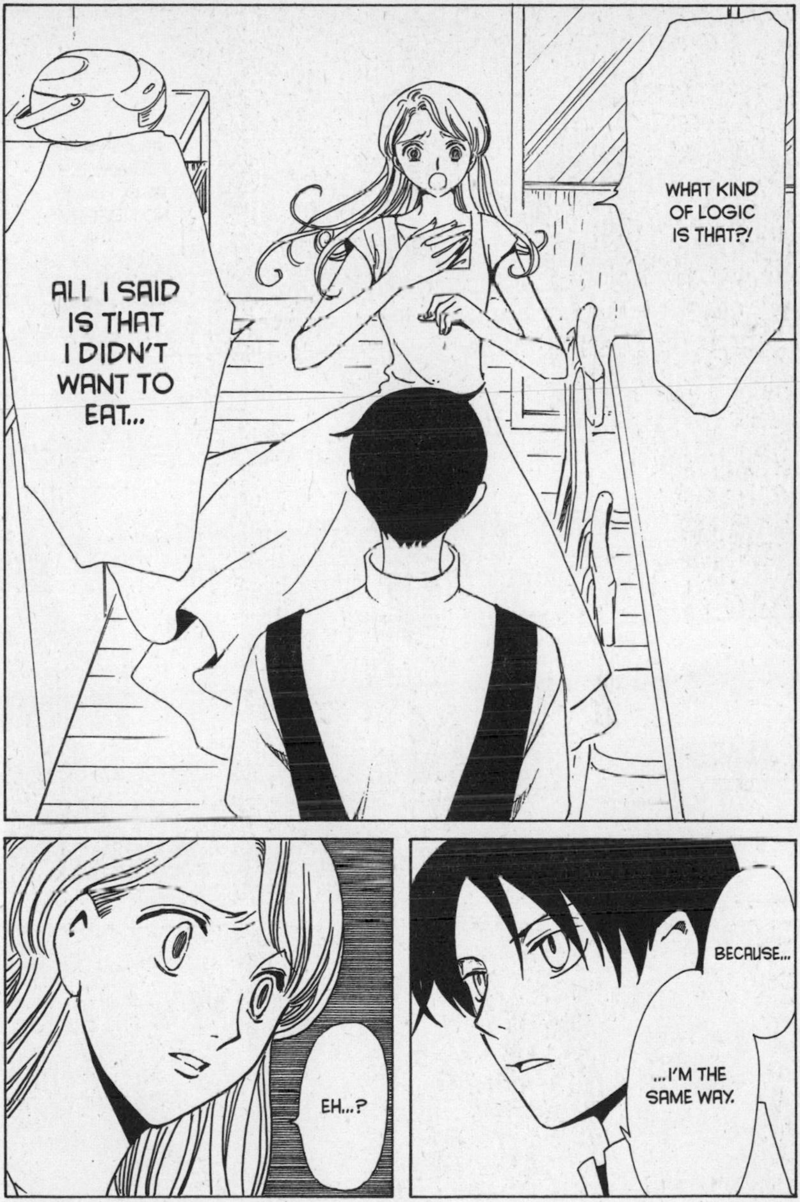
WHAT KIND OF LOGIC IS THAT?!
ALL I SAID IS THAT I DIDN'T WANT TO EAT...
BECAUSE...
...I'M THE SAME WAY.
EH...?

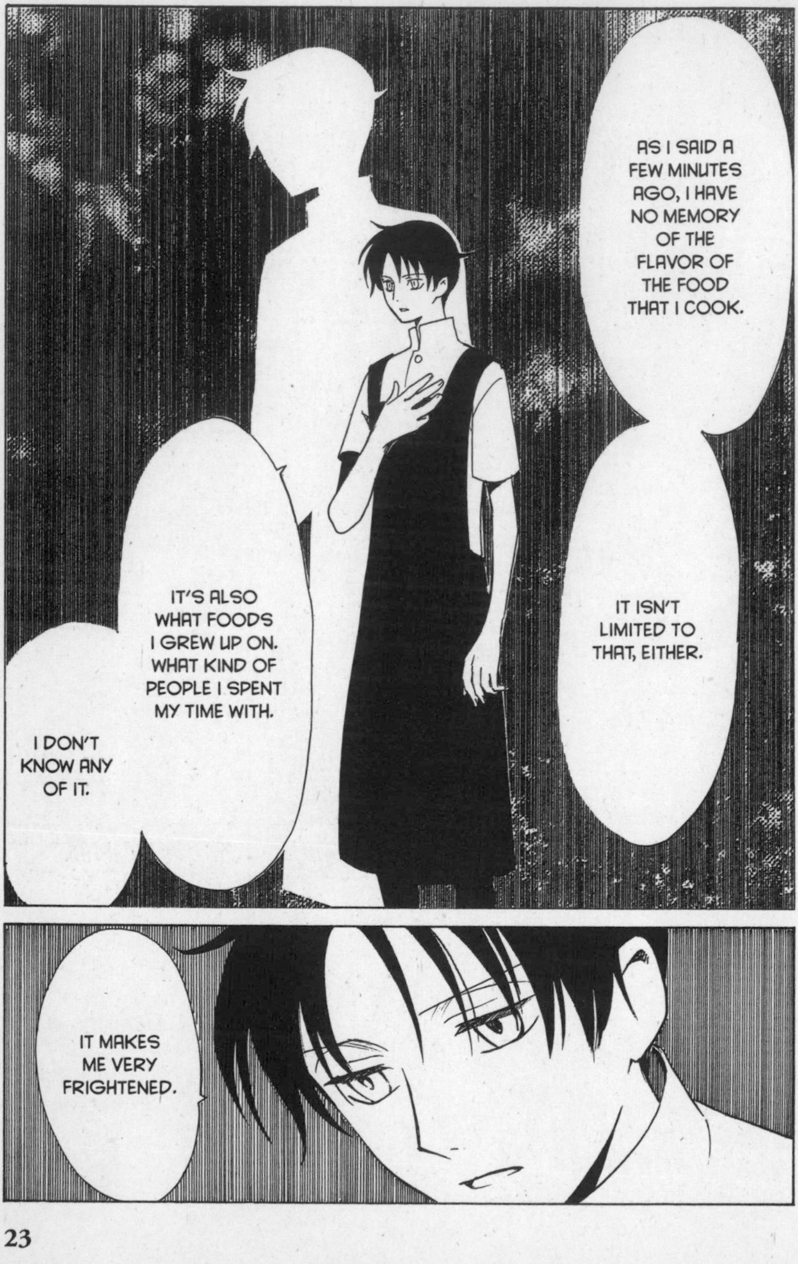
AS I SAID A FEW MINUTES AGO, I HAVE NO MEMORY OF THE FLAVOR OF THE FOOD THAT I COOK.
IT ISN'T LIMITED TO THAT, EITHER.
IT'S ALSO WHAT FOODS I GREW UP ON. WHAT KIND OF PEOPLE I SPENT MY TIME WITH.
I DON'T KNOW ANY OF IT.
IT MAKES ME VERY FRIGHTENED.

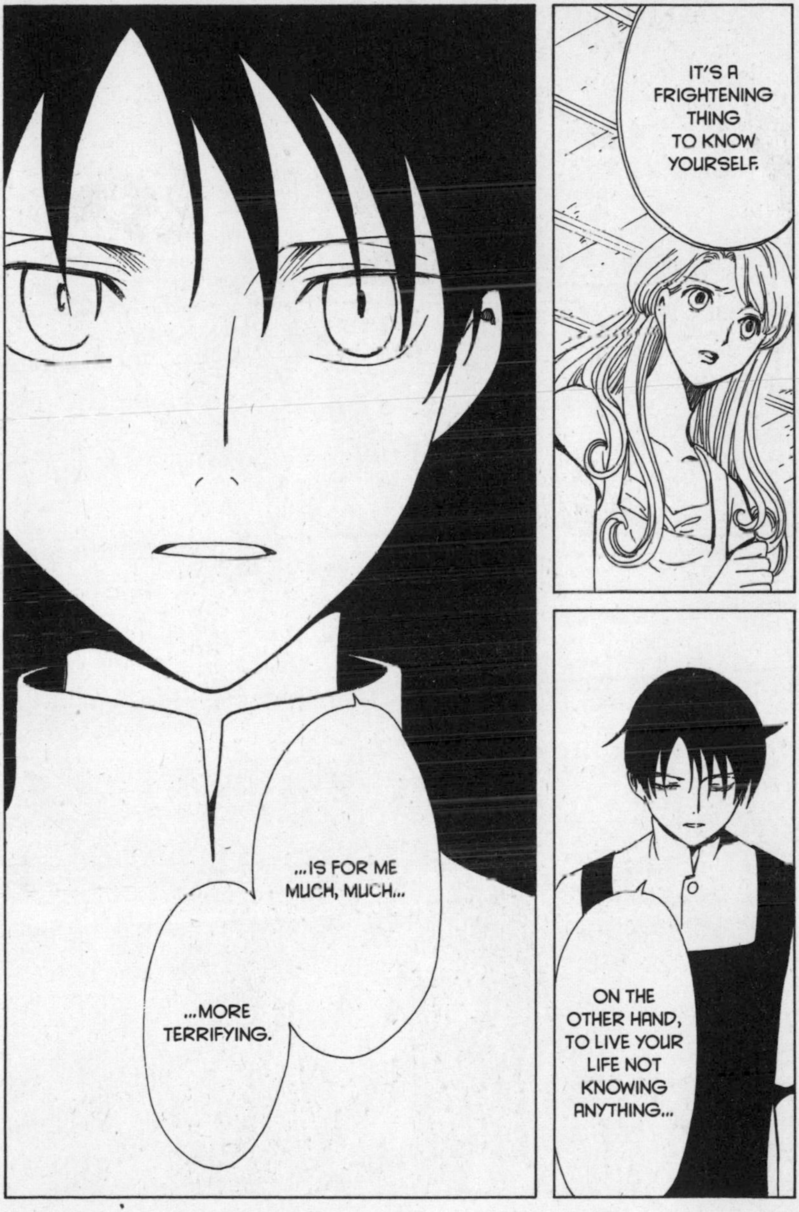
IT'S A FRIGHTENING THING TO KNOW YOURSELF.
ON THE OTHER HAND, TO LIVE YOUR LIFE NOT KNOWING ANYTHING...
...IS FOR ME MUCH, MUCH...
...MORE TERRIFYING.

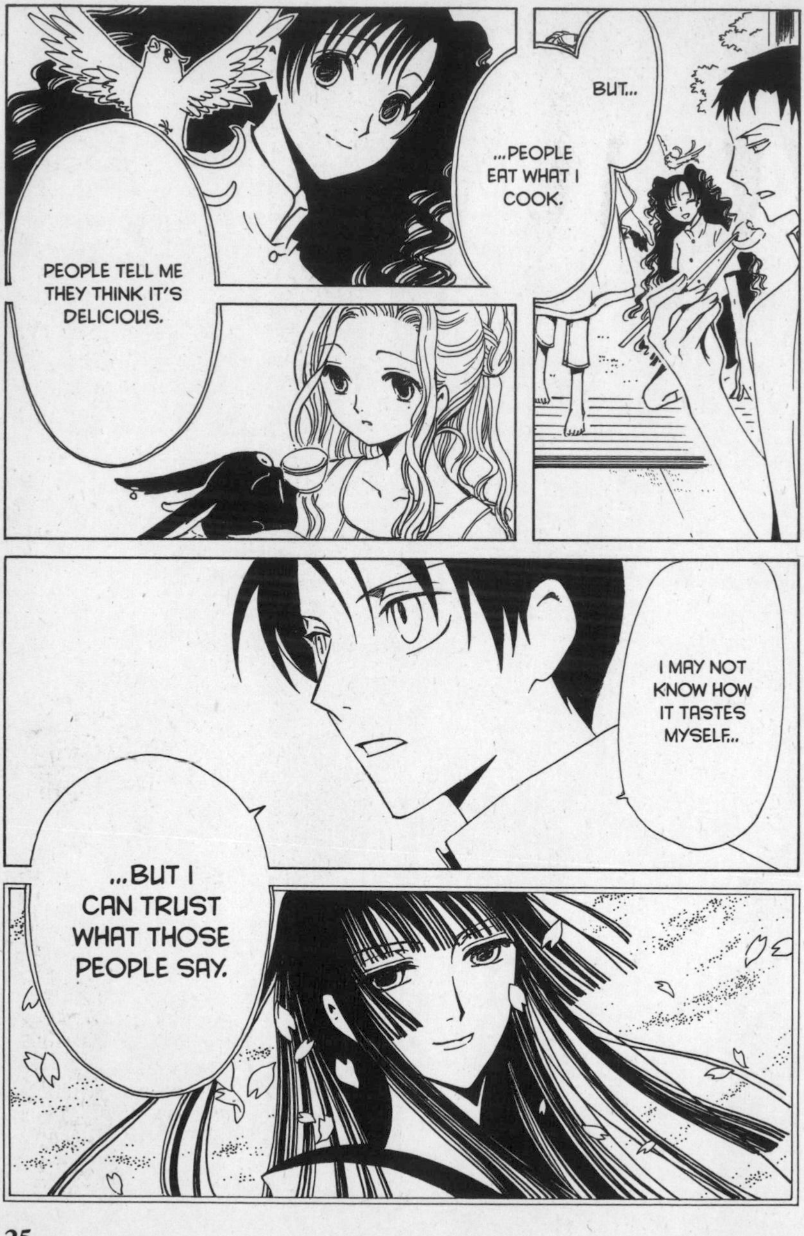
BUT...
...PEOPLE EAT WHAT I COOK.
PEOPLE TELL ME THEY THINK IT'S DELICIOUS.
I MAY NOT KNOW HOW IT TASTES MYSELF...
...BUT I CAN TRUST WHAT THOSE PEOPLE SAY.

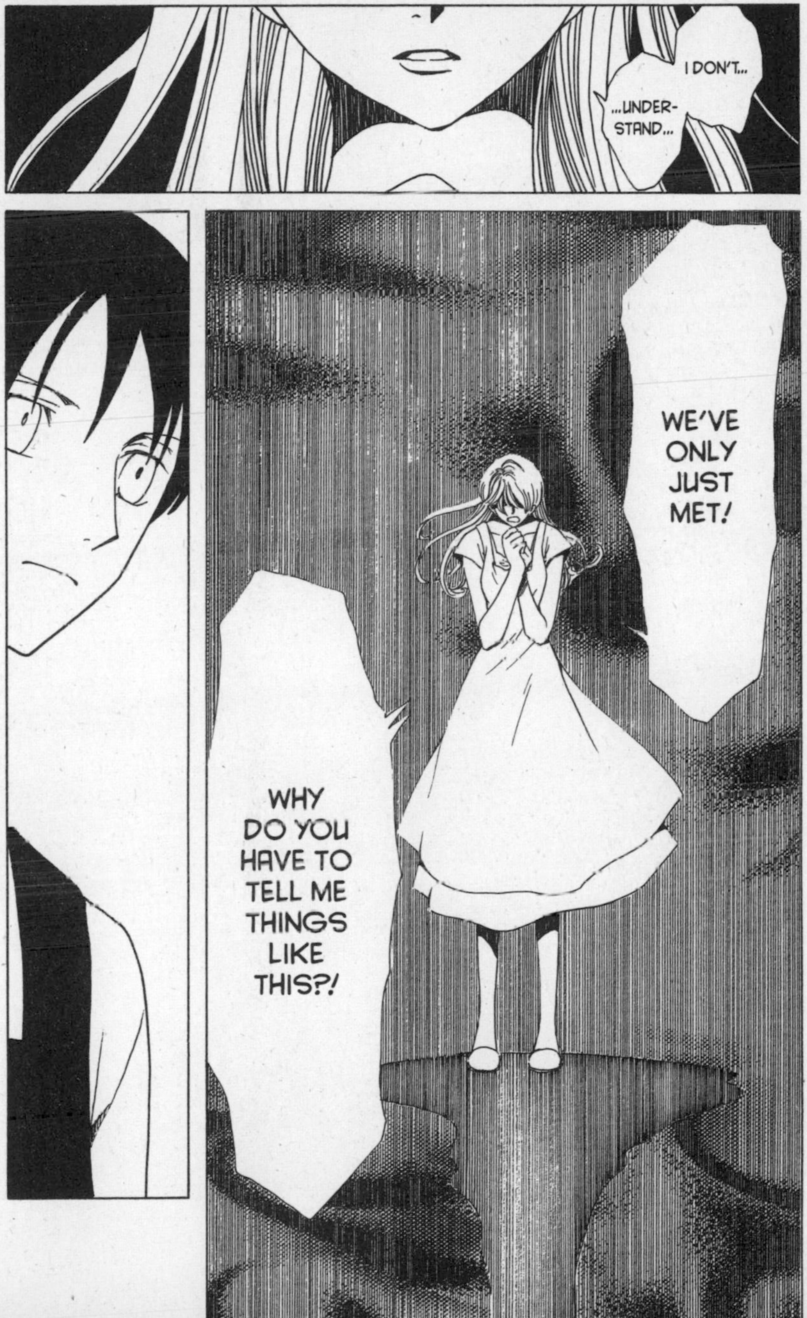
I DON'T...
...UNDER-STAND...
WE'VE ONLY JUST MET!
WHY DO YOU HAVE TO TELL ME THINGS LIKE THIS?!

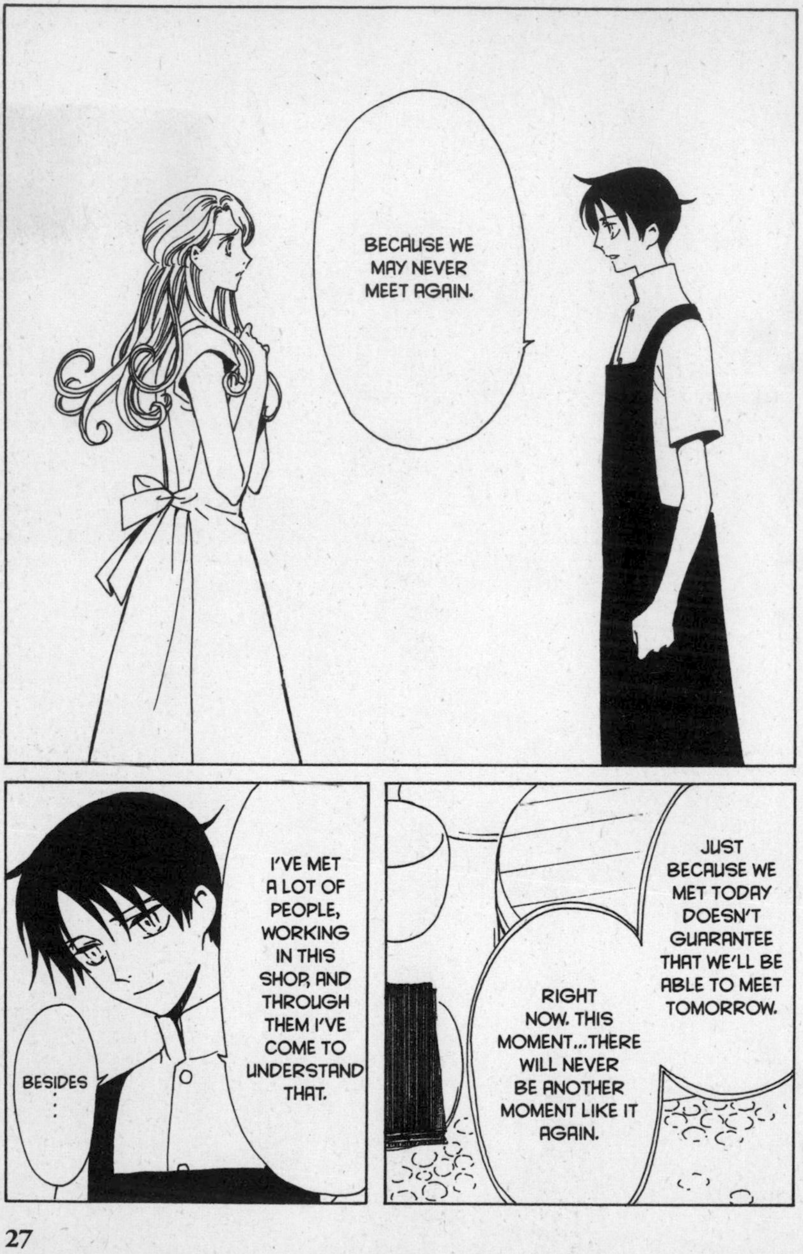
BECAUSE WE MAY NEVER MEET AGAIN.
JUST BECAUSE WE MET TODAY DOESN'T GUARANTEE THAT WE'LL BE ABLE TO MEET TOMORROW.
RIGHT NOW. THIS MOMENT...THERE WILL NEVER BE ANOTHER MOMENT LIKE IT AGAIN.
I'VE MET A LOT OF PEOPLE, WORKING IN THIS SHOP, AND THROUGH THEM I'VE COME TO UNDERSTAND THAT.
BESIDES...

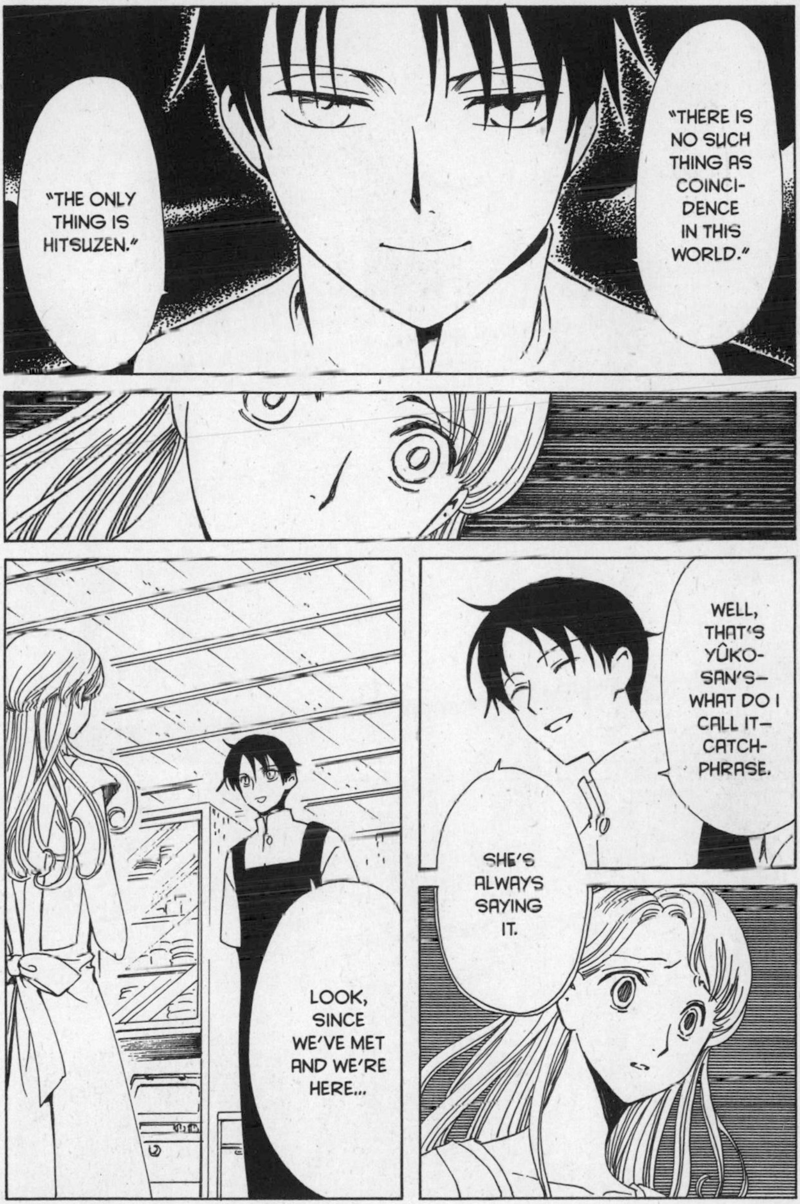
"THERE IS NO SUCH THING AS COINCIDENCE IN THIS WORLD."
"THE ONLY THING IS HITSUZEN."
WELL, THAT'S YÛKO-SAN'S—WHAT DO I CALL IT—CATCHPHRASE.
SHE'S ALWAYS SAYING IT.
LOOK, SINCE WE'VE MET AND WE'RE HERE...

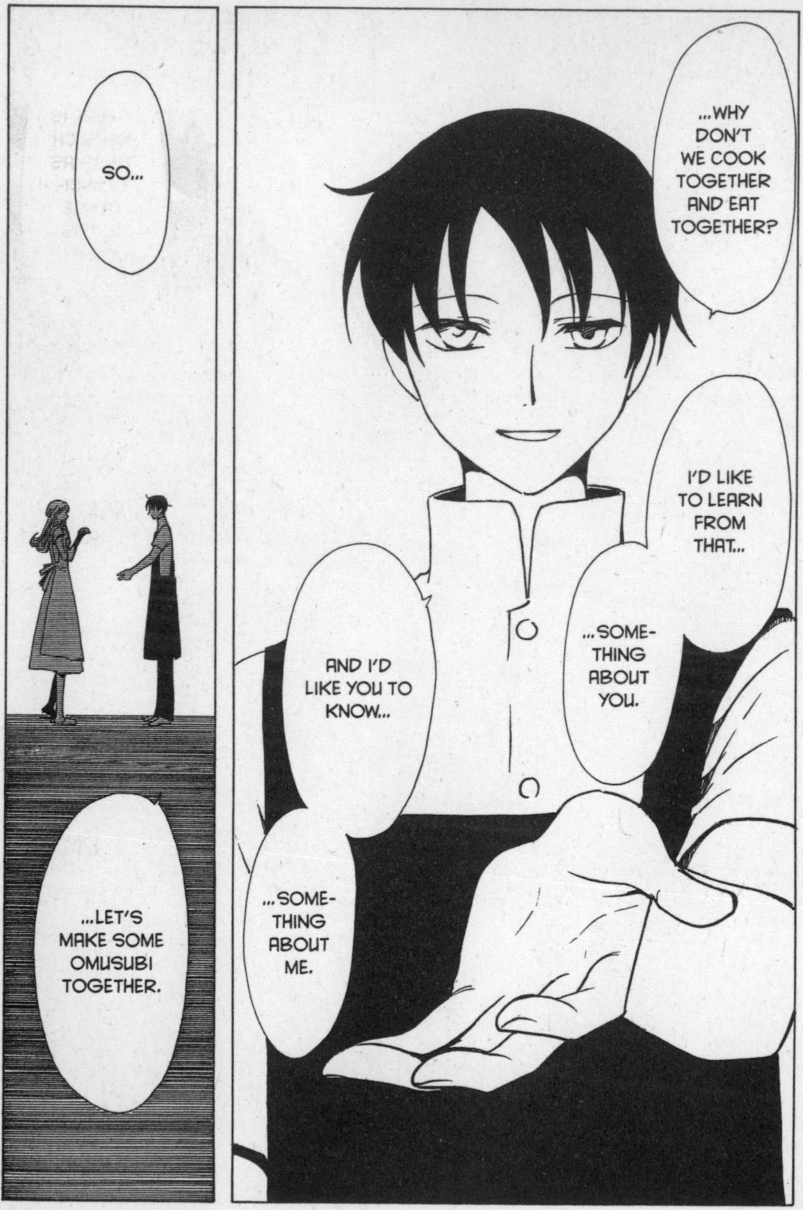
...WHY DON'T WE COOK TOGETHER AND EAT TOGETHER?
I'D LIKE TO LEARN FROM THAT...
...SOME-THING ABOUT YOU.
AND I'D LIKE YOU TO KNOW...
...SOME-THING ABOUT ME.
SO...
...LET'S MAKE SOME OMUSUBI TOGETHER.

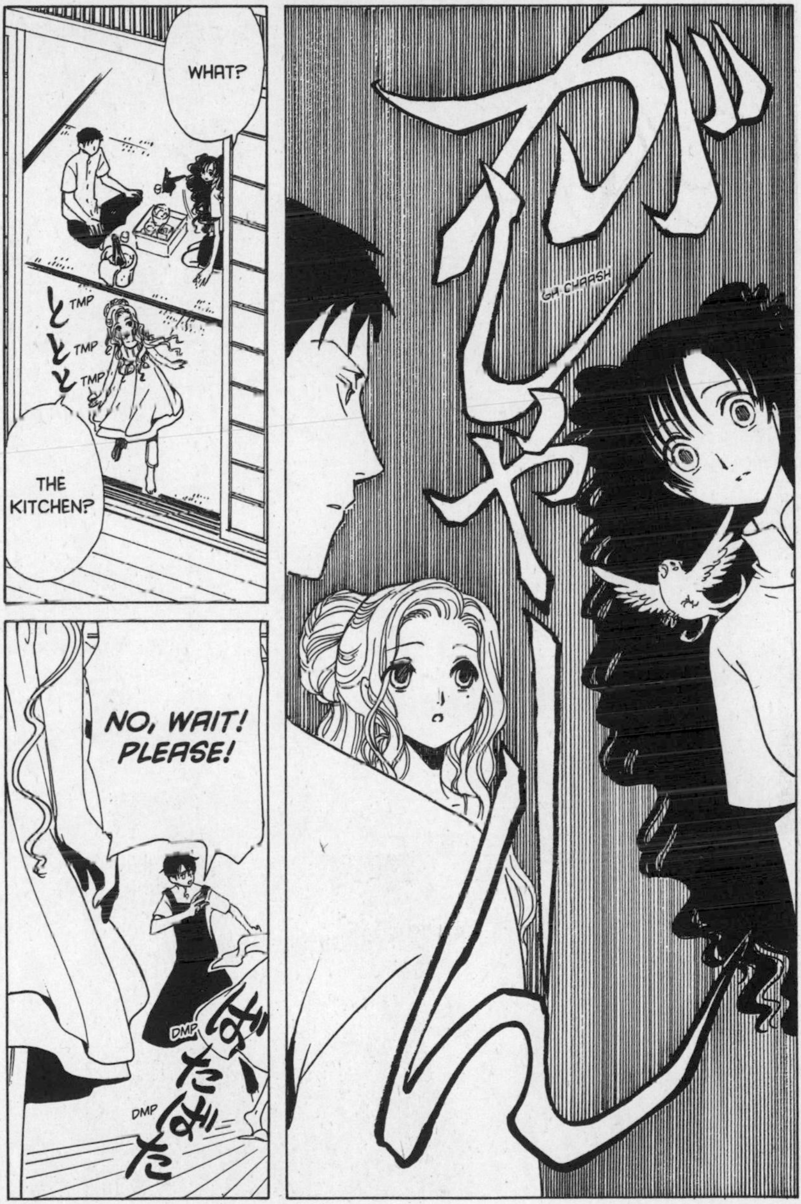
がしゃん
GA CHAASH
WHAT?
とととTMP TMP TMP
THE KITCHEN?
NO, WAIT! PLEASE!
ぱたぱた DMP DMP

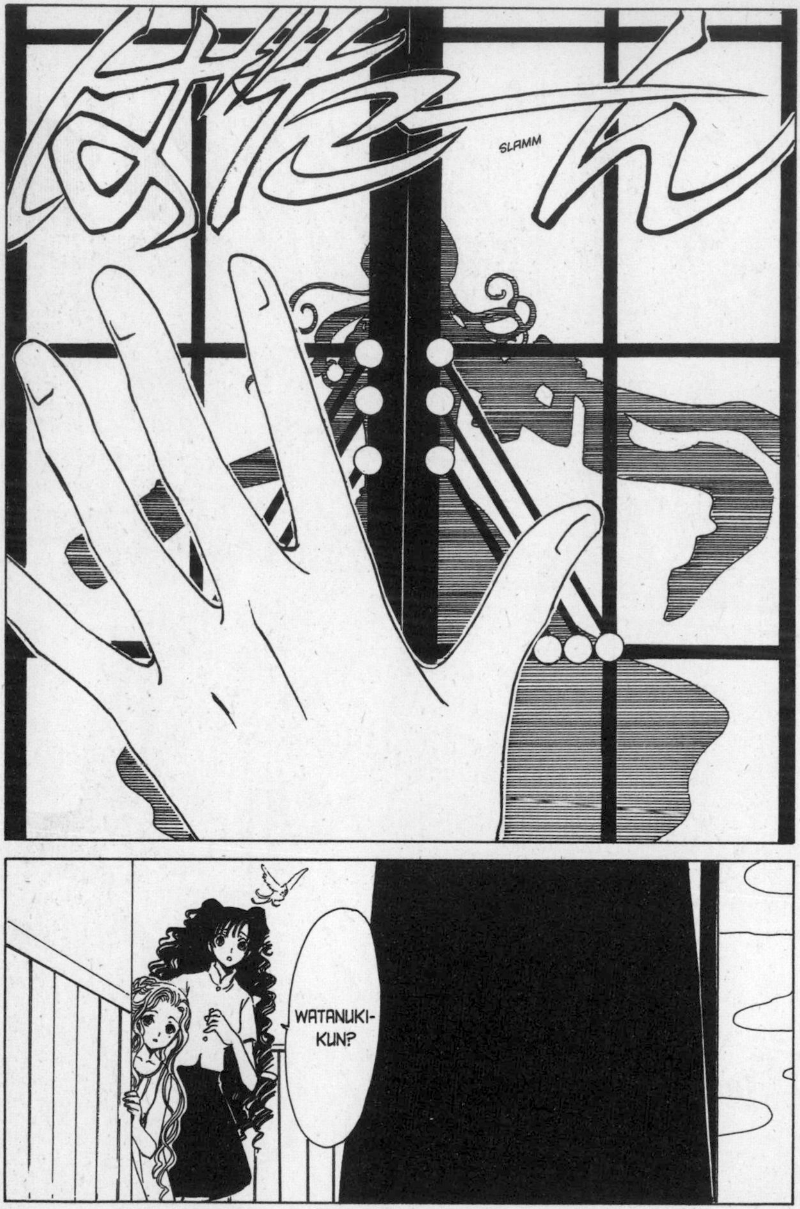
SLAMM
WATANUKI-KUN?

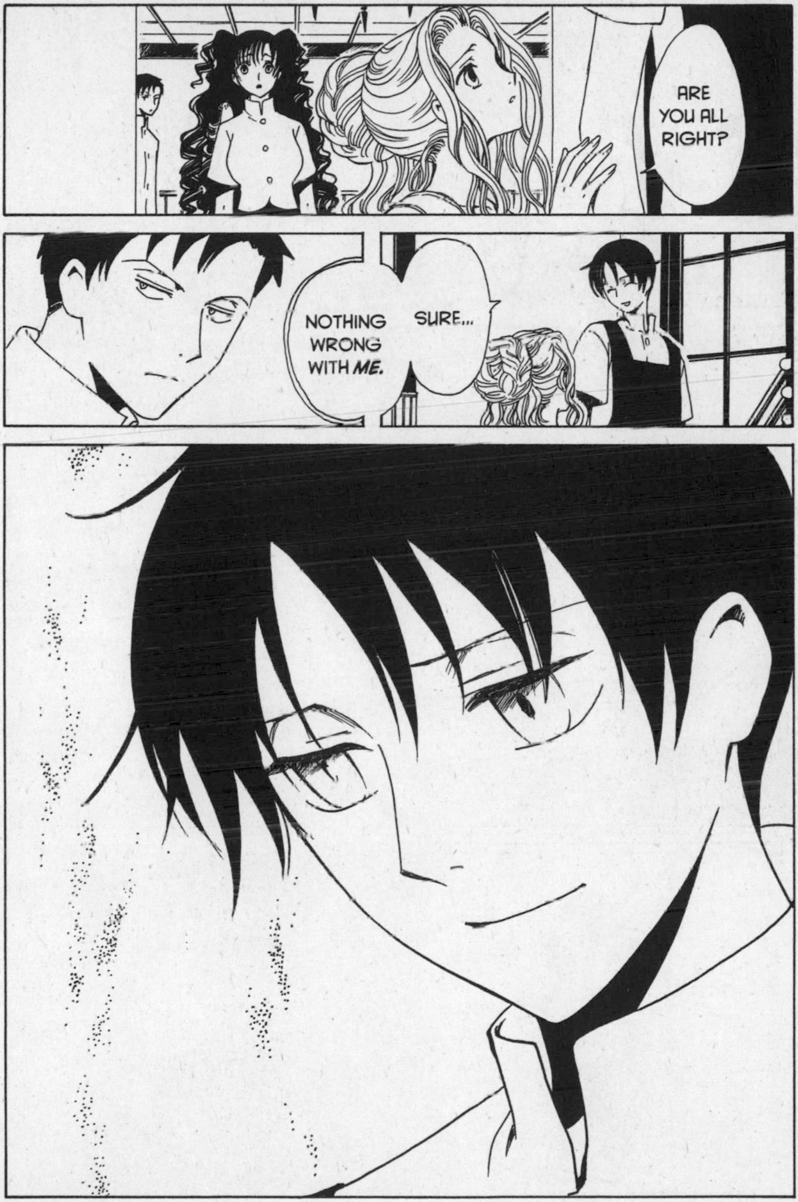
ARE YOU ALL RIGHT?
SURE...
NOTHING WRONG WITH *ME.*

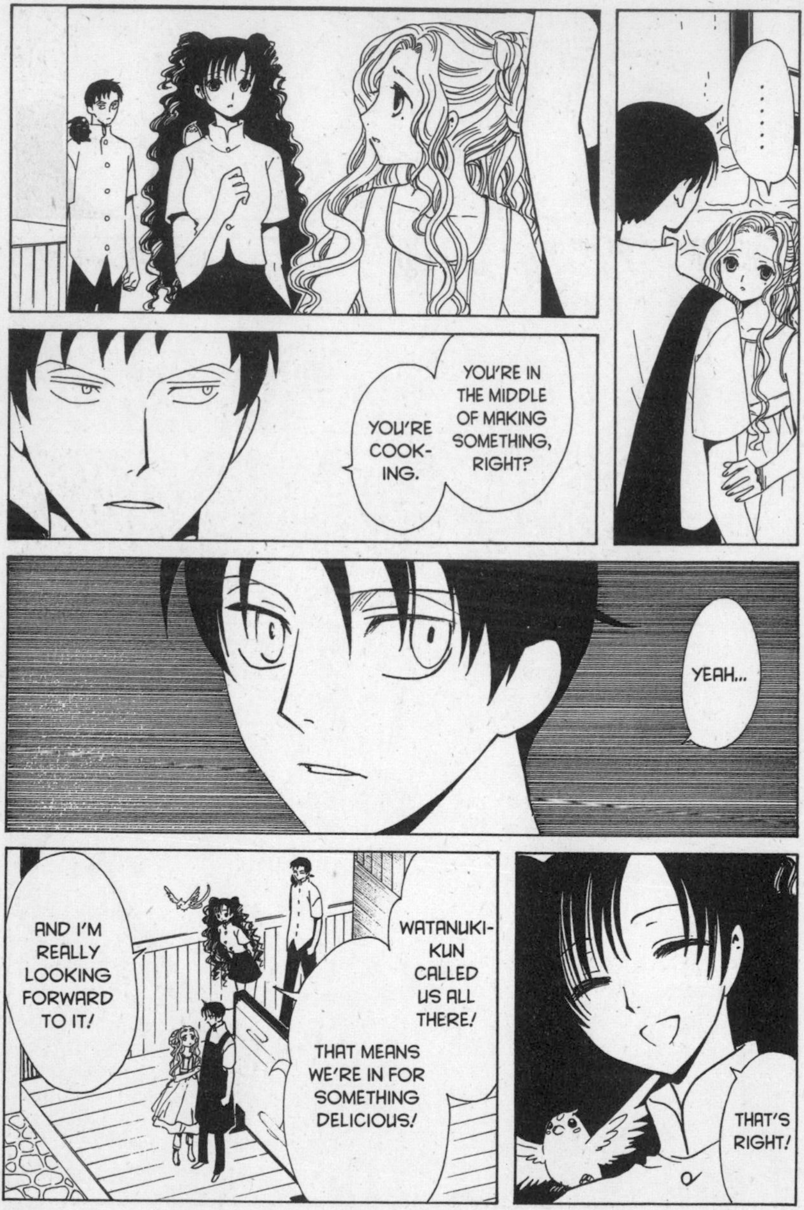
......
YOU'RE IN THE MIDDLE OF MAKING SOMETHING, RIGHT?
YOU'RE COOKING.
YEAH...
THAT'S RIGHT!
WATANUKI-KUN CALLED US ALL THERE!
THAT MEANS WE'RE IN FOR SOMETHING DELICIOUS!
AND I'M REALLY LOOKING FORWARD TO IT!

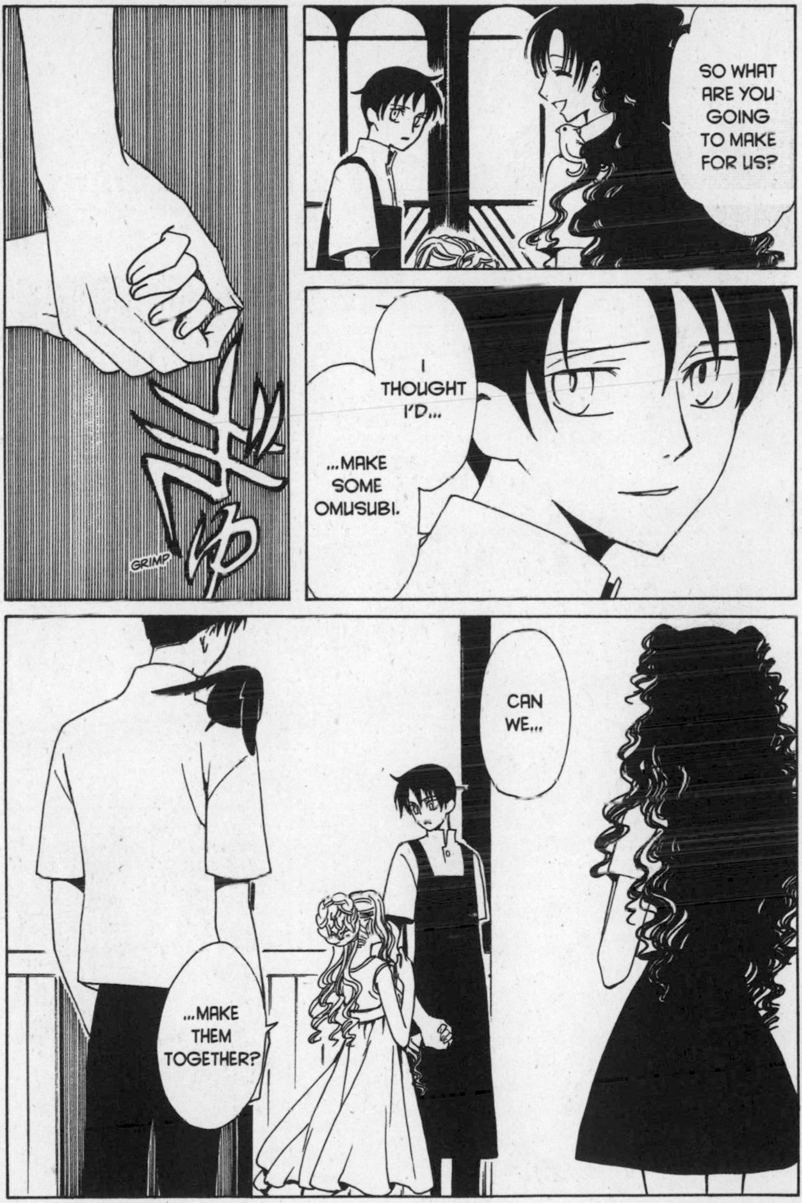
SO WHAT ARE YOU GOING TO MAKE FOR US?
I THOUGHT I'D...
...MAKE SOME OMUSUBI.
GRIMP
CAN WE...
...MAKE THEM TOGETHER?

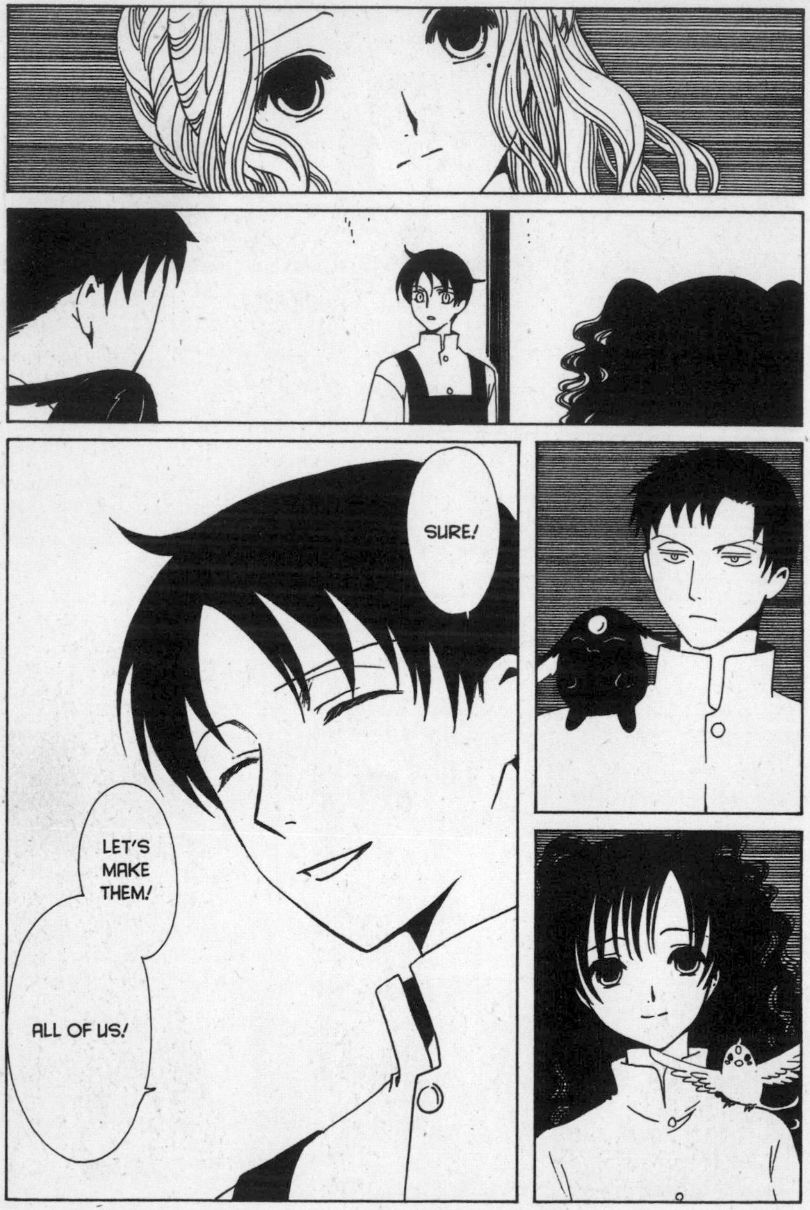
SURE!
LET'S MAKE THEM!
ALL OF US!

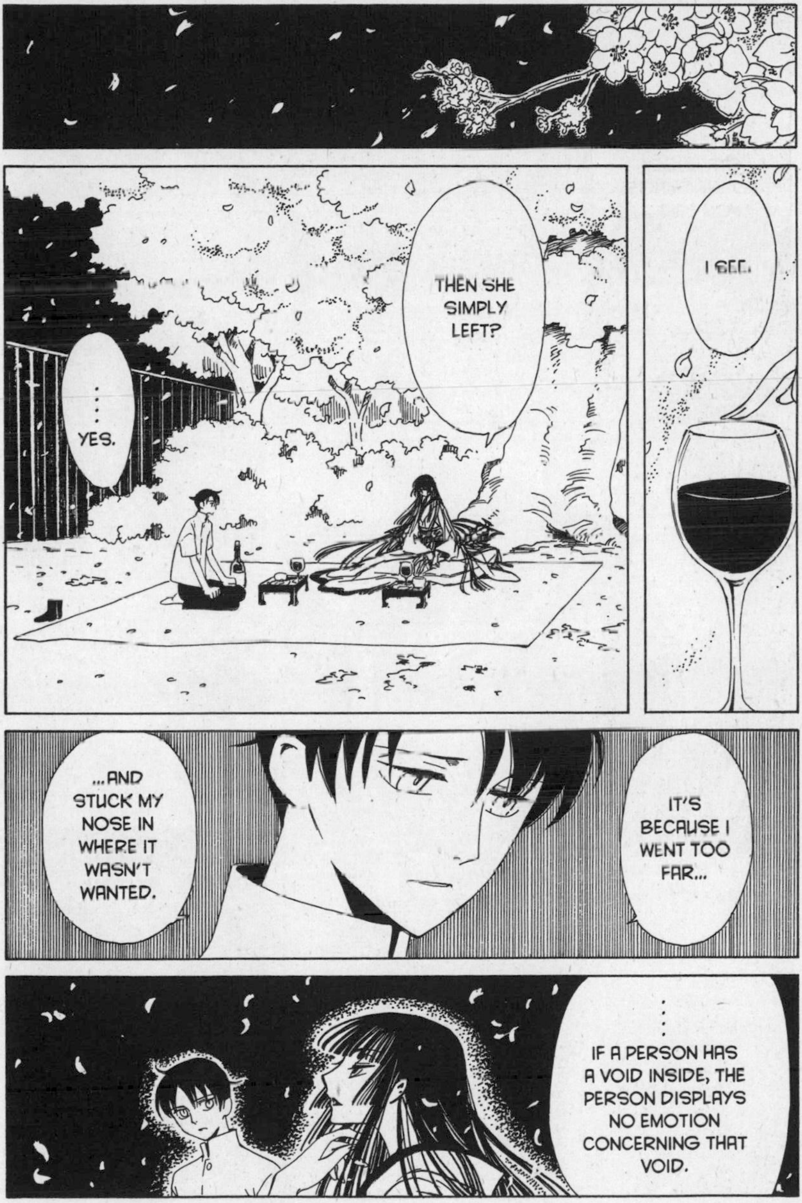
I SEE.
THEN SHE SIMPLY LEFT?
...YES.
IT'S BECAUSE I WENT TOO FAR...
...AND STUCK MY NOSE IN WHERE IT WASN'T WANTED.
... IF A PERSON HAS A VOID INSIDE, THE PERSON DISPLAYS NO EMOTION CONCERNING THAT VOID.

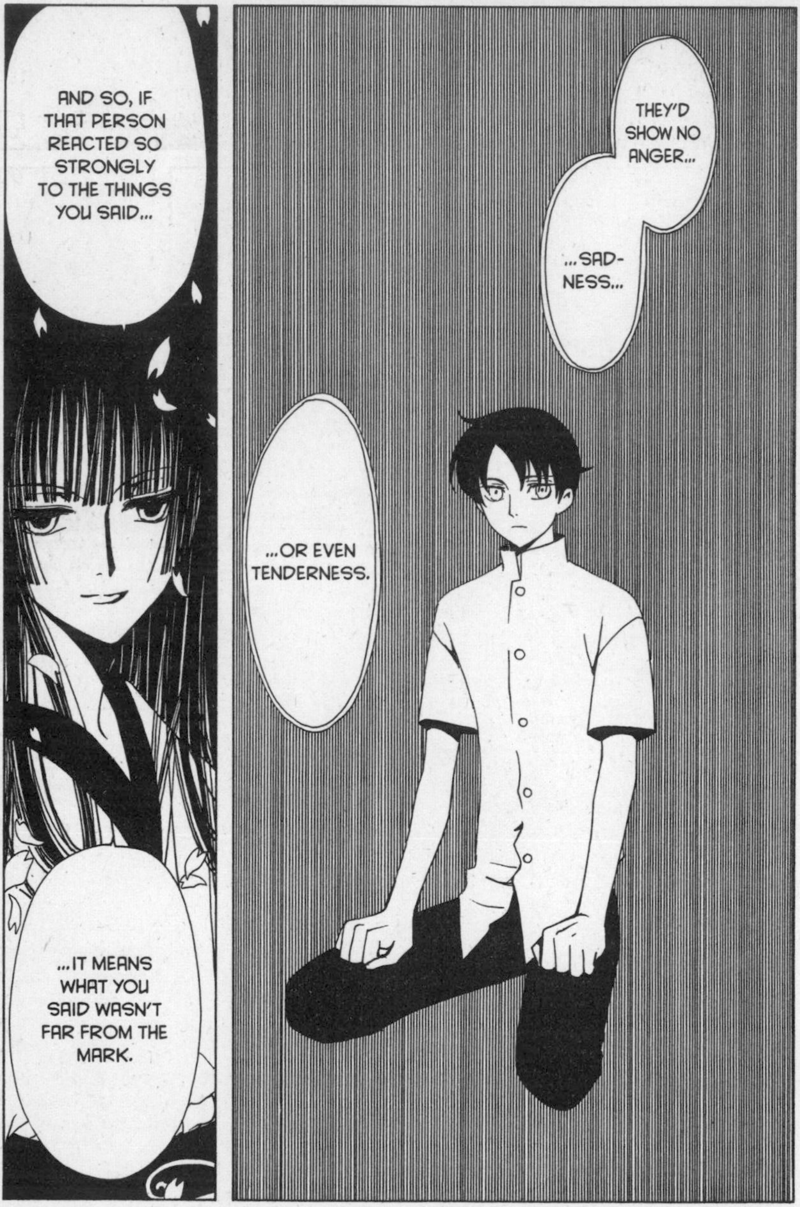
THEY'D SHOW NO ANGER...
...SAD-NESS...
...OR EVEN TENDERNESS.
AND SO, IF THAT PERSON REACTED SO STRONGLY TO THE THINGS YOU SAID...
...IT MEANS WHAT YOU SAID WASN'T FAR FROM THE MARK.

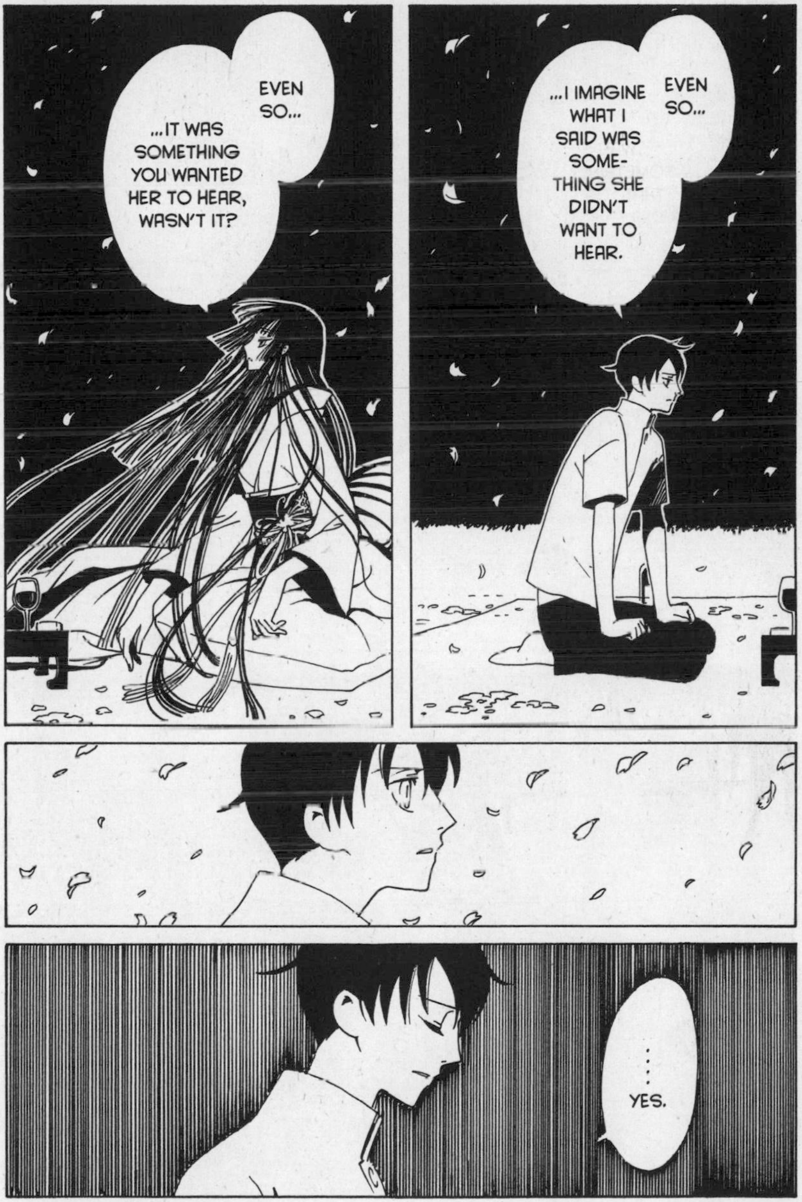
EVEN SO... ...I IMAGINE WHAT I SAID WAS SOME-THING SHE DIDN'T WANT TO HEAR.
EVEN SO... ...IT WAS SOMETHING YOU WANTED HER TO HEAR, WASN'T IT?
.... YES.

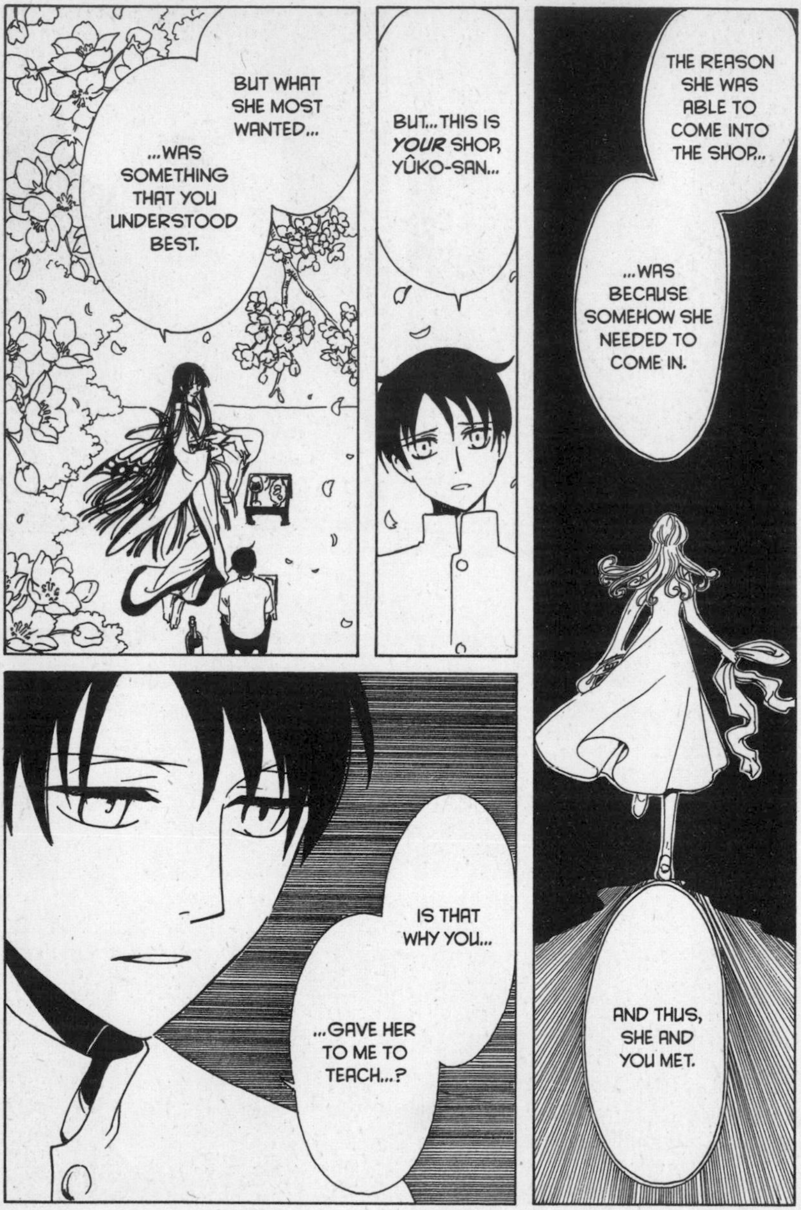
THE REASON SHE WAS ABLE TO COME INTO THE SHOP...
...WAS BECAUSE SOMEHOW SHE NEEDED TO COME IN.
AND THUS, SHE AND YOU MET.
BUT...THIS IS *YOUR* SHOP, YÛKO-SAN...
BUT WHAT SHE MOST WANTED...
...WAS SOMETHING THAT YOU UNDERSTOOD BEST.
IS THAT WHY YOU...
...GAVE HER TO ME TO TEACH...?

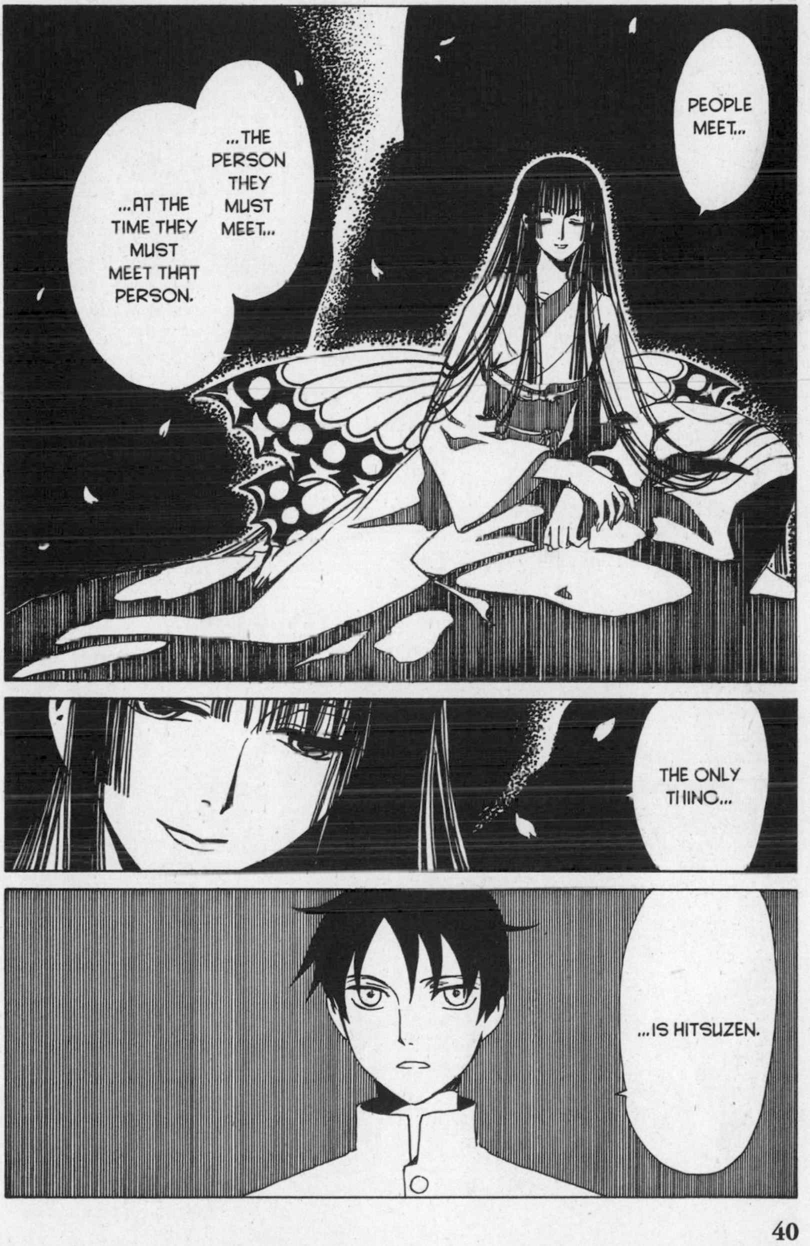
PEOPLE MEET...
...THE PERSON THEY MUST MEET...
...AT THE TIME THEY MUST MEET THAT PERSON.
THE ONLY THING...
...IS HITSUZEN.

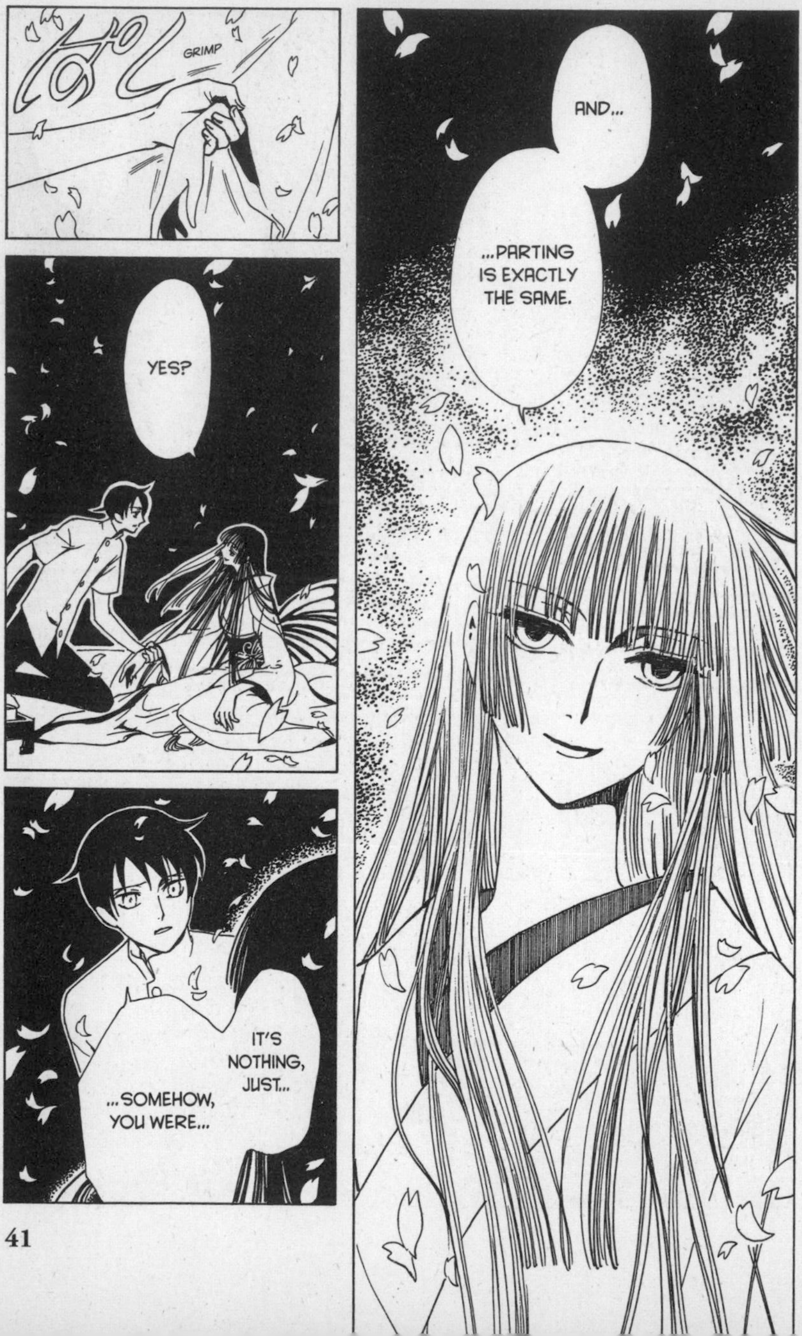
AND...
...PARTING IS EXACTLY THE SAME.
GRIMP
YES?
IT'S NOTHING, JUST...
...SOMEHOW, YOU WERE...

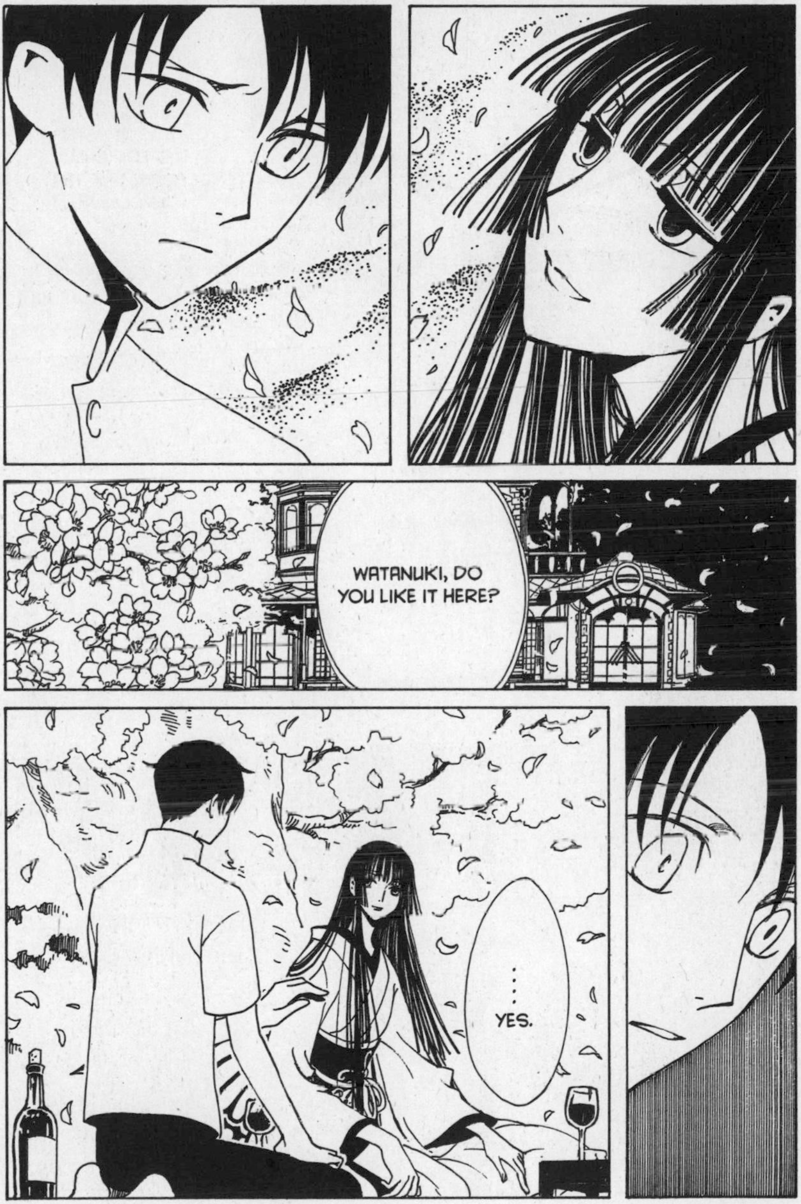
WATANUKI, DO YOU LIKE IT HERE?
... YES.

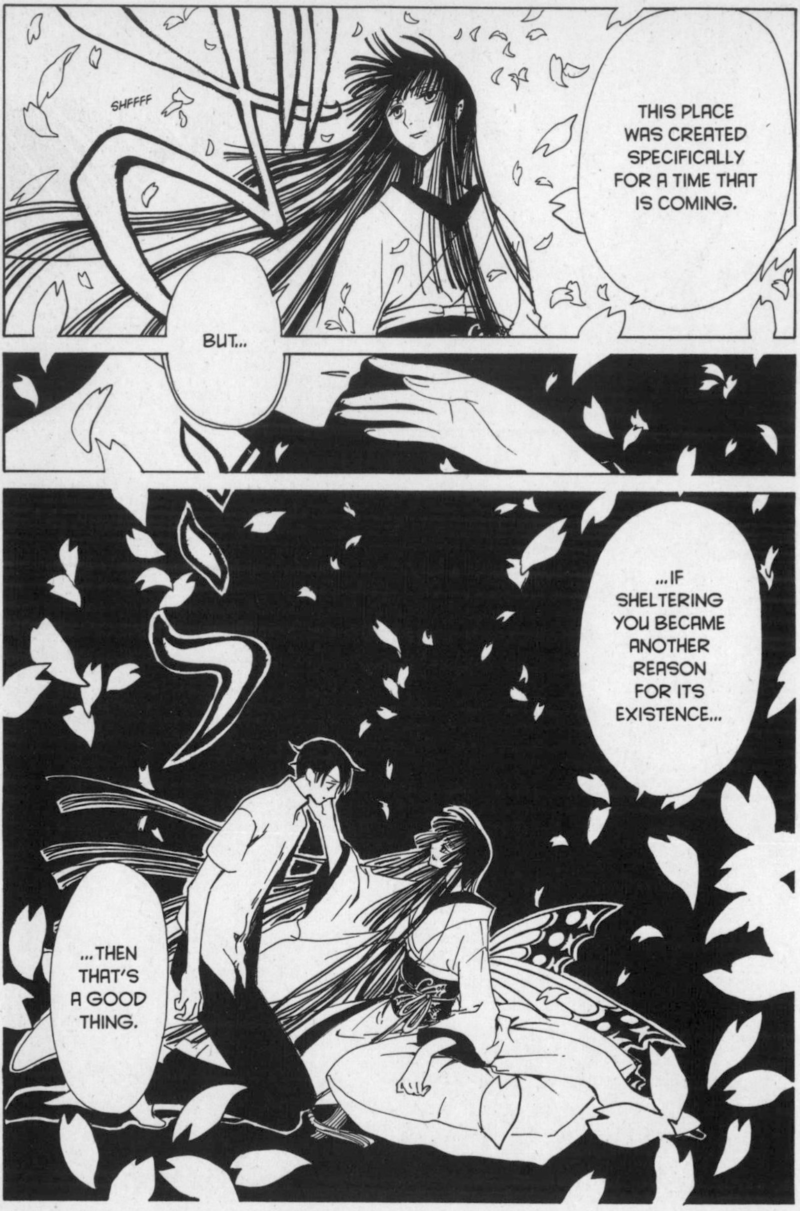
THIS PLACE WAS CREATED SPECIFICALLY FOR A TIME THAT IS COMING.
SHFFFF
BUT...
...IF SHELTERING YOU BECAME ANOTHER REASON FOR ITS EXISTENCE...
...THEN THAT'S A GOOD THING.

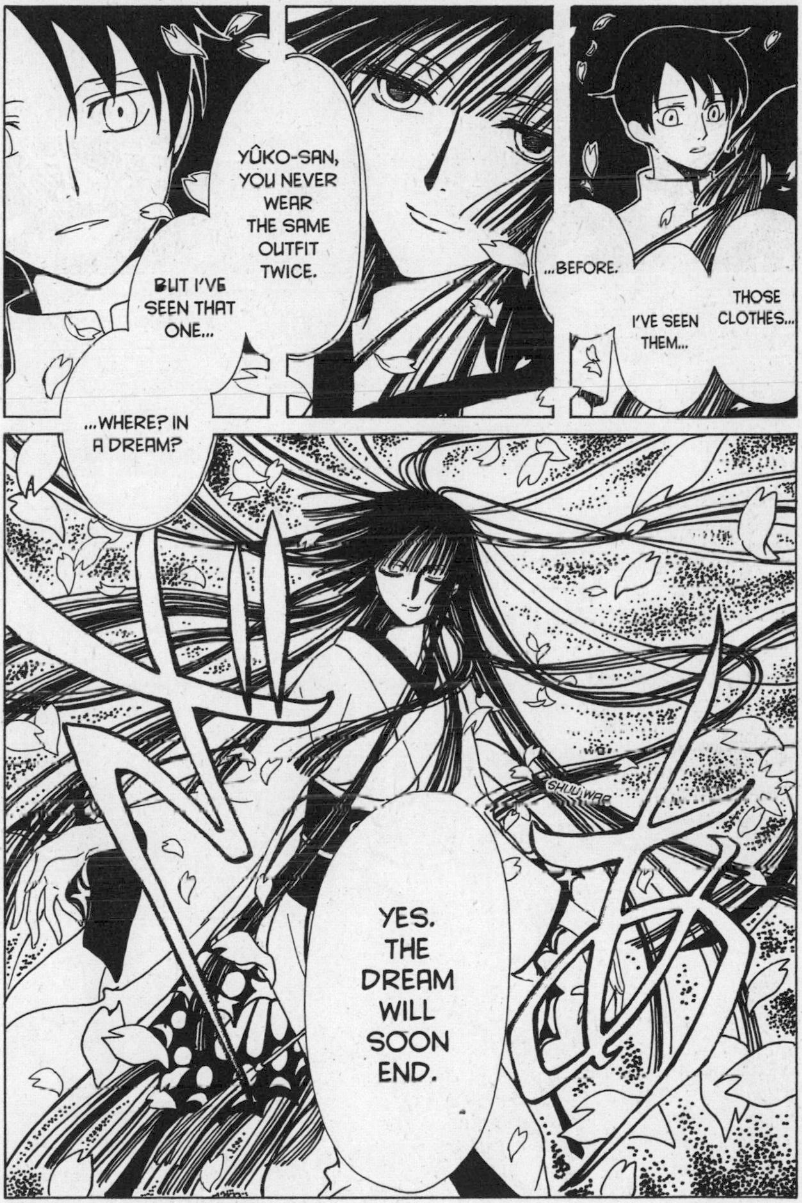
THOSE CLOTHES...
I'VE SEEN THEM...
...BEFORE.
YÛKO-SAN, YOU NEVER WEAR THE SAME OUTFIT TWICE.
BUT I'VE SEEN THAT ONE...
...WHERE? IN A DREAM?
SHUU WAA
YES. THE DREAM WILL SOON END.

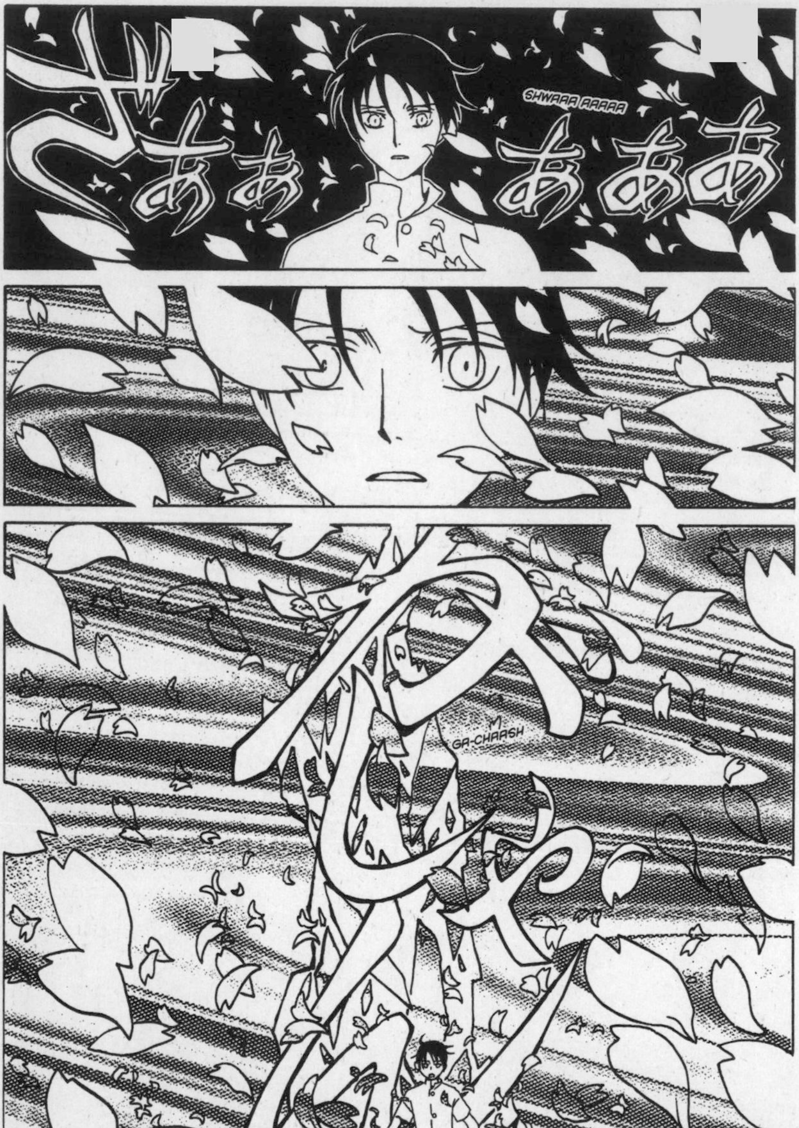
ざあああ
あああ
SHWAAA AAAAA
GA-CHAASH

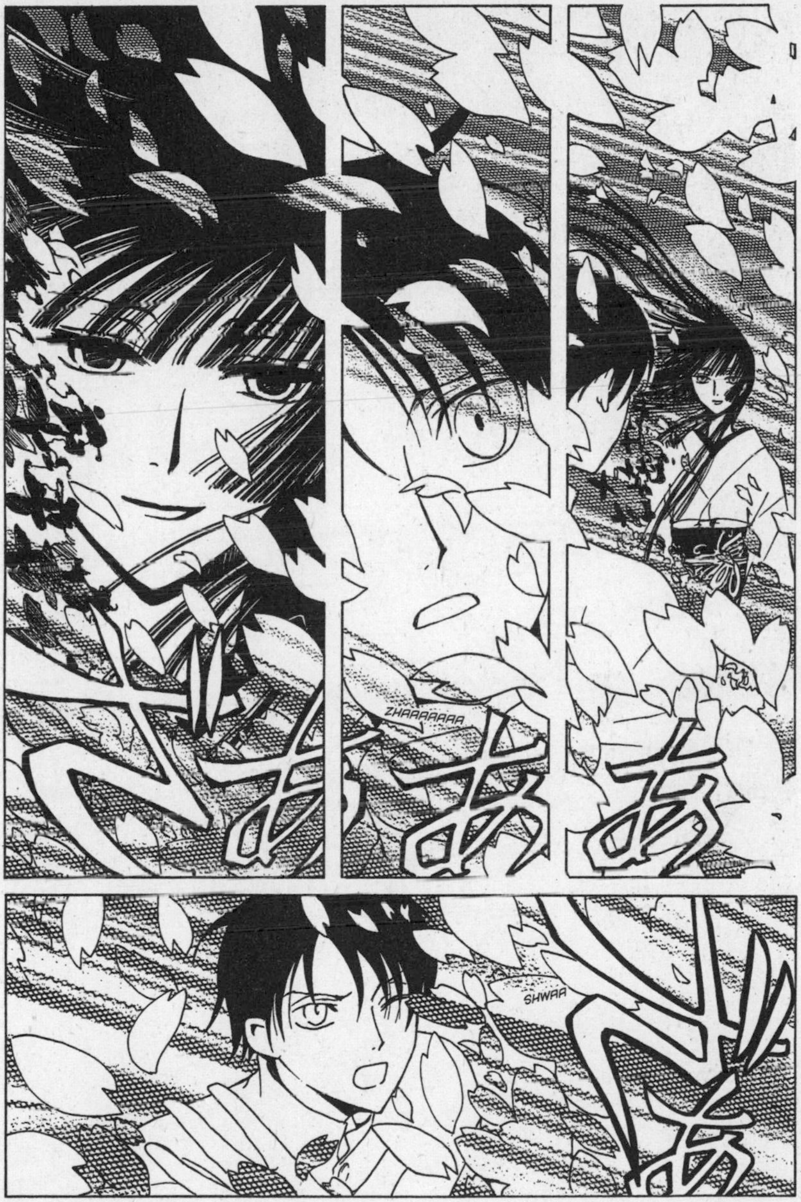

ZHAAAAAAAA
SHWAA

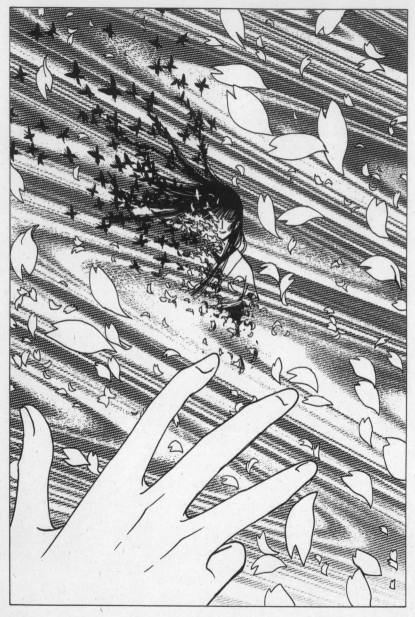

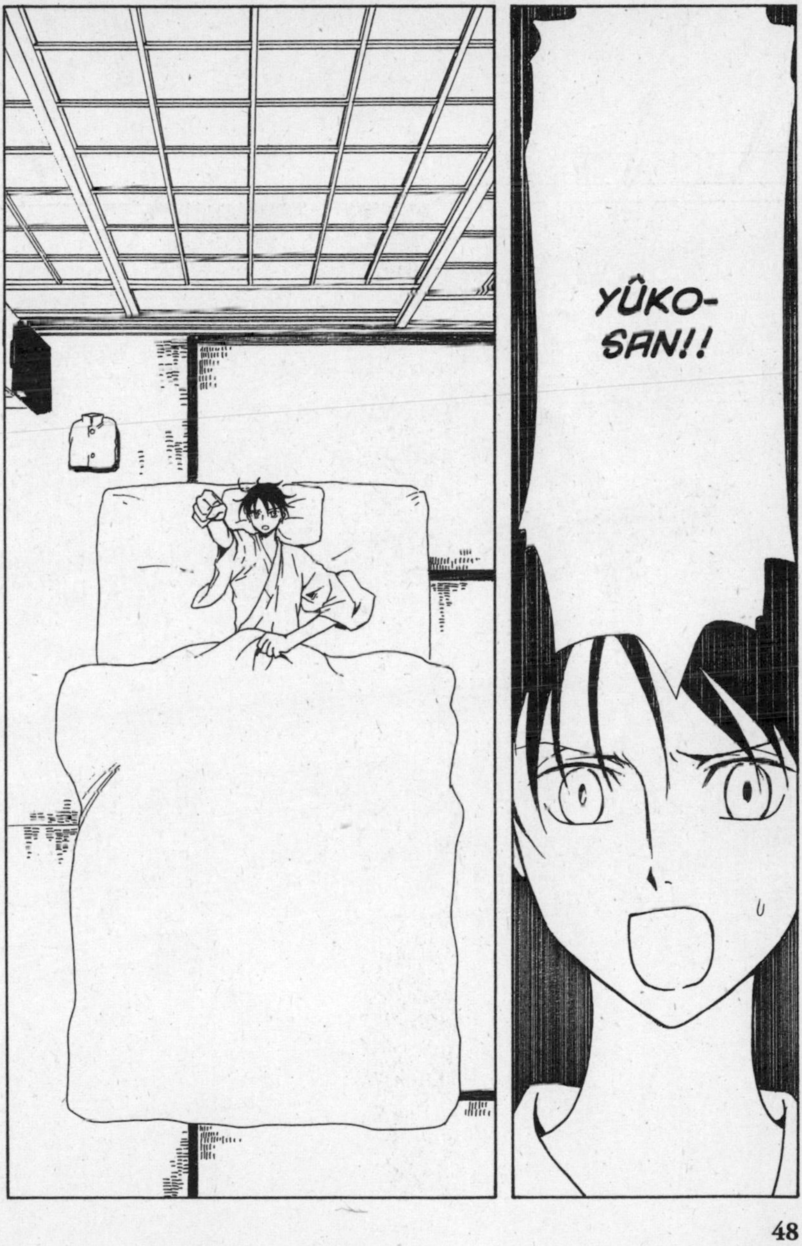
YÛKO-
SAN!!

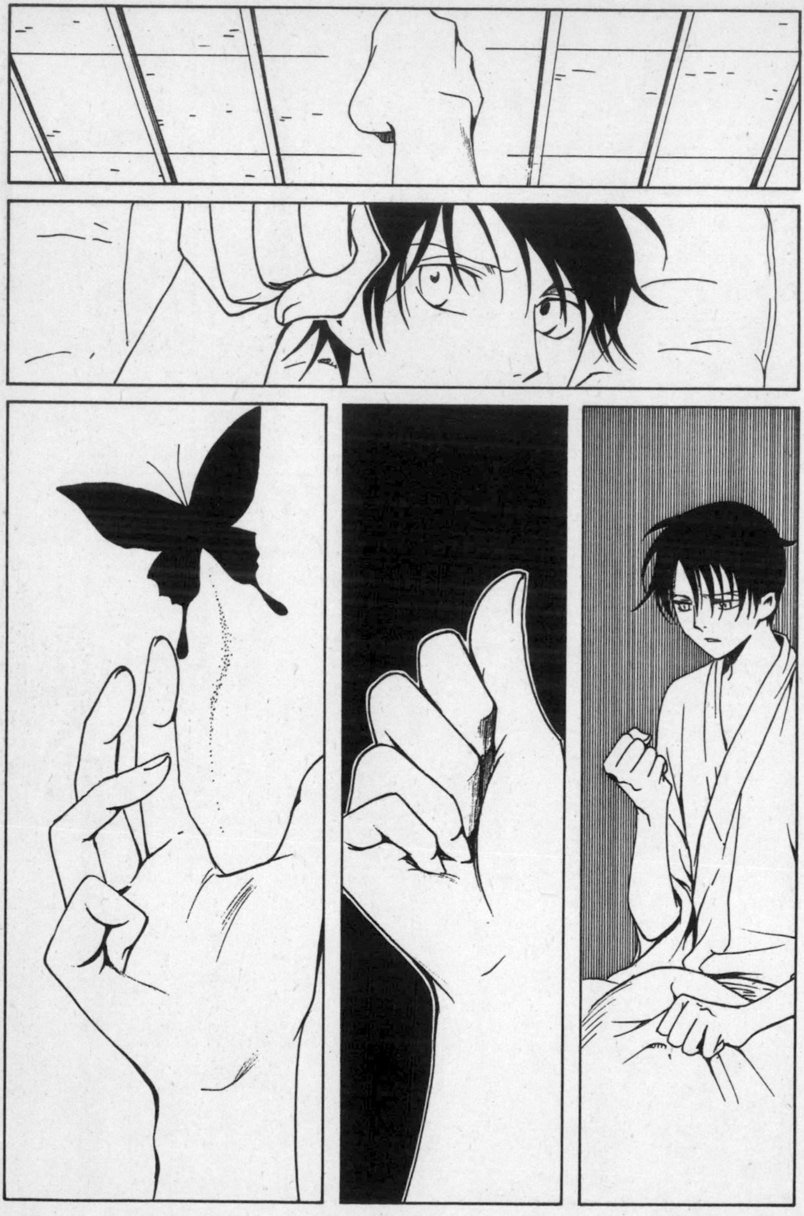

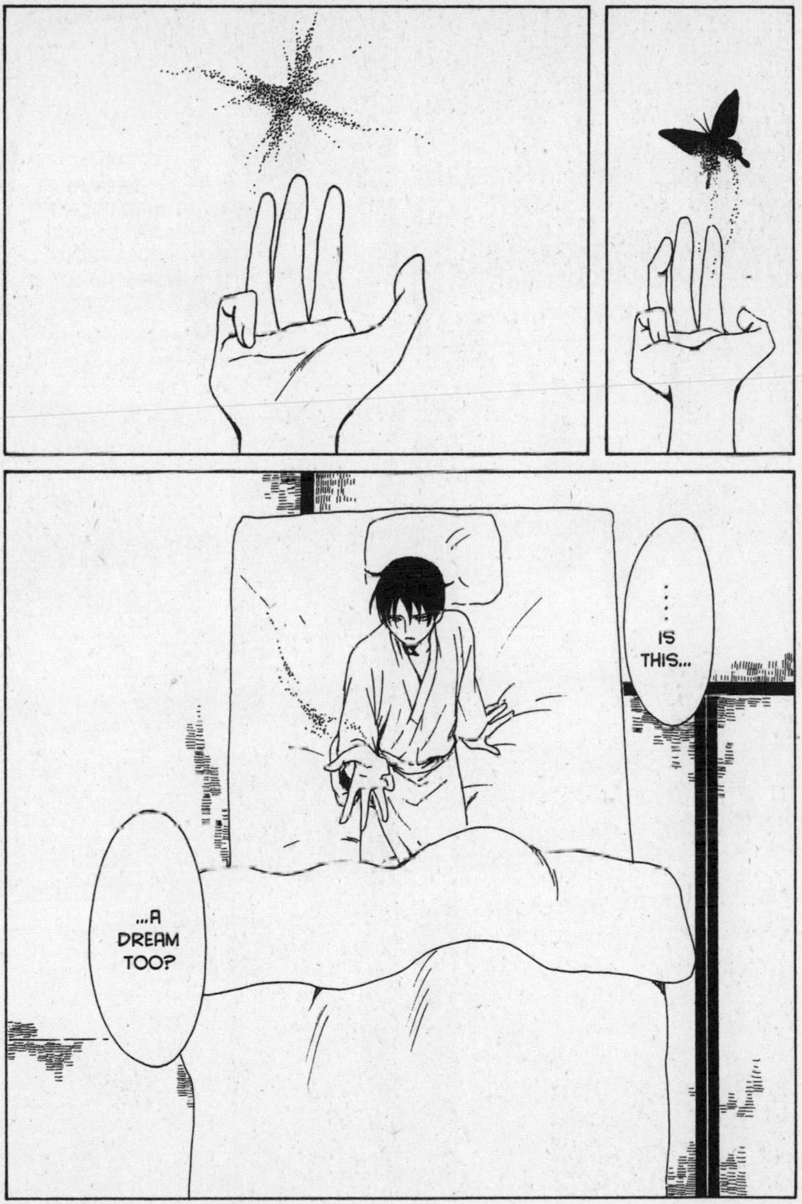
... IS THIS...
...A DREAM TOO?

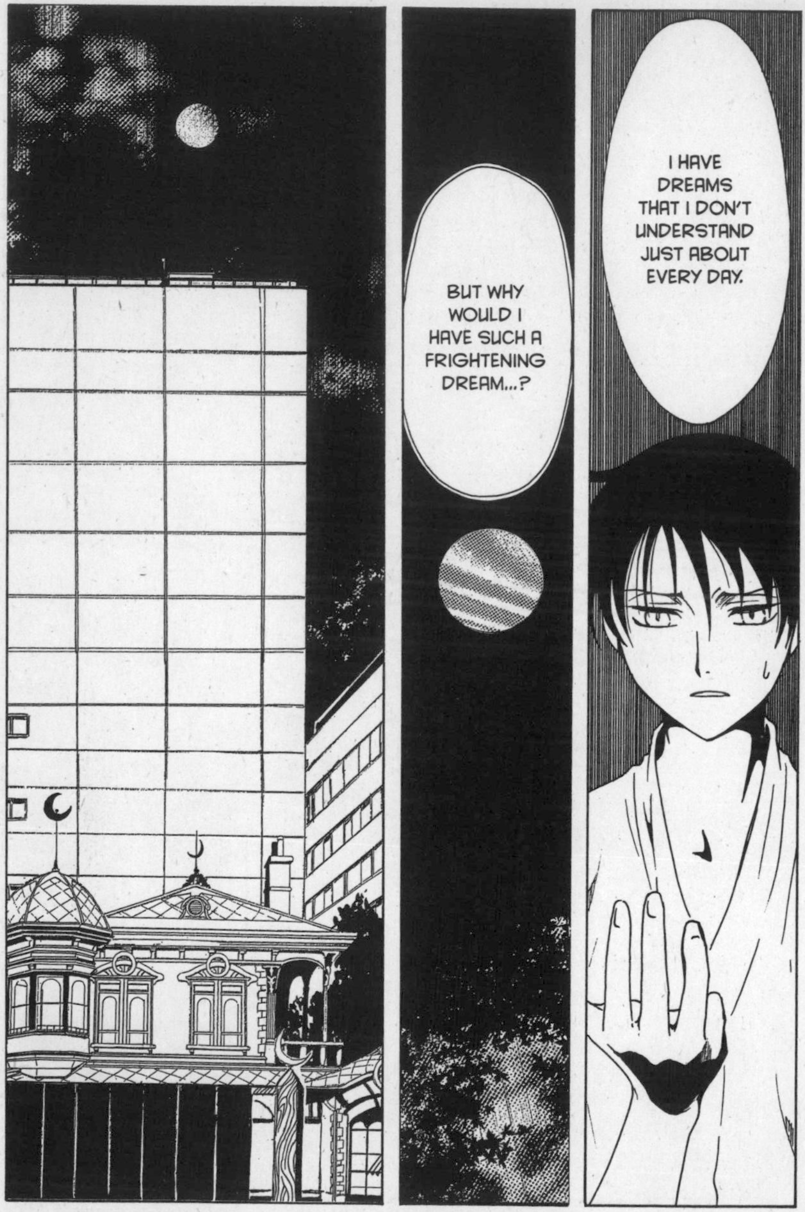
I HAVE DREAMS THAT I DON'T UNDERSTAND JUST ABOUT EVERY DAY.
BUT WHY WOULD I HAVE SUCH A FRIGHTENING DREAM...?

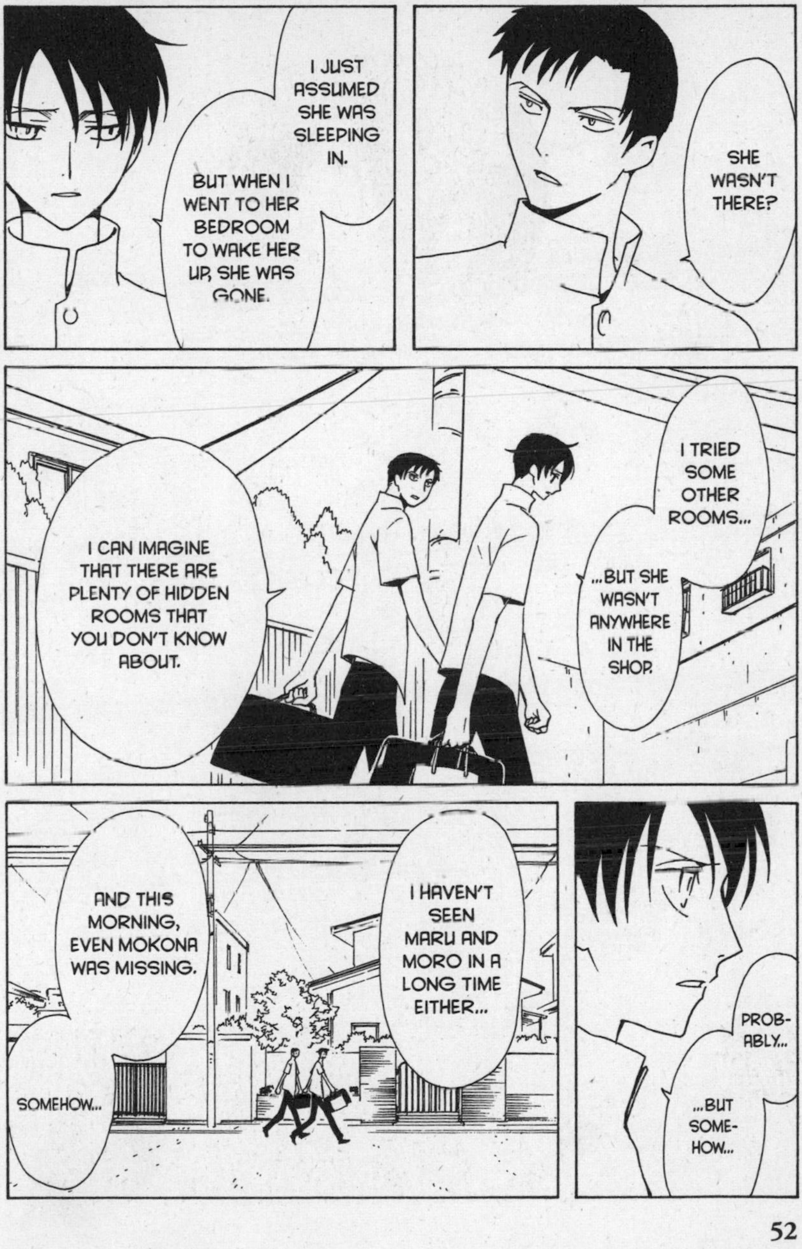
SHE WASN'T THERE?
I JUST ASSUMED SHE WAS SLEEPING IN.
BUT WHEN I WENT TO HER BEDROOM TO WAKE HER UP, SHE WAS GONE.
I TRIED SOME OTHER ROOMS...
...BUT SHE WASN'T ANYWHERE IN THE SHOP.
I CAN IMAGINE THAT THERE ARE PLENTY OF HIDDEN ROOMS THAT YOU DON'T KNOW ABOUT.
PROB-ABLY...
...BUT SOME-HOW...
I HAVEN'T SEEN MARU AND MORO IN A LONG TIME EITHER...
AND THIS MORNING, EVEN MOKONA WAS MISSING.
SOMEHOW...

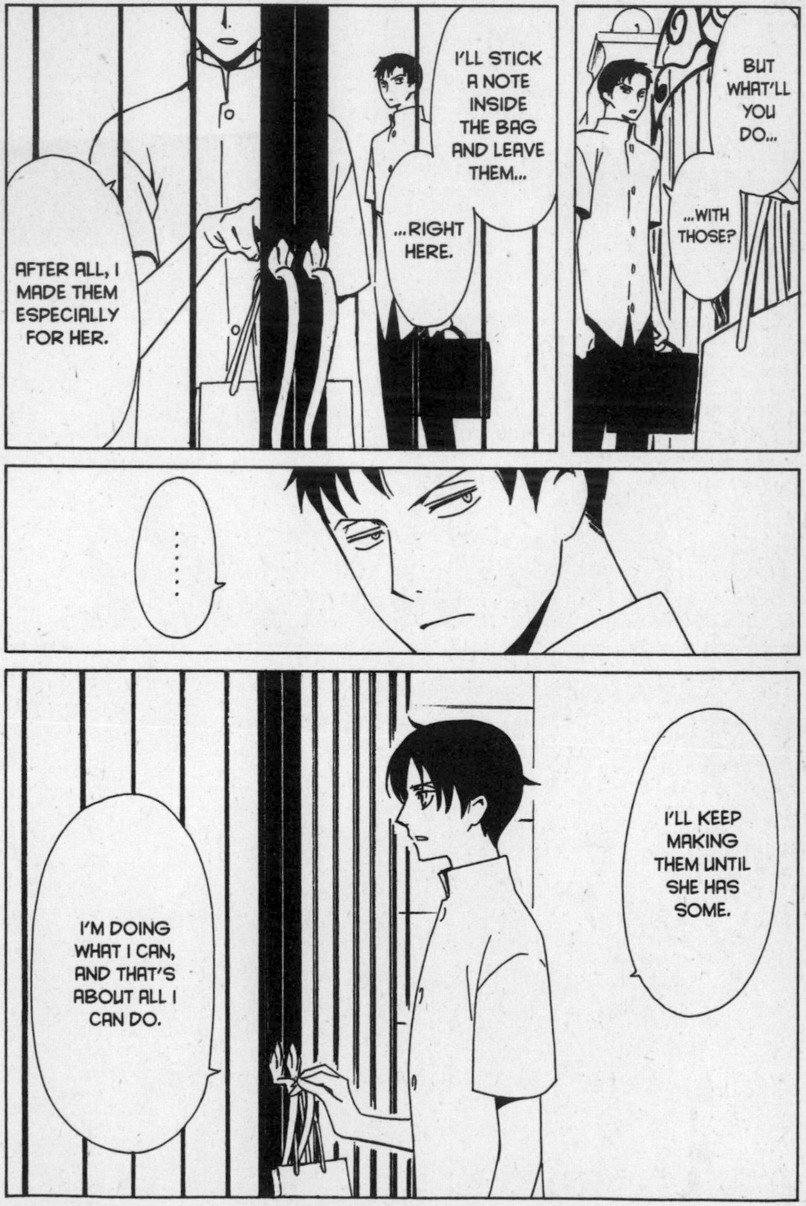
BUT WHAT'LL YOU DO...
...WITH THOSE?
I'LL STICK A NOTE INSIDE THE BAG AND LEAVE THEM...
...RIGHT HERE.
AFTER ALL, I MADE THEM ESPECIALLY FOR HER.
......
I'LL KEEP MAKING THEM UNTIL SHE HAS SOME.
I'M DOING WHAT I CAN, AND THAT'S ABOUT ALL I CAN DO.

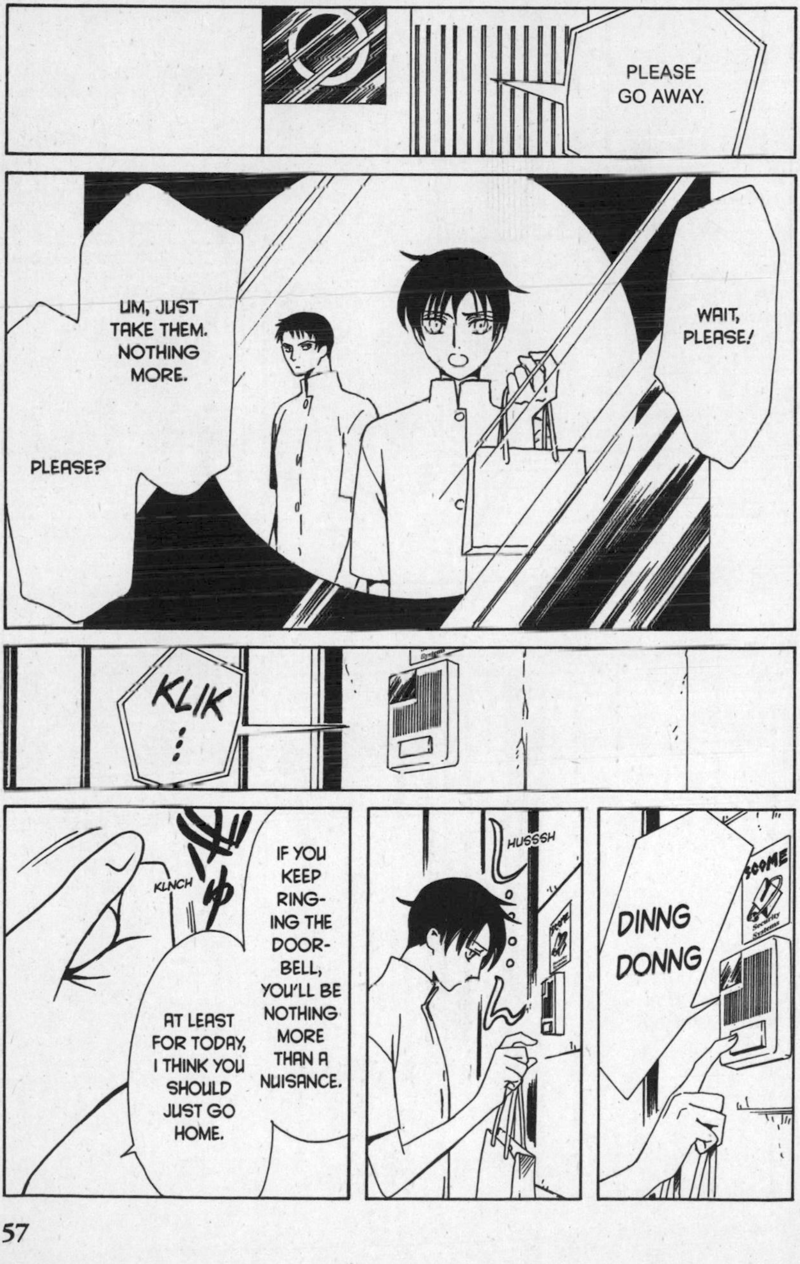
PLEASE GO AWAY.
WAIT, PLEASE!
UM, JUST TAKE THEM. NOTHING MORE.
PLEASE?
KLIK
DINNG DONNG
HUSSSH
KLNCH
IF YOU KEEP RING-ING THE DOOR-BELL, YOU'LL BE NOTHING MORE THAN A NUISANCE.
AT LEAST FOR TODAY, I THINK YOU SHOULD JUST GO HOME.

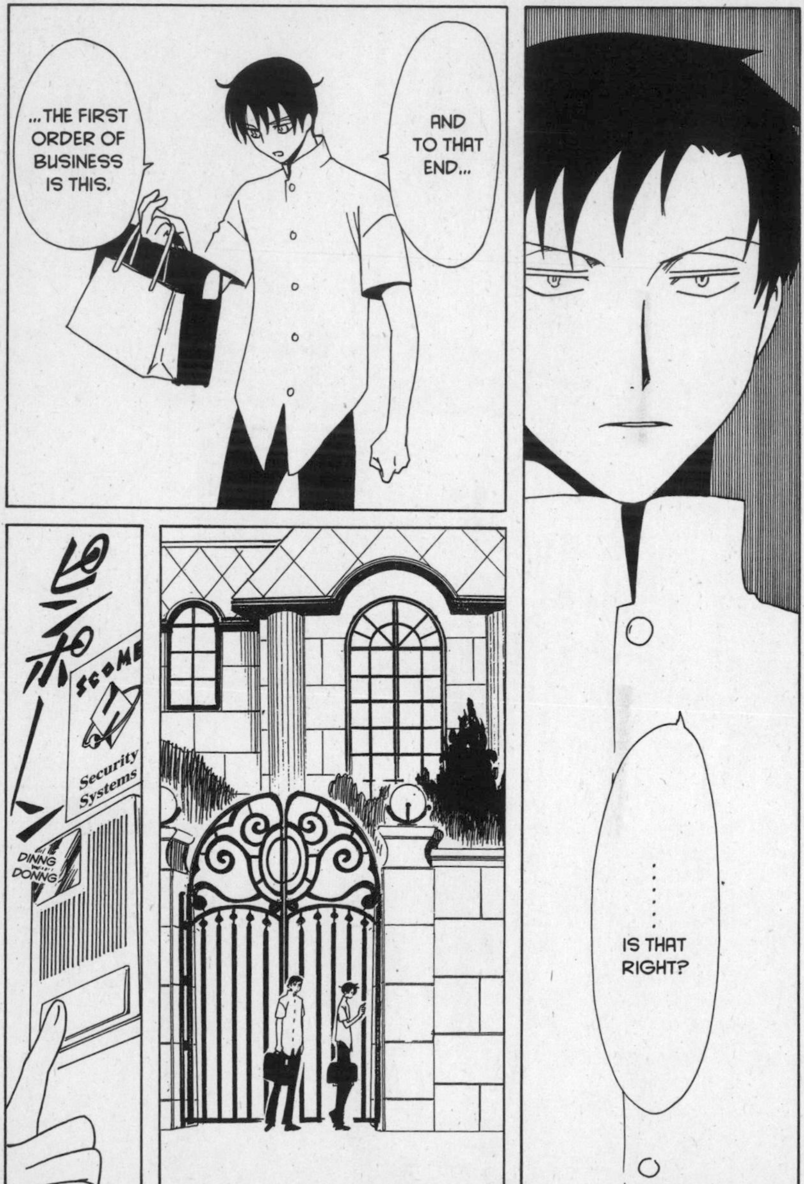
......
IS THAT RIGHT?
AND TO THAT END...
...THE FIRST ORDER OF BUSINESS IS THIS.
ピンポーン
DINNG DONNG
Security Systems

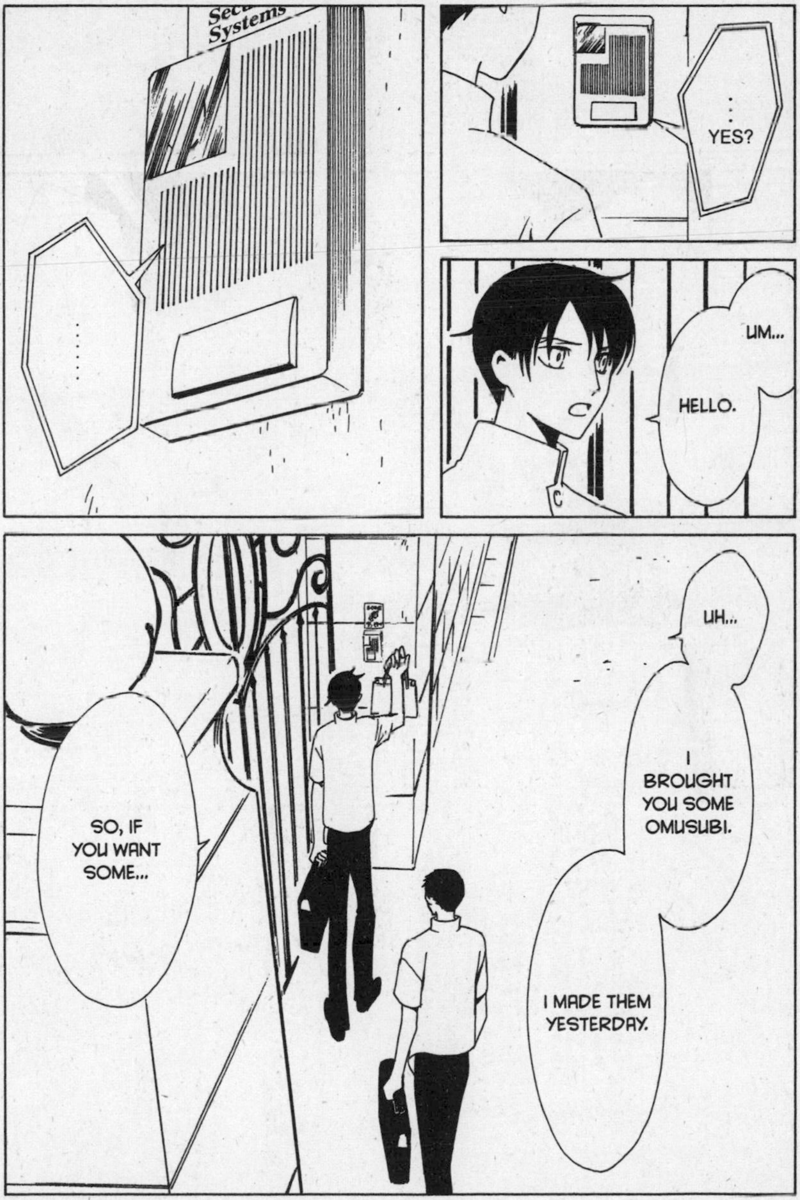
Systems
...YES?
UM...
HELLO.
......
UH...
I BROUGHT YOU SOME OMUSUBI.
I MADE THEM YESTERDAY.
SO, IF YOU WANT SOME...

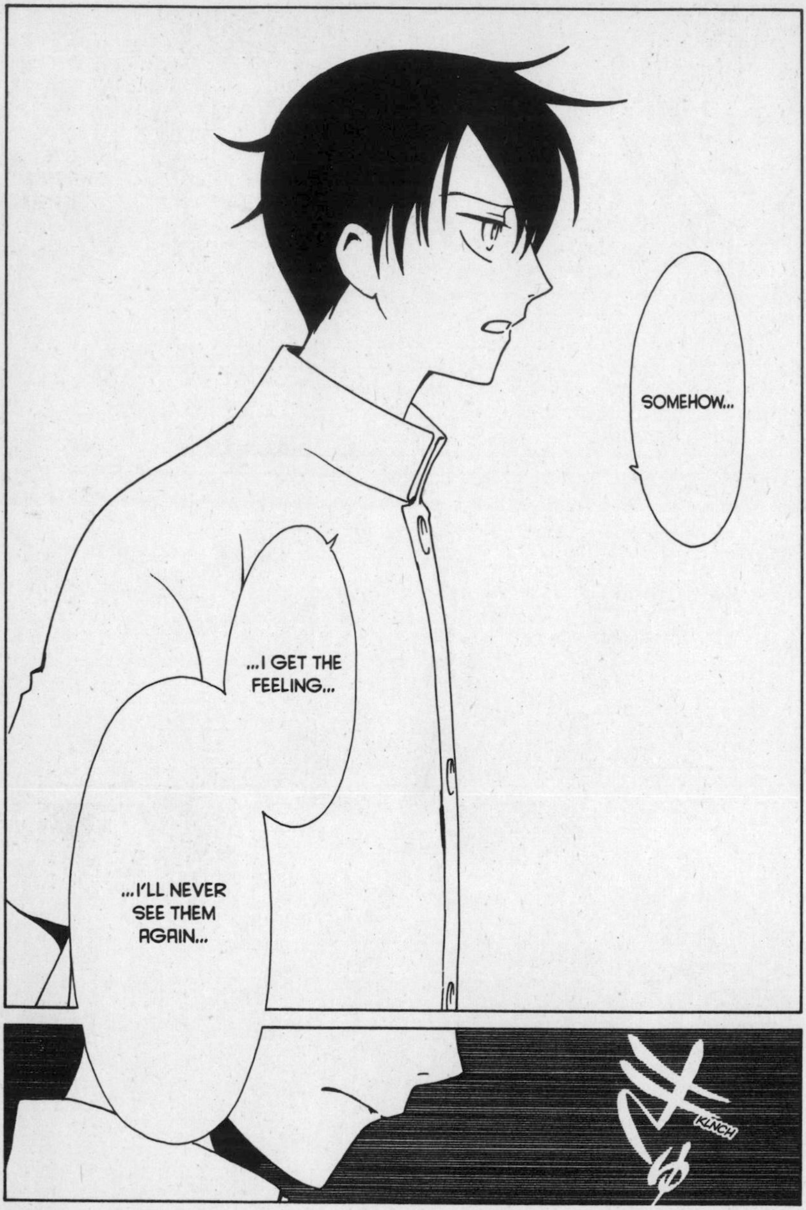
SOMEHOW...
...I GET THE FEELING...
...I'LL NEVER SEE THEM AGAIN...
KLNCH

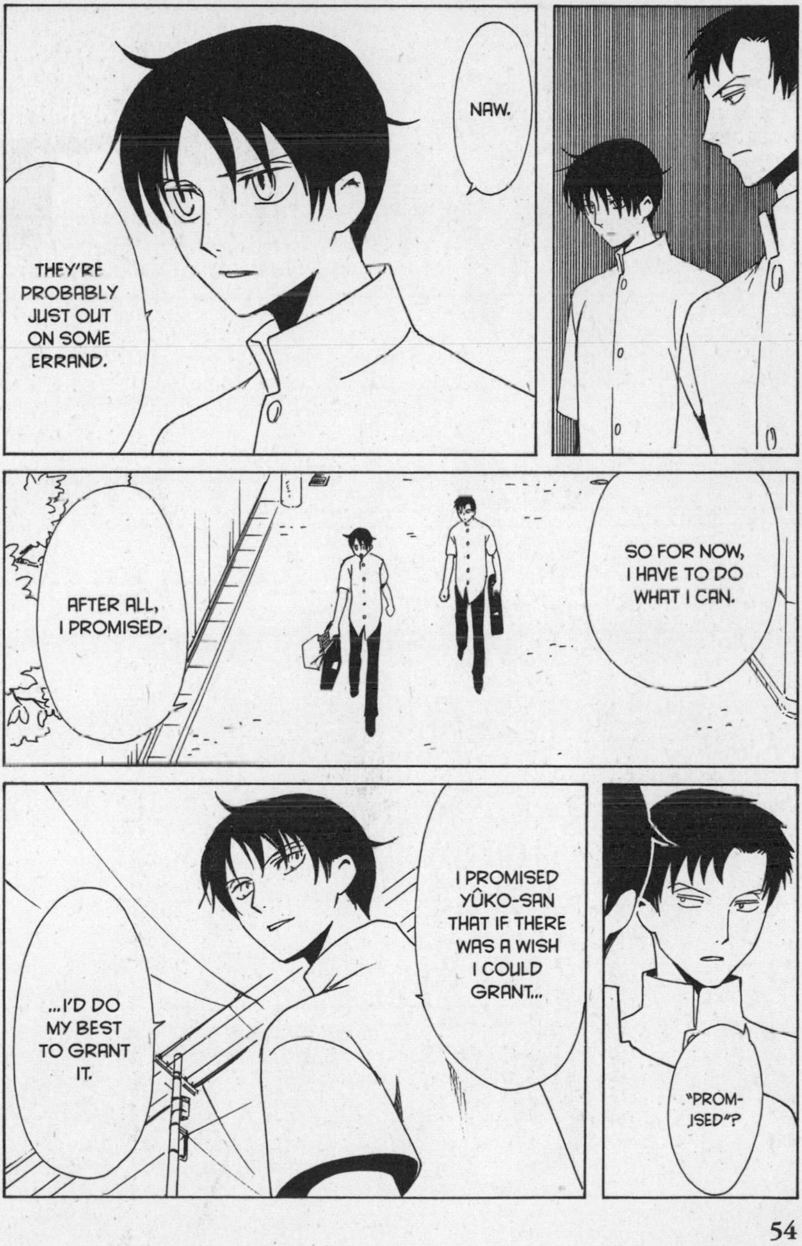
NAW.
THEY'RE PROBABLY JUST OUT ON SOME ERRAND.
SO FOR NOW, I HAVE TO DO WHAT I CAN.
AFTER ALL, I PROMISED.
"PROM-ISED"?
I PROMISED YÛKO-SAN THAT IF THERE WAS A WISH I COULD GRANT...
...I'D DO MY BEST TO GRANT IT.

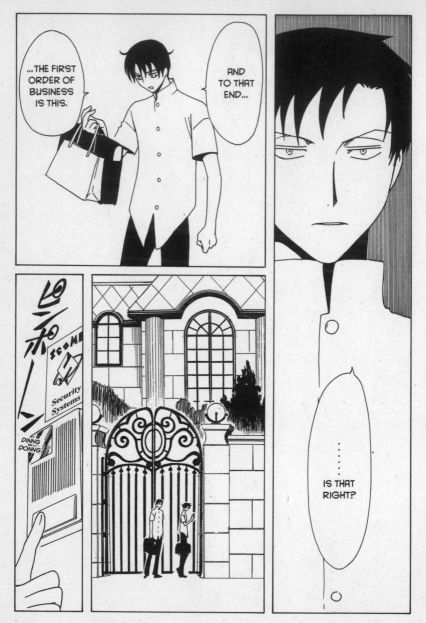

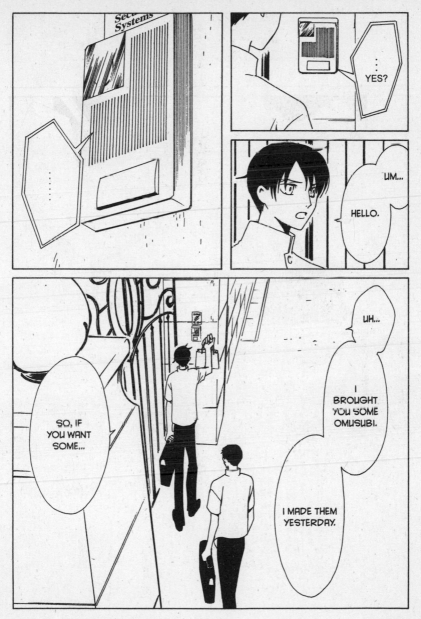

Secu
Systems

......

: ...
YES?

UM...

HELLO.

UH...

I
BROUGHT
YOU SOME
OMUSUBI.

SO, IF
YOU WANT
SOME...

I MADE THEM
YESTERDAY.

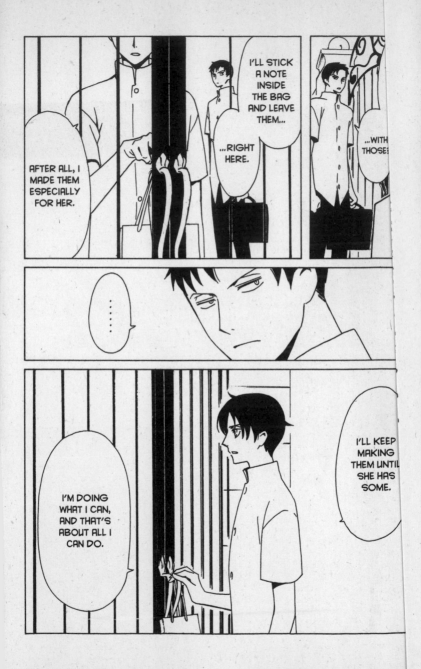

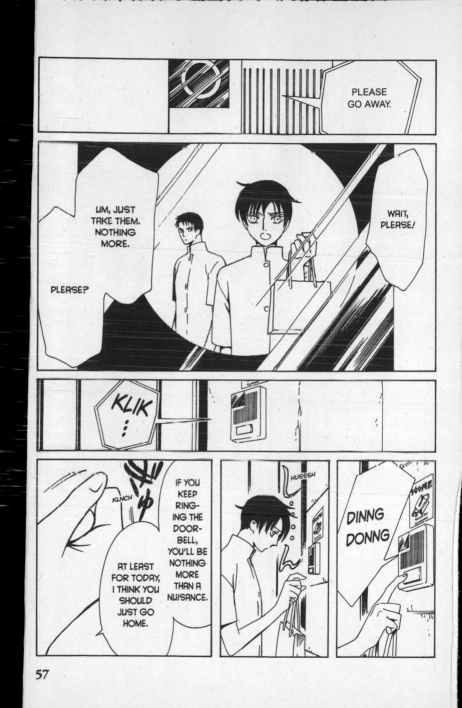

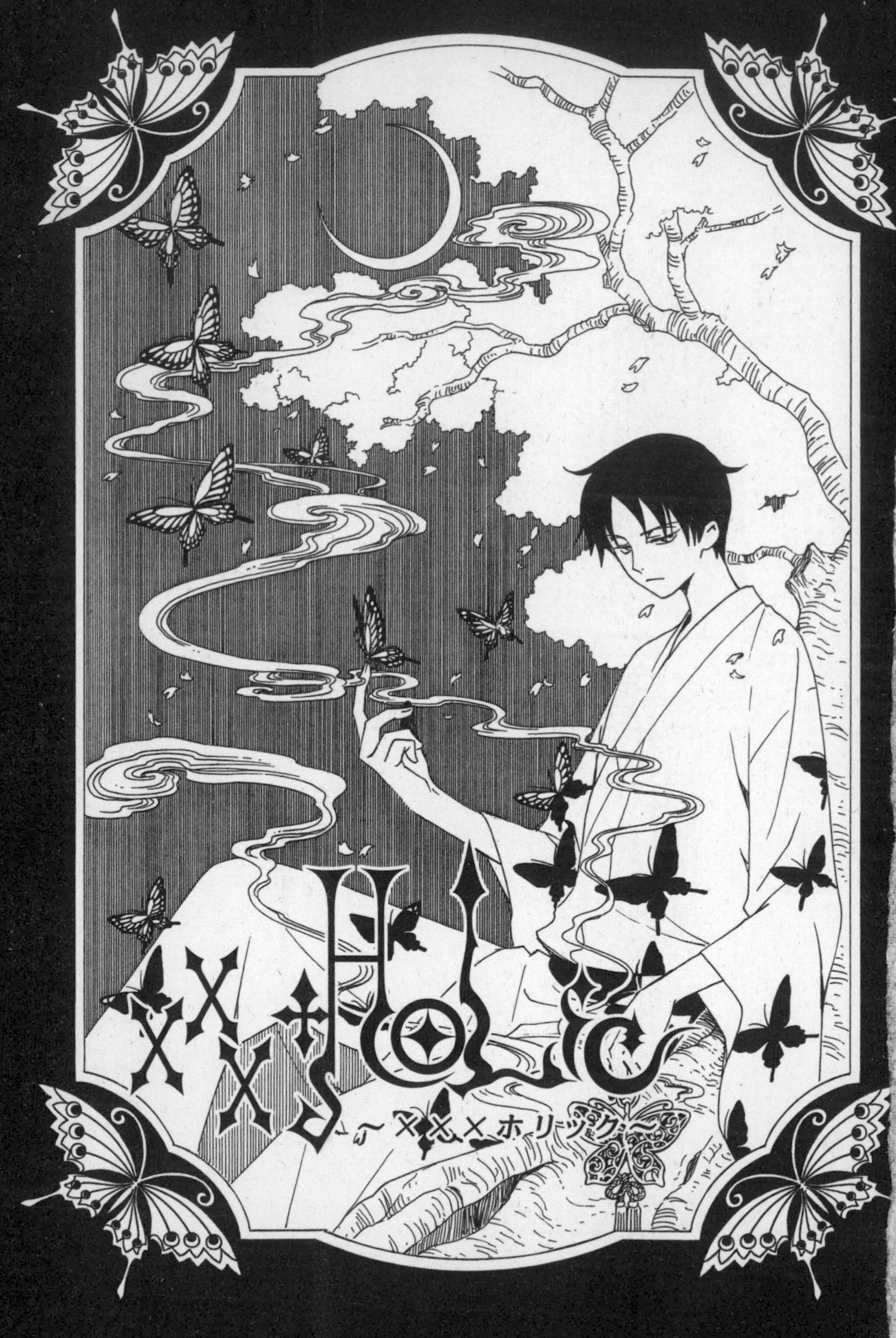
xxxHOLiC
〜×××ホリック〜

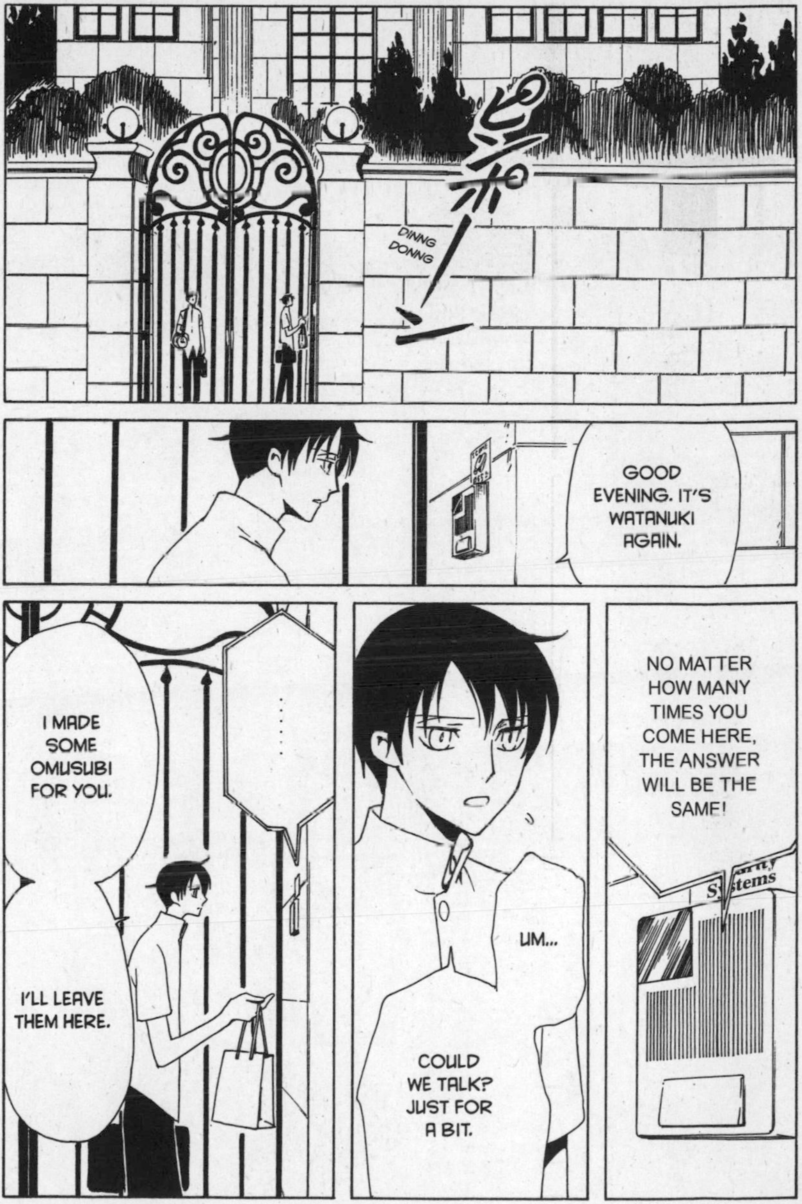
ピンポーン
DINNG DONNG
GOOD EVENING. IT'S WATANUKI AGAIN.
NO MATTER HOW MANY TIMES YOU COME HERE, THE ANSWER WILL BE THE SAME!
UM...
COULD WE TALK? JUST FOR A BIT.
......
I MADE SOME OMUSUBI FOR YOU.
I'LL LEAVE THEM HERE.

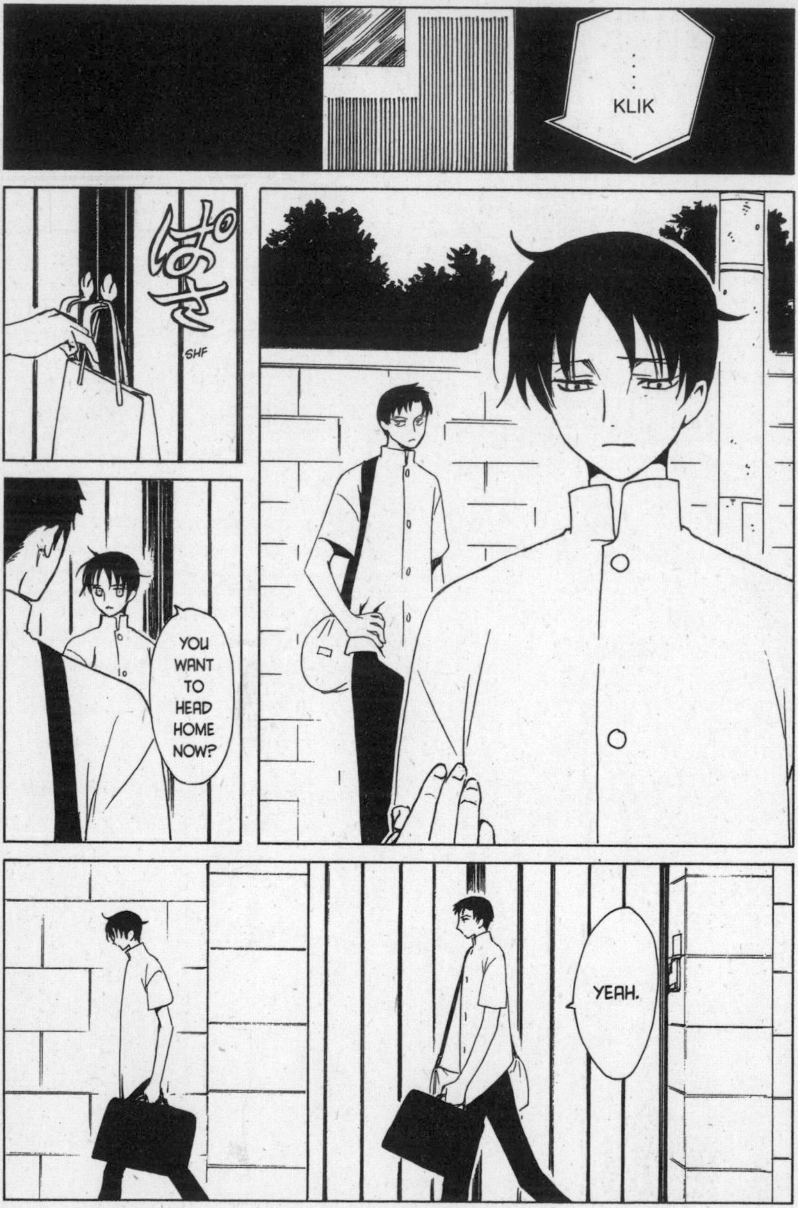
....
KLIK
ぱさ
SHF
YOU WANT TO HEAD HOME NOW?
YEAH.

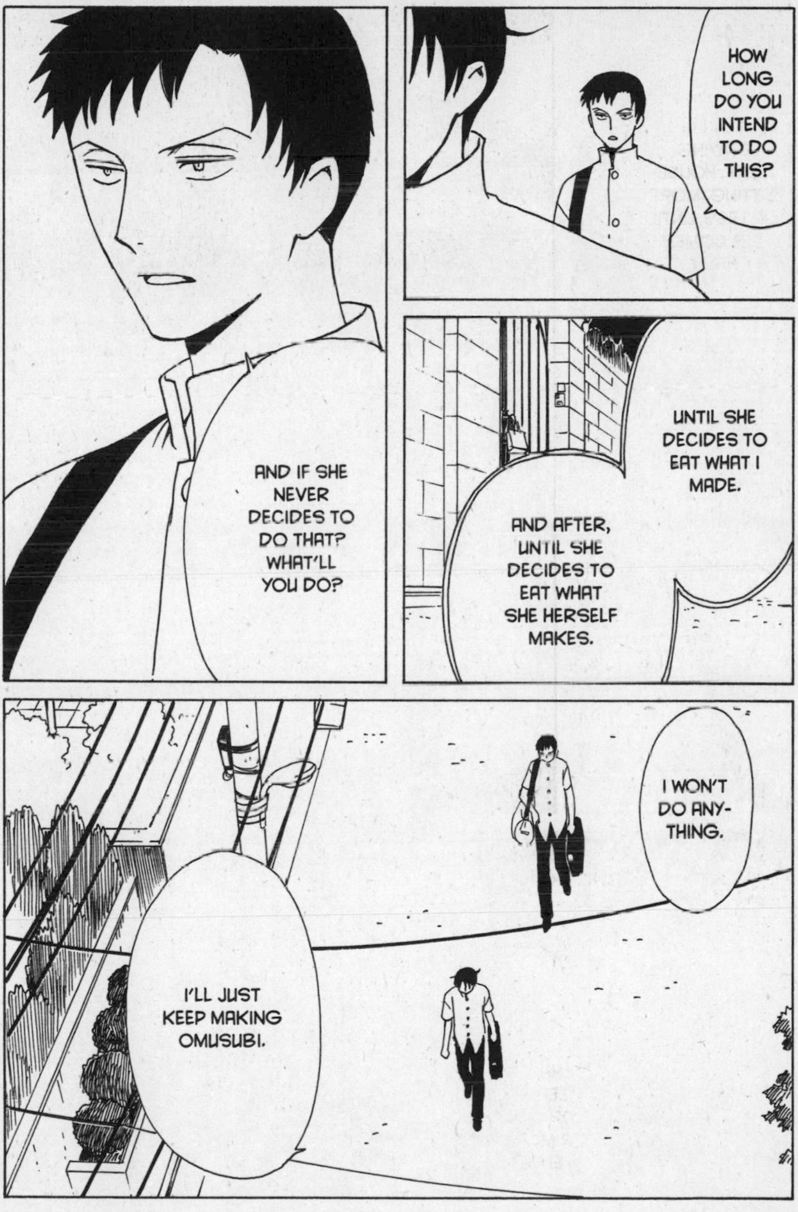
HOW LONG DO YOU INTEND TO DO THIS?
UNTIL SHE DECIDES TO EAT WHAT I MADE.
AND AFTER, UNTIL SHE DECIDES TO EAT WHAT SHE HERSELF MAKES.
AND IF SHE NEVER DECIDES TO DO THAT? WHAT'LL YOU DO?
I WON'T DO ANY-THING.
I'LL JUST KEEP MAKING OMUSUBI.

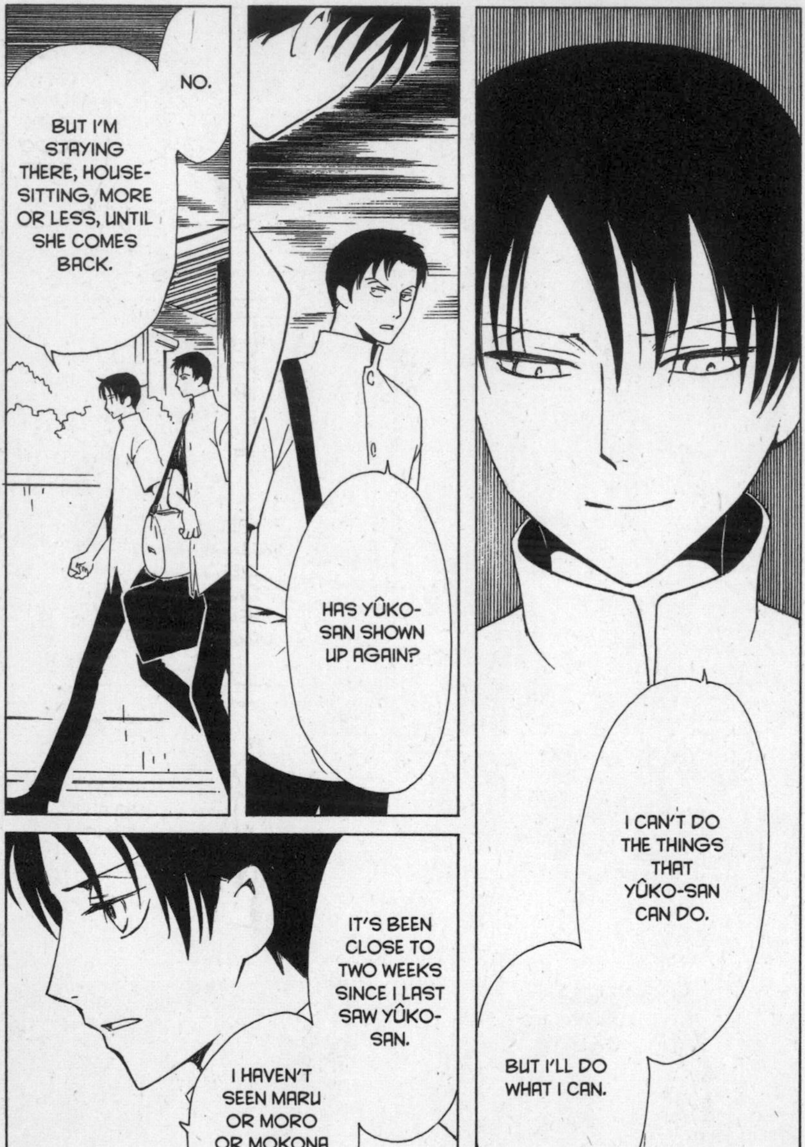
I CAN'T DO THE THINGS THAT YÛKO-SAN CAN DO.
BUT I'LL DO WHAT I CAN.
HAS YÛKO-SAN SHOWN UP AGAIN?
NO.
BUT I'M STAYING THERE, HOUSE-SITTING, MORE OR LESS, UNTIL SHE COMES BACK.
IT'S BEEN CLOSE TO TWO WEEKS SINCE I LAST SAW YÛKO-SAN.
I HAVEN'T SEEN MARU OR MORO OR MOKONA EITHER.

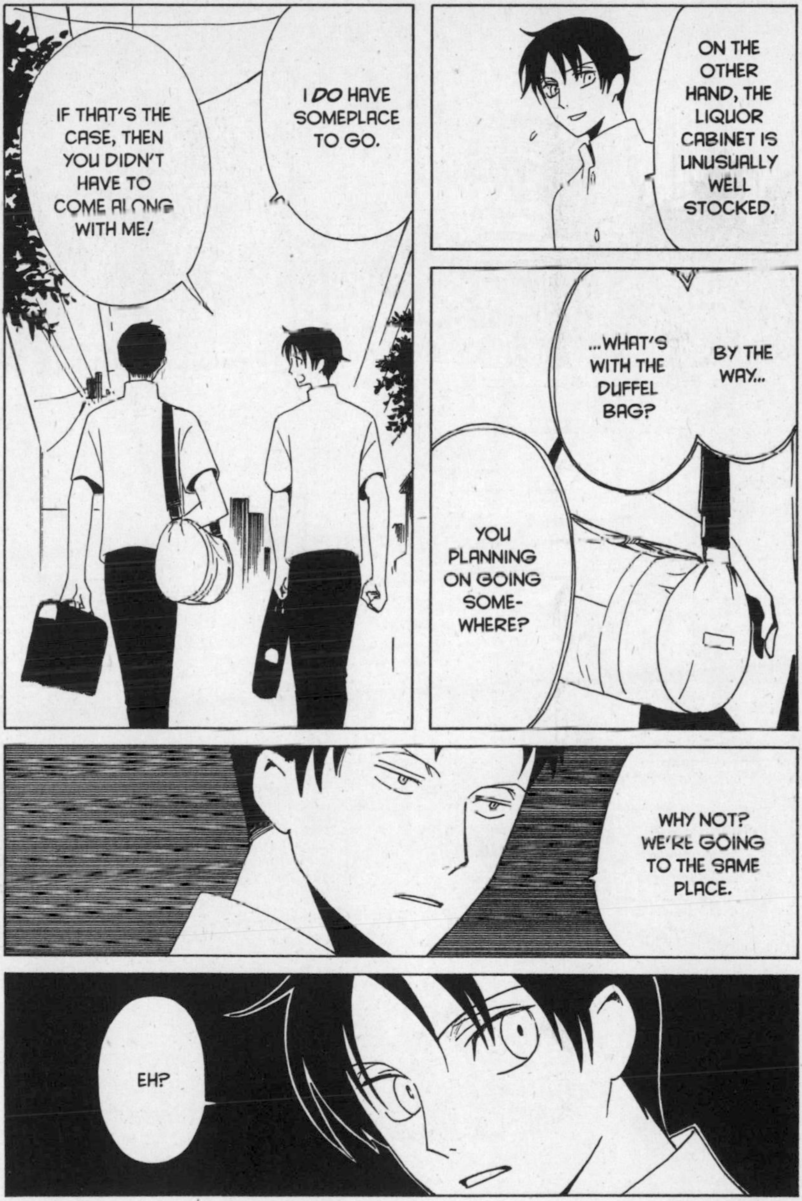
ON THE OTHER HAND, THE LIQUOR CABINET IS UNUSUALLY WELL STOCKED.
BY THE WAY...
...WHAT'S WITH THE DUFFEL BAG?
YOU PLANNING ON GOING SOME-WHERE?
I *DO* HAVE SOMEPLACE TO GO.
IF THAT'S THE CASE, THEN YOU DIDN'T HAVE TO COME ALONG WITH ME!
WHY NOT? WE'RE GOING TO THE SAME PLACE.
EH?

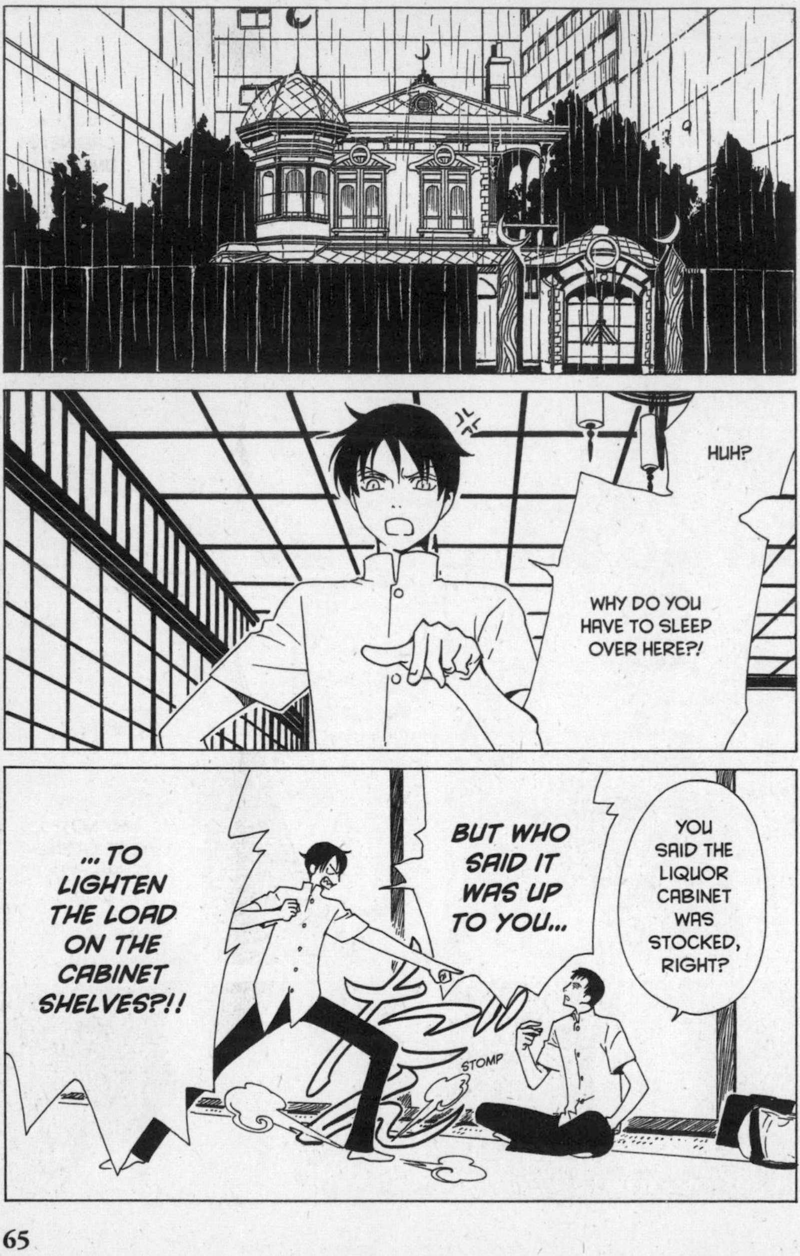
HUH?
WHY DO YOU HAVE TO SLEEP OVER HERE?!
YOU SAID THE LIQUOR CABINET WAS STOCKED, RIGHT?
BUT WHO SAID IT WAS UP TO YOU...
...TO LIGHTEN THE LOAD ON THE CABINET SHELVES?!!
STOMP

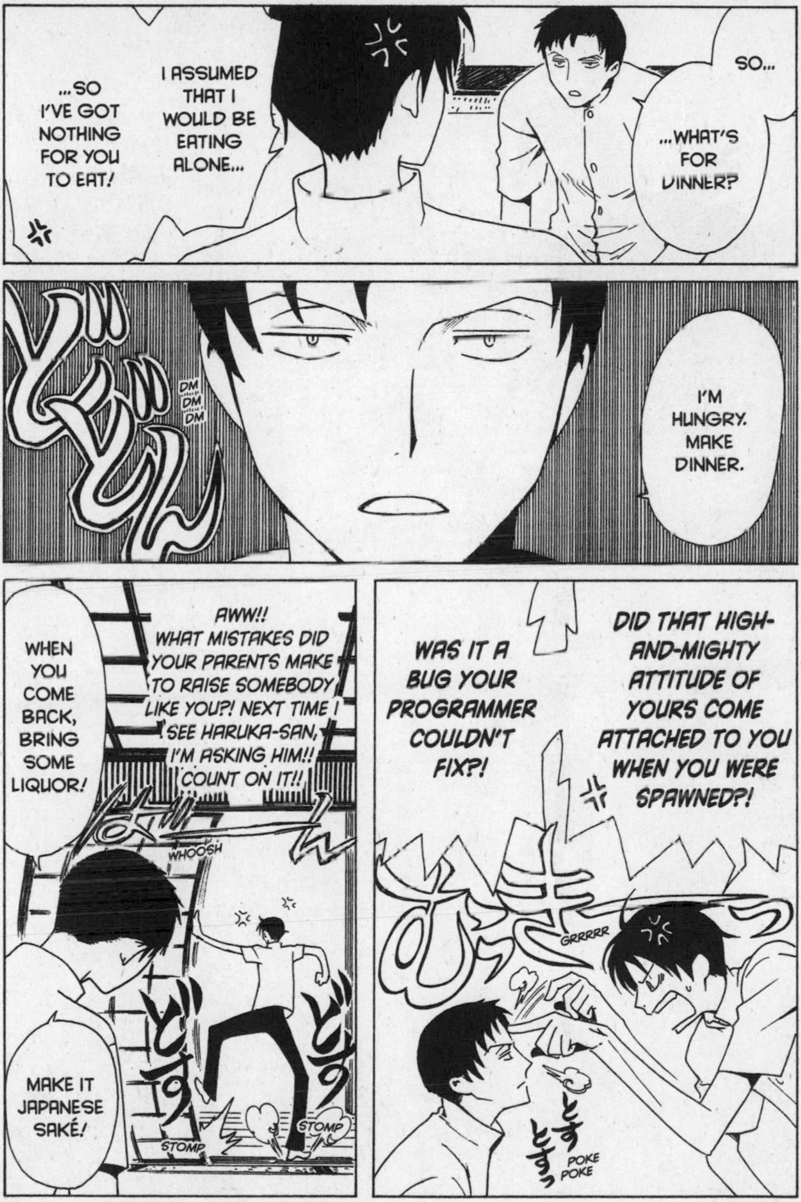
SO...
...WHAT'S FOR DINNER?
I ASSUMED THAT I WOULD BE EATING ALONE...
...SO I'VE GOT NOTHING FOR YOU TO EAT!
I'M HUNGRY. MAKE DINNER.
DM DM DM
DID THAT HIGH-AND-MIGHTY ATTITUDE OF YOURS COME ATTACHED TO YOU WHEN YOU WERE SPAWNED?!
WAS IT A BUG YOUR PROGRAMMER COULDN'T FIX?!
GRRRRR
POKE POKE
AWW!! WHAT MISTAKES DID YOUR PARENTS MAKE TO RAISE SOMEBODY LIKE YOU?! NEXT TIME I SEE HARUKA-SAN, I'M ASKING HIM!! COUNT ON IT!!
WHEN YOU COME BACK, BRING SOME LIQUOR!
WHOOSH
STOMP
STOMP
MAKE IT JAPANESE SAKÉ!

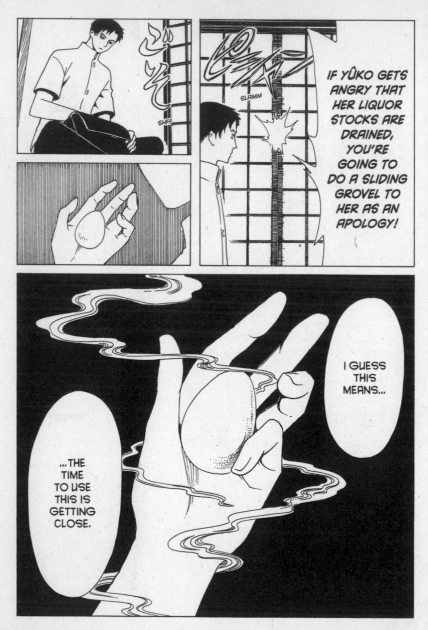

SHFF

SLAMM

IF YÛKO GETS ANGRY THAT HER LIQUOR STOCKS ARE DRAINED, YOU'RE GOING TO DO A SLIDING GROVEL TO HER AS AN APOLOGY!

I GUESS THIS MEANS...

...THE TIME TO USE THIS IS GETTING CLOSE.

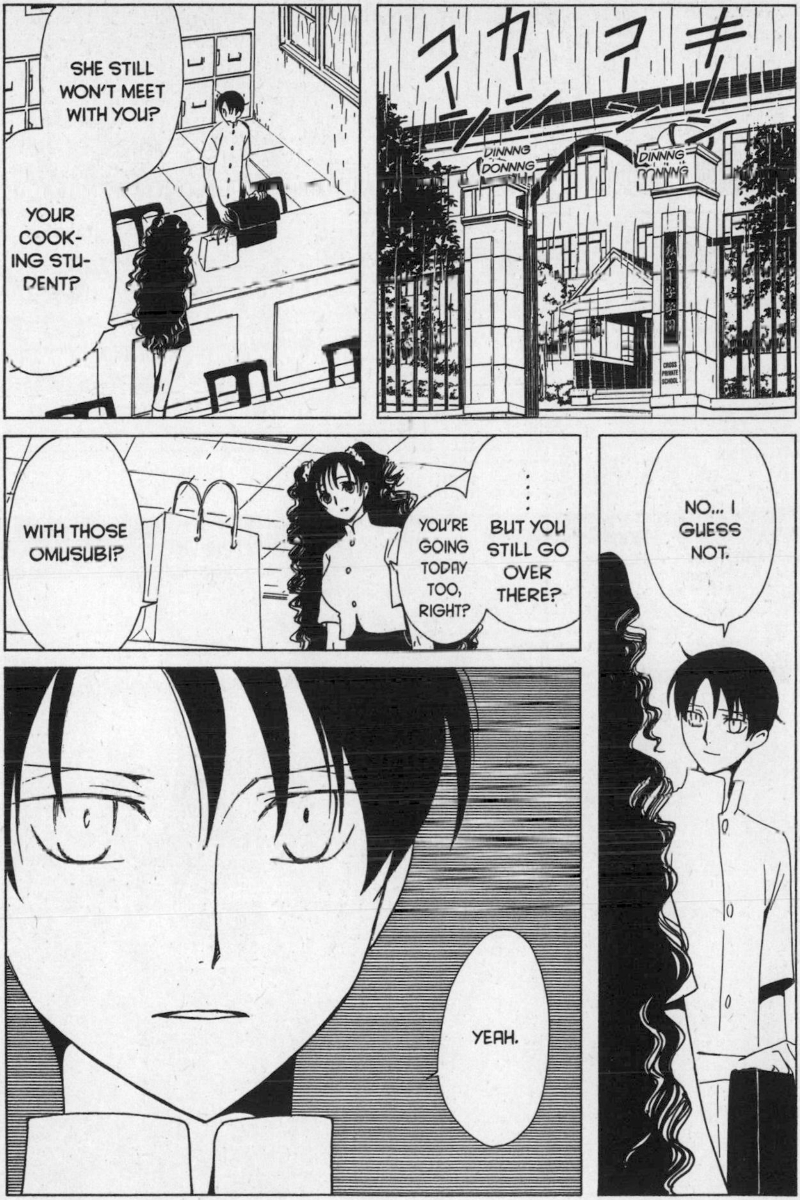
DINNNG DONNNG
DINNNG DONNNG
CROSS PRIVATE SCHOOL
SHE STILL WON'T MEET WITH YOU?
YOUR COOK-ING STU-DENT?
NO... I GUESS NOT.
...
BUT YOU STILL GO OVER THERE?
YOU'RE GOING TODAY TOO, RIGHT?
WITH THOSE OMUSUBI?
YEAH.

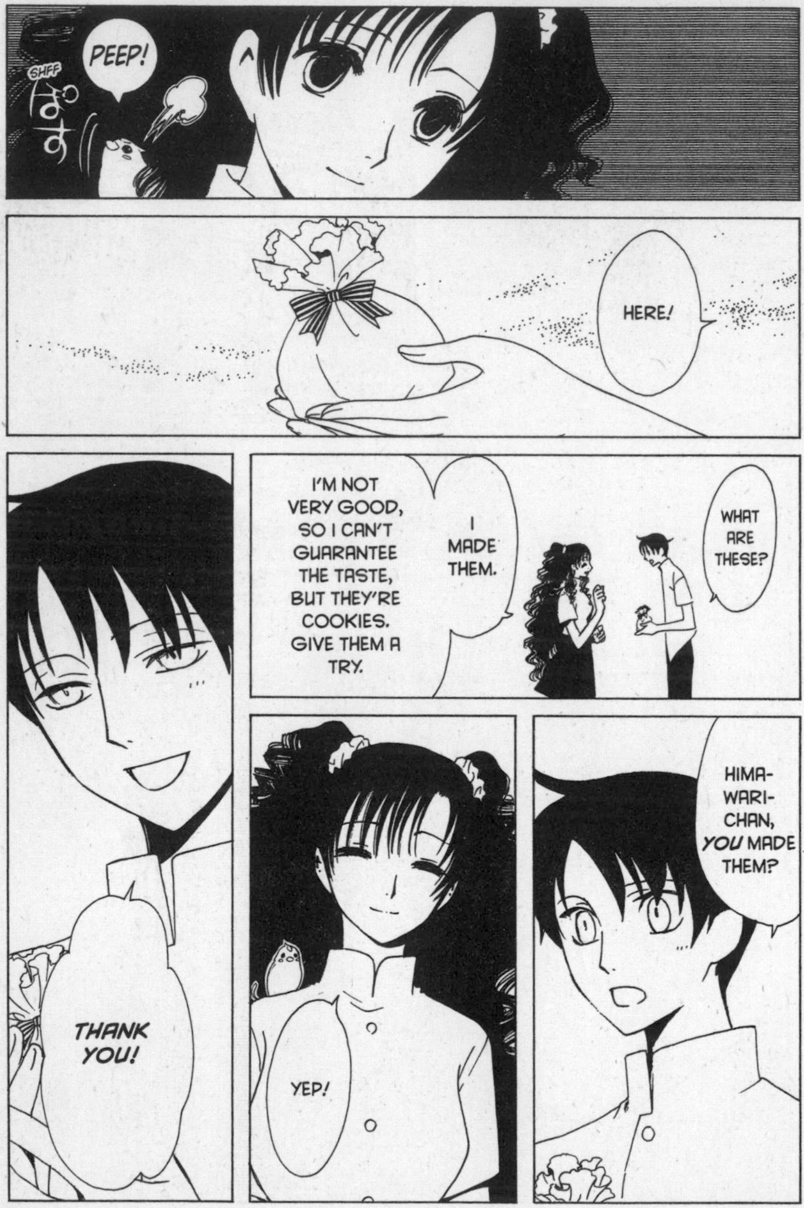

PEEP!
SHFF
ぱす
HERE!
WHAT ARE THESE?
I MADE THEM.
I'M NOT VERY GOOD, SO I CAN'T GUARANTEE THE TASTE, BUT THEY'RE COOKIES. GIVE THEM A TRY.
HIMA-WARI-CHAN, *YOU* MADE THEM?
YEP!
THANK YOU!

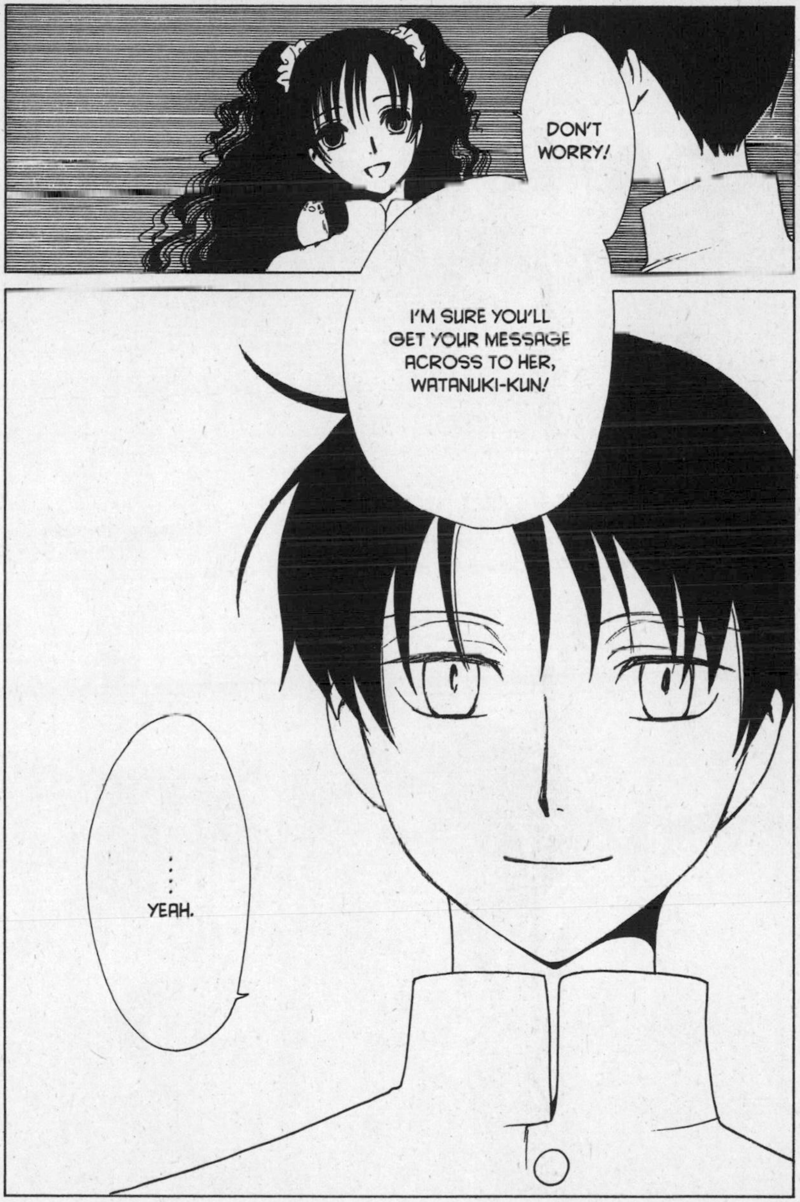
DON'T WORRY!
I'M SURE YOU'LL GET YOUR MESSAGE ACROSS TO HER, WATANUKI-KUN!
..... YEAH.

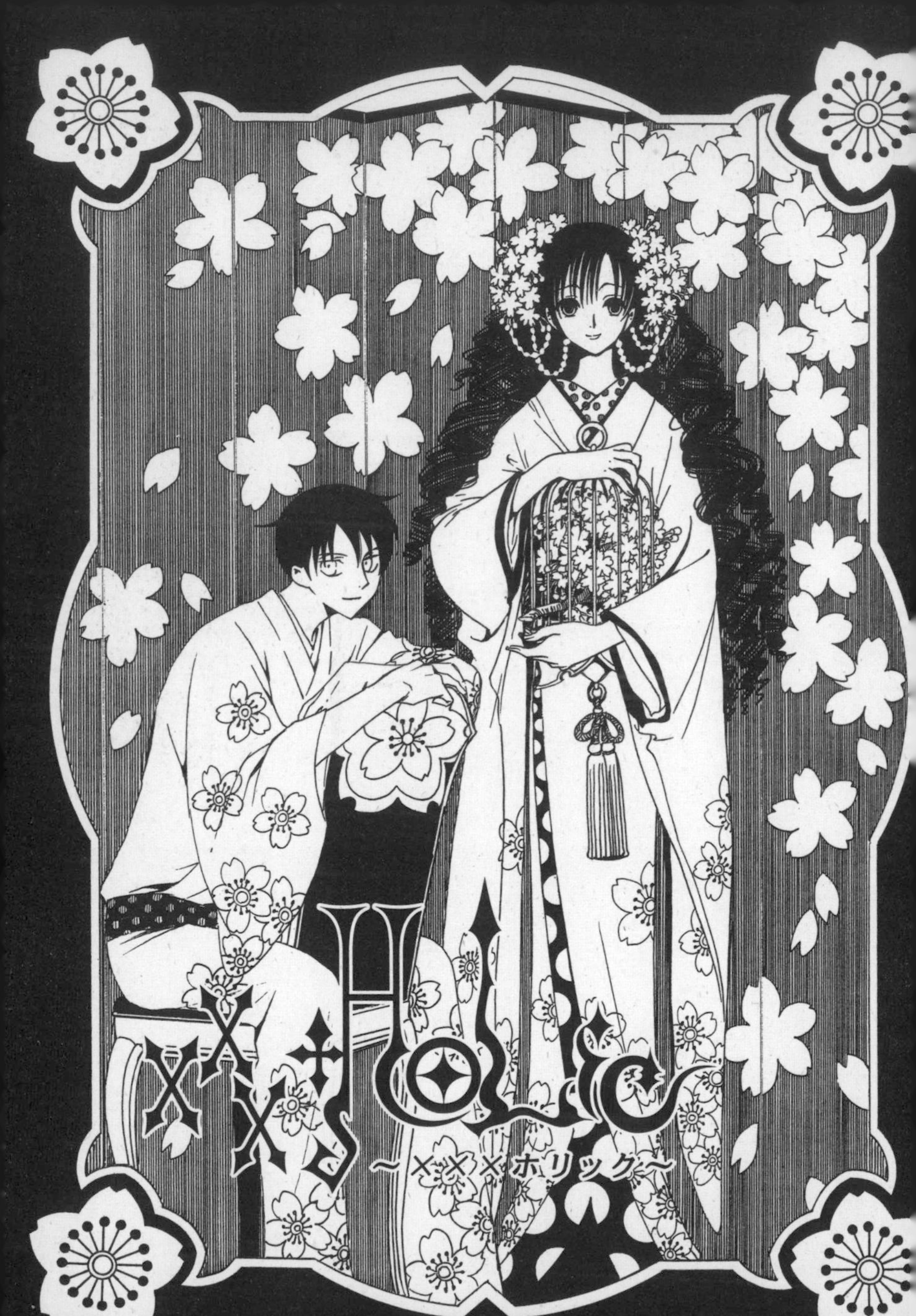
xxxHOLiC
〜×××ホリック〜

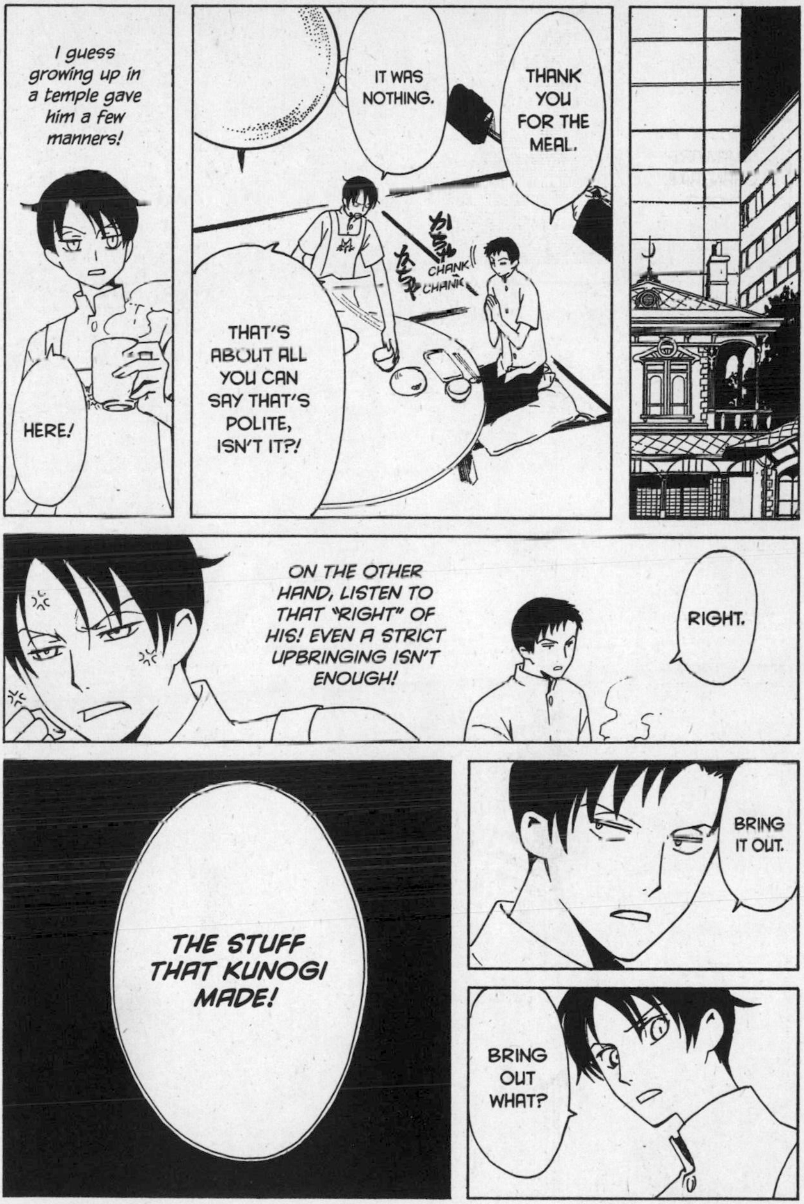
THANK YOU FOR THE MEAL.
IT WAS NOTHING.
CHANK CHANK
THAT'S ABOUT ALL YOU CAN SAY THAT'S POLITE, ISN'T IT?!
I guess growing up in a temple gave him a few manners!
HERE!
RIGHT.
ON THE OTHER HAND, LISTEN TO THAT "RIGHT" OF HIS! EVEN A STRICT UPBRINGING ISN'T ENOUGH!
BRING IT OUT.
BRING OUT WHAT?
THE STUFF THAT KUNOGI MADE!

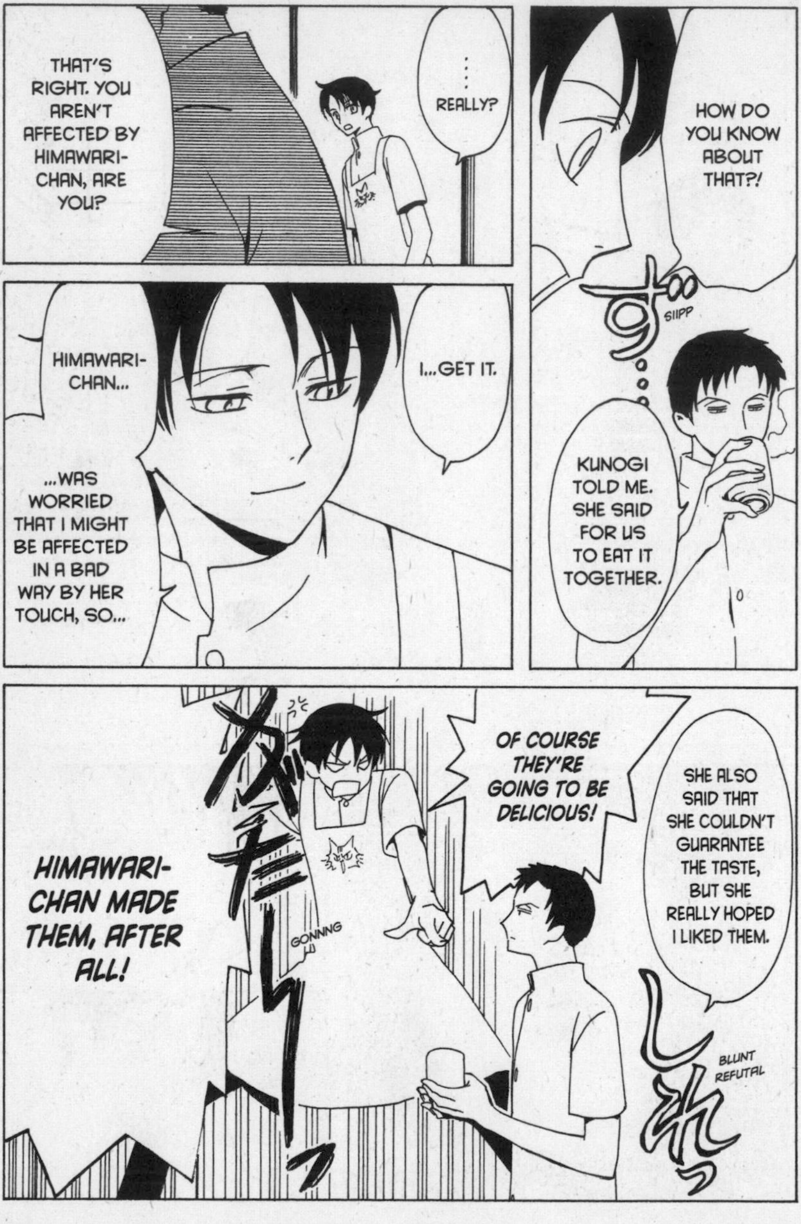
HOW DO YOU KNOW ABOUT THAT?!
SIIPP
KUNOGI TOLD ME. SHE SAID FOR US TO EAT IT TOGETHER.
......REALLY?
THAT'S RIGHT. YOU AREN'T AFFECTED BY HIMAWARI-CHAN, ARE YOU?
I...GET IT.
HIMAWARI-CHAN...
...WAS WORRIED THAT I MIGHT BE AFFECTED IN A BAD WAY BY HER TOUCH, SO...
SHE ALSO SAID THAT SHE COULDN'T GUARANTEE THE TASTE, BUT SHE REALLY HOPED I LIKED THEM.
BLUNT REFUTAL
OF COURSE THEY'RE GOING TO BE DELICIOUS!
GONNNG
HIMAWARI-CHAN MADE THEM, AFTER ALL!

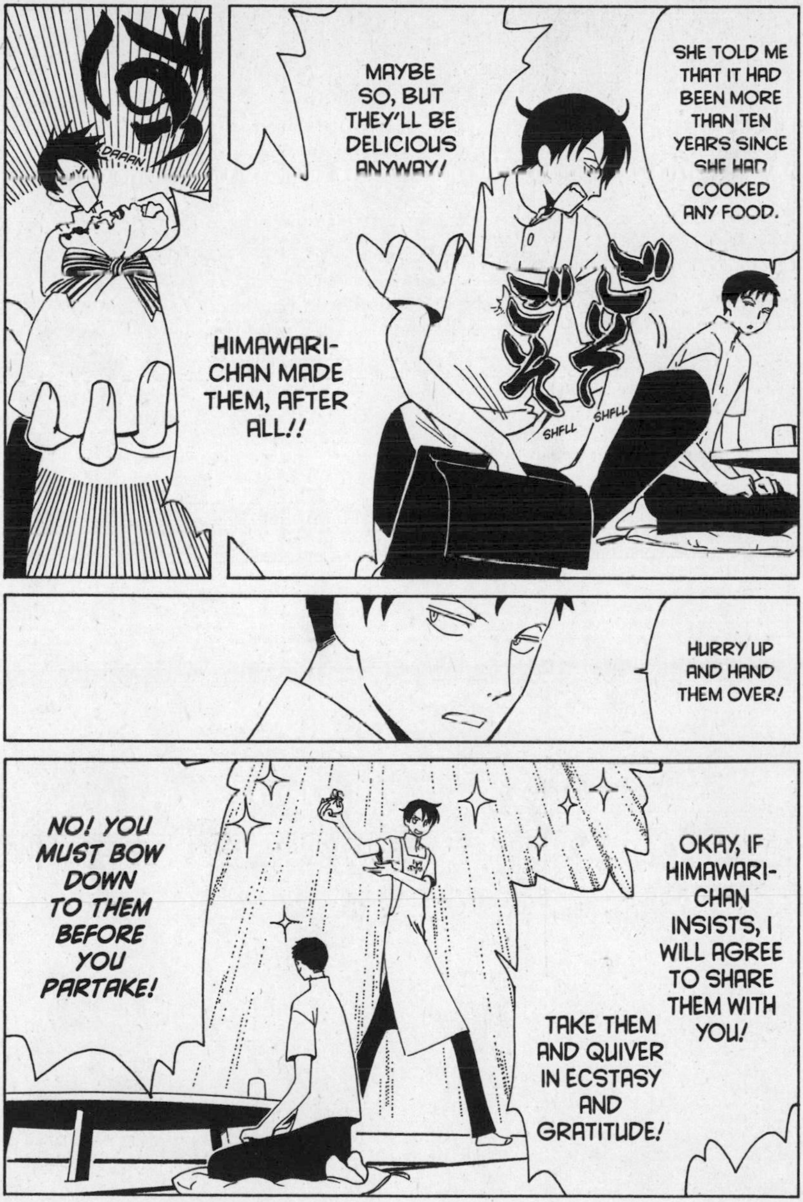
SHE TOLD ME THAT IT HAD BEEN MORE THAN TEN YEARS SINCE SHE HAD COOKED ANY FOOD.
MAYBE SO, BUT THEY'LL BE DELICIOUS ANYWAY!
HIMAWARI-CHAN MADE THEM, AFTER ALL!!
SHFLL
SHFLL
DRAAN
HURRY UP AND HAND THEM OVER!
OKAY, IF HIMAWARI-CHAN INSISTS, I WILL AGREE TO SHARE THEM WITH YOU!
TAKE THEM AND QUIVER IN ECSTASY AND GRATITUDE!
NO! YOU MUST BOW DOWN TO THEM BEFORE YOU PARTAKE!

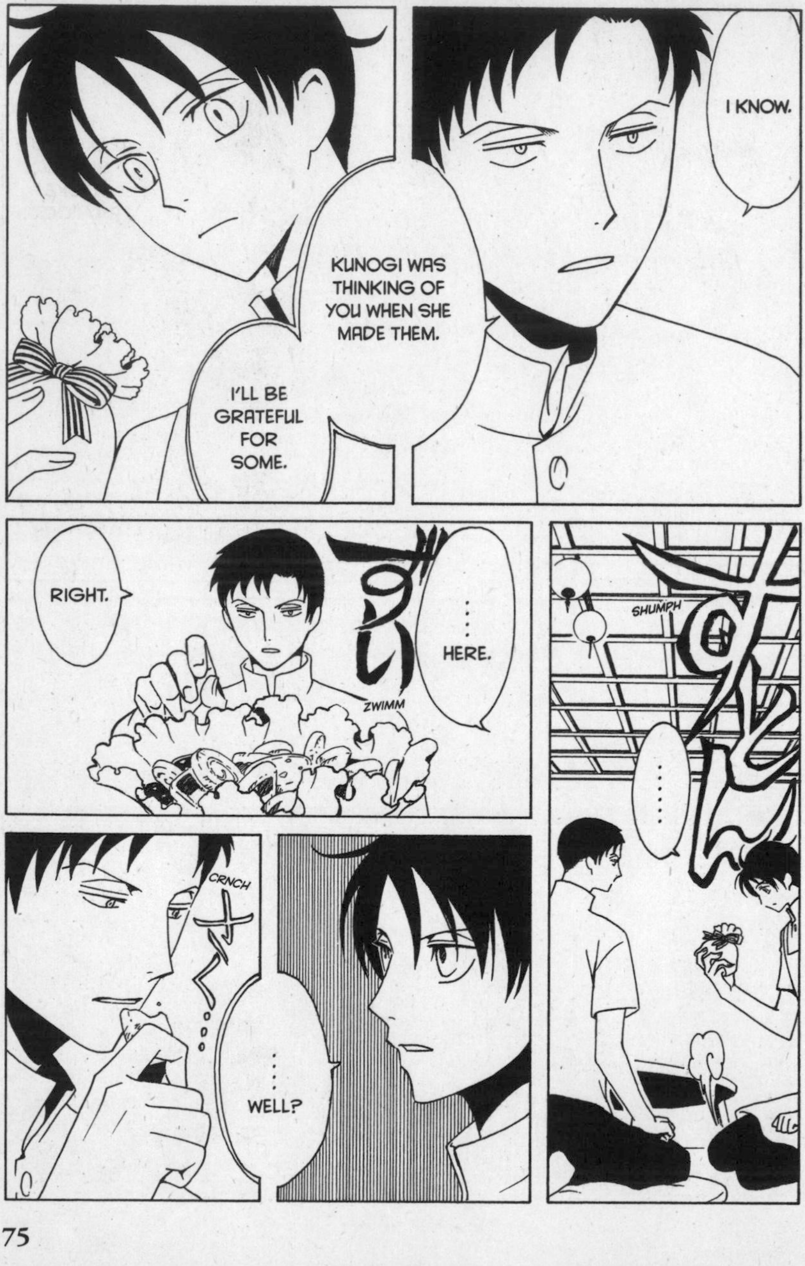

I KNOW.
KUNOGI WAS THINKING OF YOU WHEN SHE MADE THEM.
I'LL BE GRATEFUL FOR SOME.
SHUMPH
......
... HERE.
ZWIMM
RIGHT.
... WELL?
CRNCH

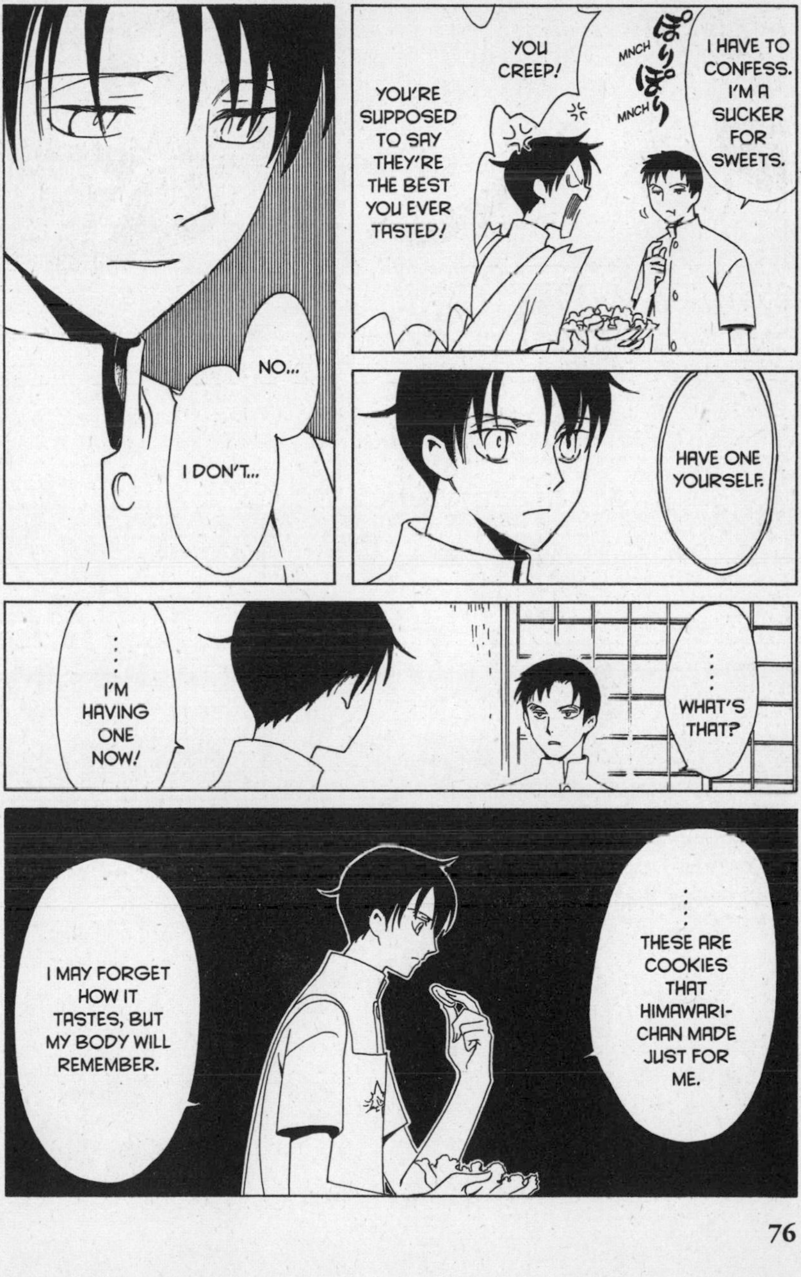
I HAVE TO CONFESS. I'M A SUCKER FOR SWEETS.
ぽりぽり
MNCH
MNCH
YOU CREEP!
YOU'RE SUPPOSED TO SAY THEY'RE THE BEST YOU EVER TASTED!
HAVE ONE YOURSELF.
NO...
I DON'T...
...WHAT'S THAT?
...I'M HAVING ONE NOW!
...THESE ARE COOKIES THAT HIMAWARI-CHAN MADE JUST FOR ME.
I MAY FORGET HOW IT TASTES, BUT MY BODY WILL REMEMBER.

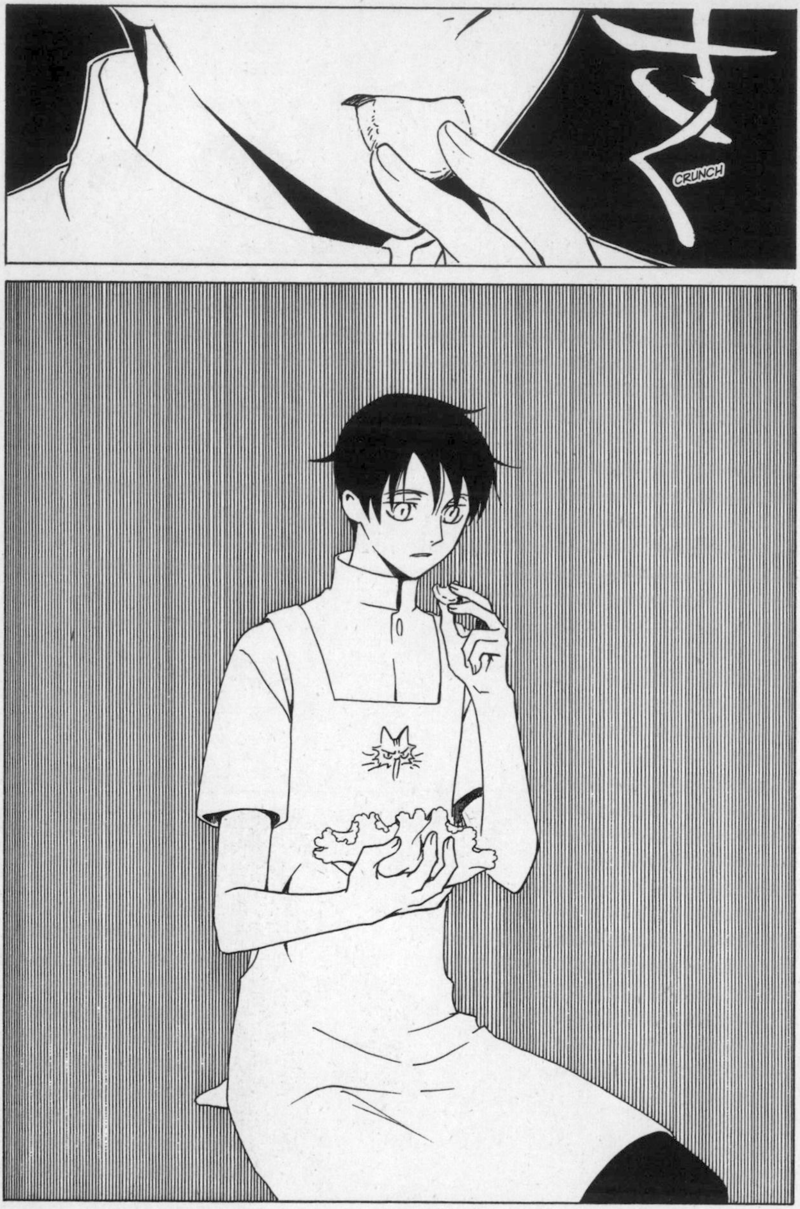
さく
CRUNCH

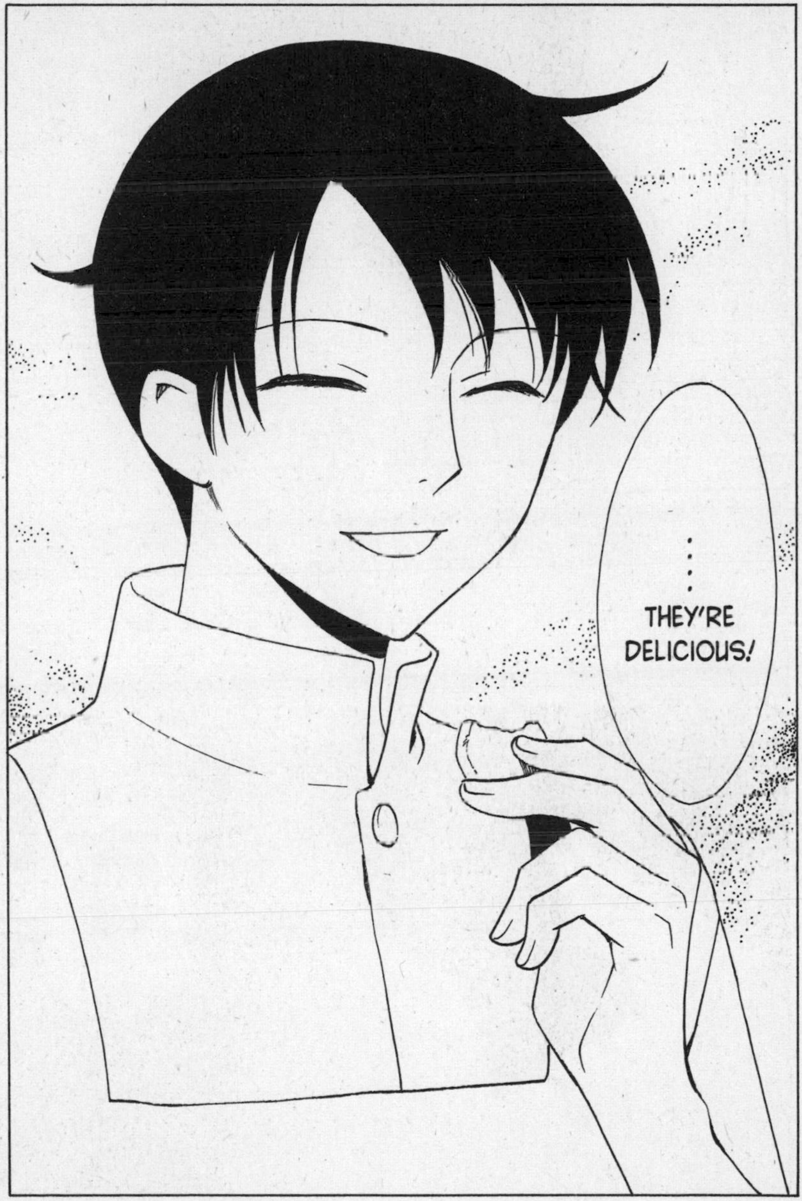
...THEY'RE DELICIOUS!

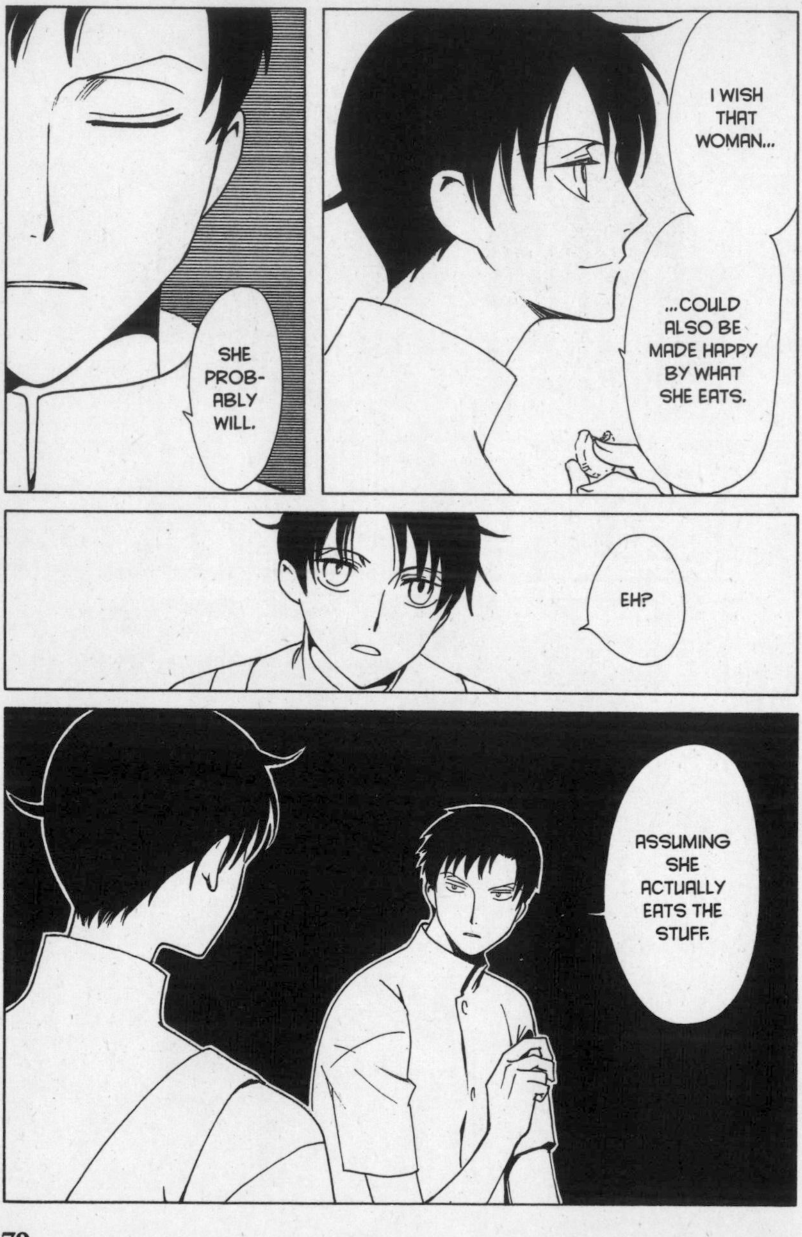
I WISH THAT WOMAN...
...COULD ALSO BE MADE HAPPY BY WHAT SHE EATS.
SHE PROBABLY WILL.
EH?
ASSUMING SHE ACTUALLY EATS THE STUFF.

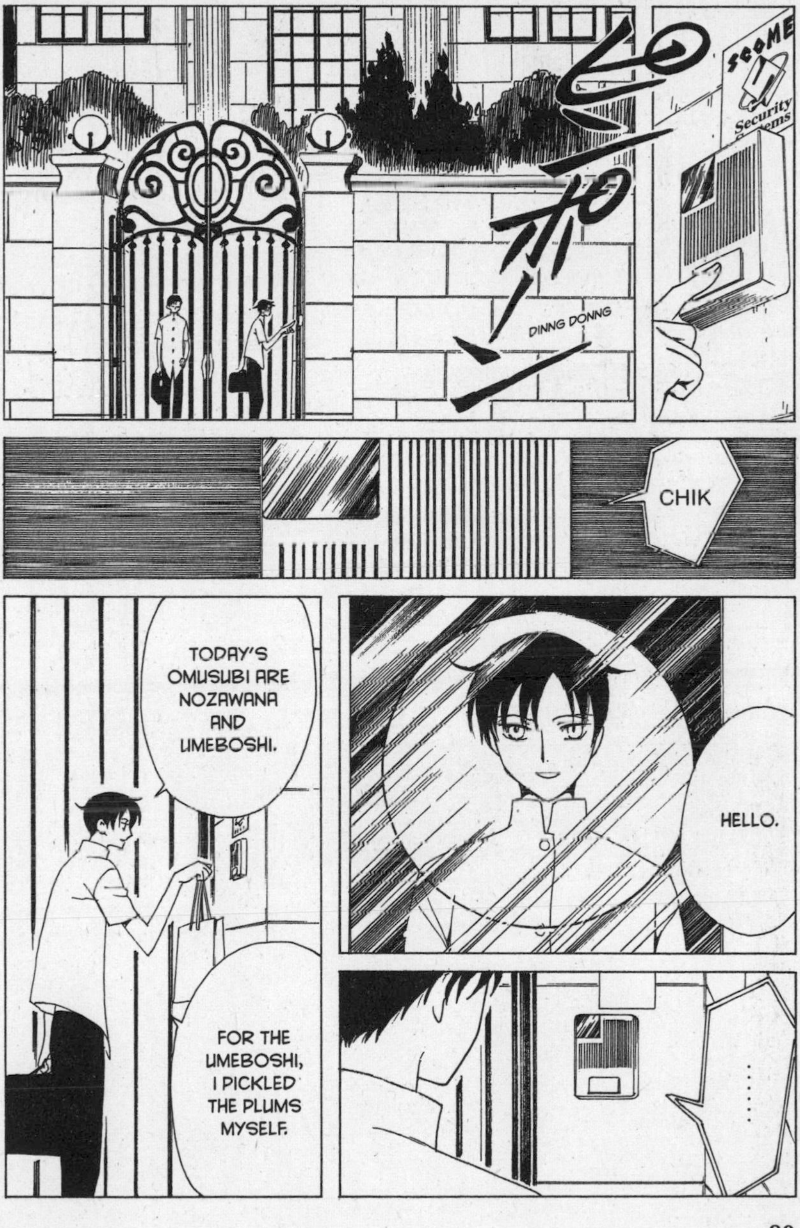

SECOME
Security
DINNG DONNG
CHIK
HELLO.
......
TODAY'S OMUSUBI ARE NOZAWANA AND UMEBOSHI.
FOR THE UMEBOSHI, I PICKLED THE PLUMS MYSELF.

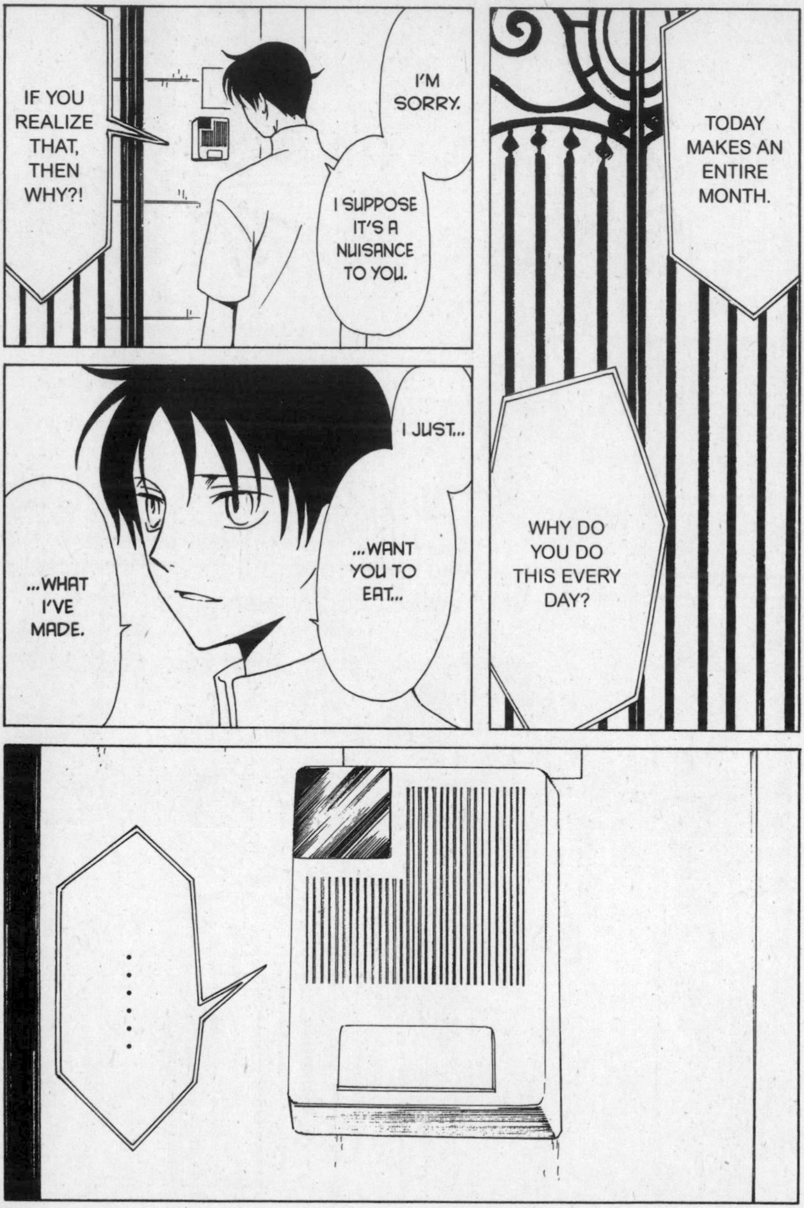
TODAY MAKES AN ENTIRE MONTH.
WHY DO YOU DO THIS EVERY DAY?
I'M SORRY.
I SUPPOSE IT'S A NUISANCE TO YOU.
IF YOU REALIZE THAT, THEN WHY?!
I JUST...
...WANT YOU TO EAT...
...WHAT I'VE MADE.
......

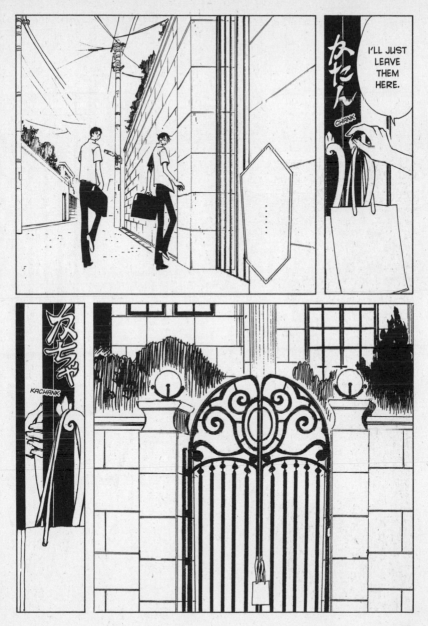

I'LL JUST LEAVE THEM HERE.

CHANK

KACHANK

82

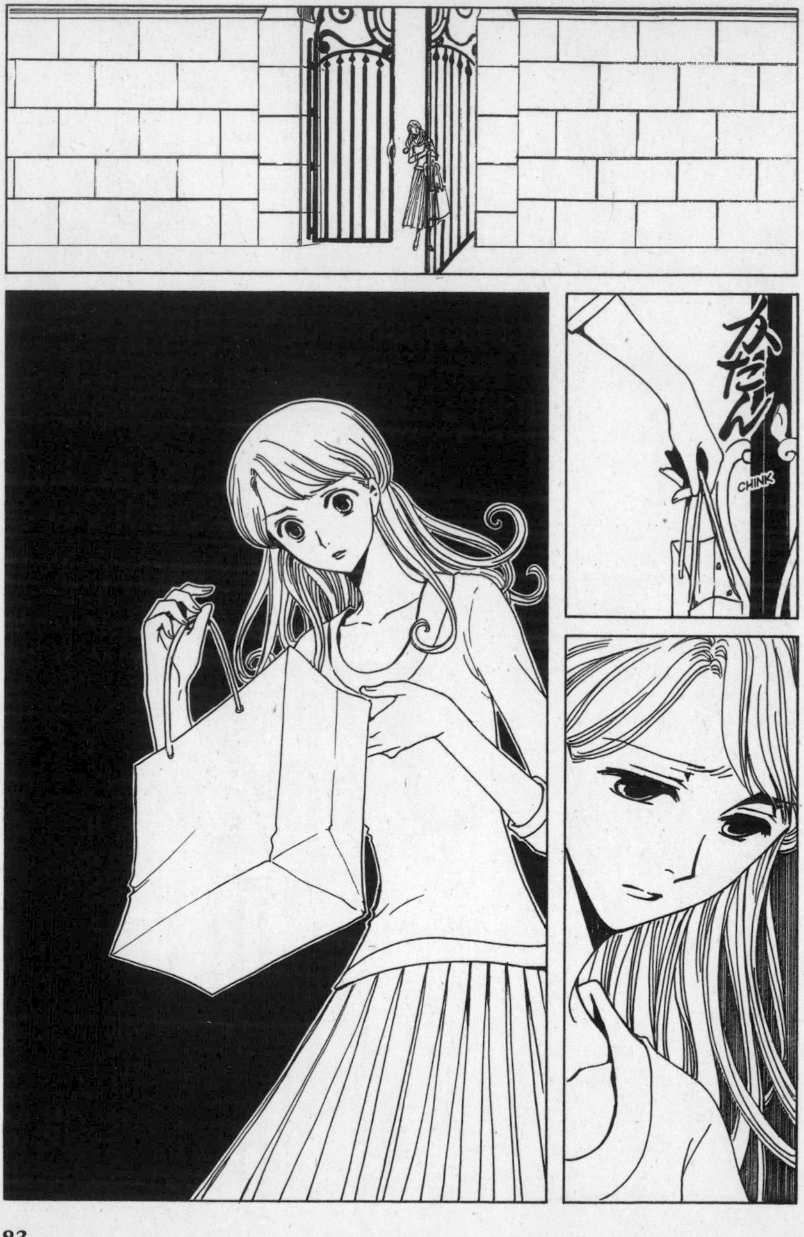
かたん
CHINK

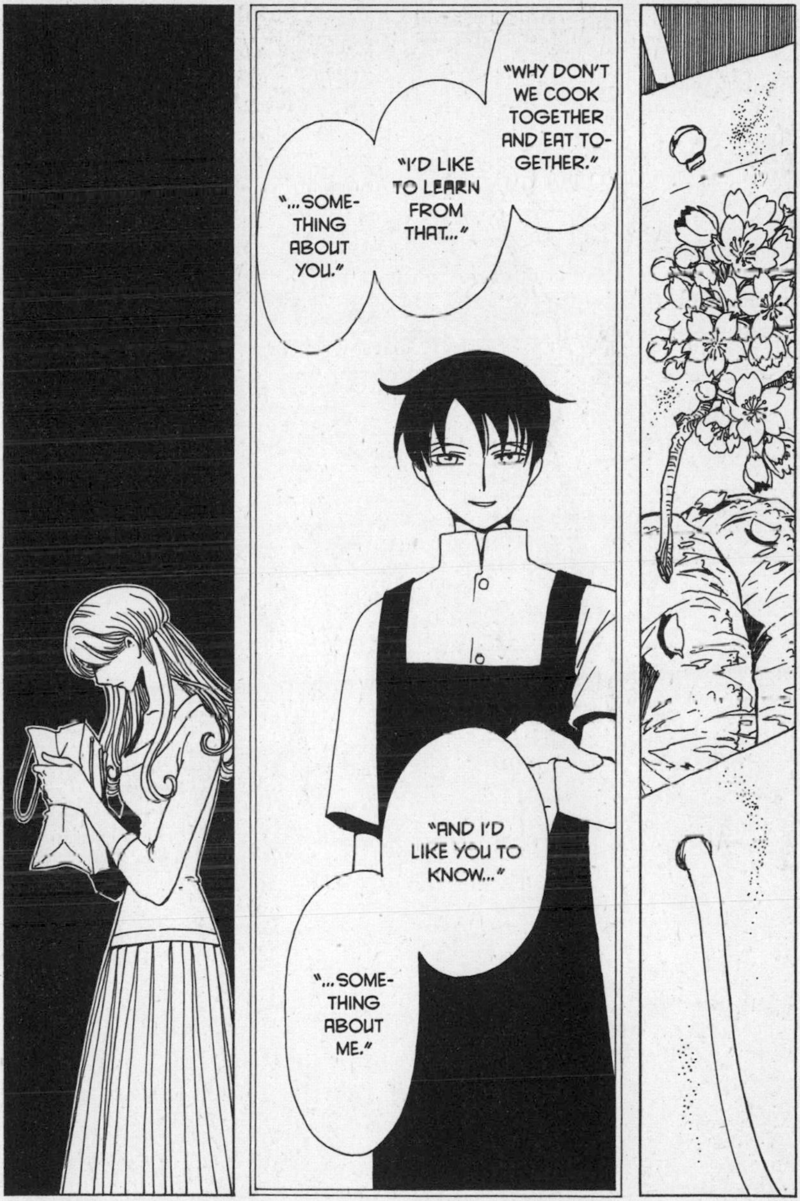
"WHY DON'T WE COOK TOGETHER AND EAT TO-GETHER."
"I'D LIKE TO LEARN FROM THAT..."
"...SOME-THING ABOUT YOU."
"AND I'D LIKE YOU TO KNOW..."
"...SOME-THING ABOUT ME."

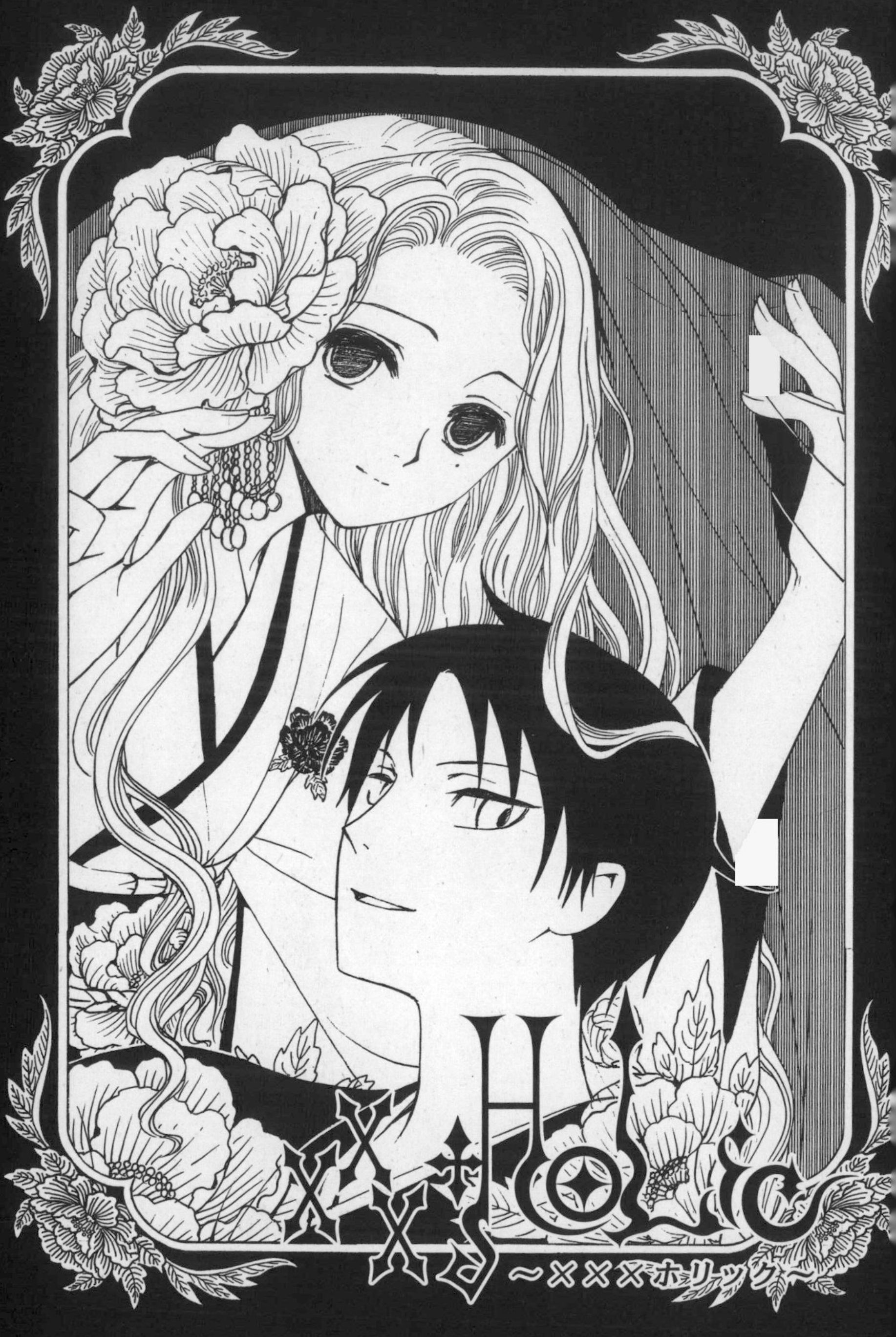
xxxHOLiC
〜×××ホリック〜

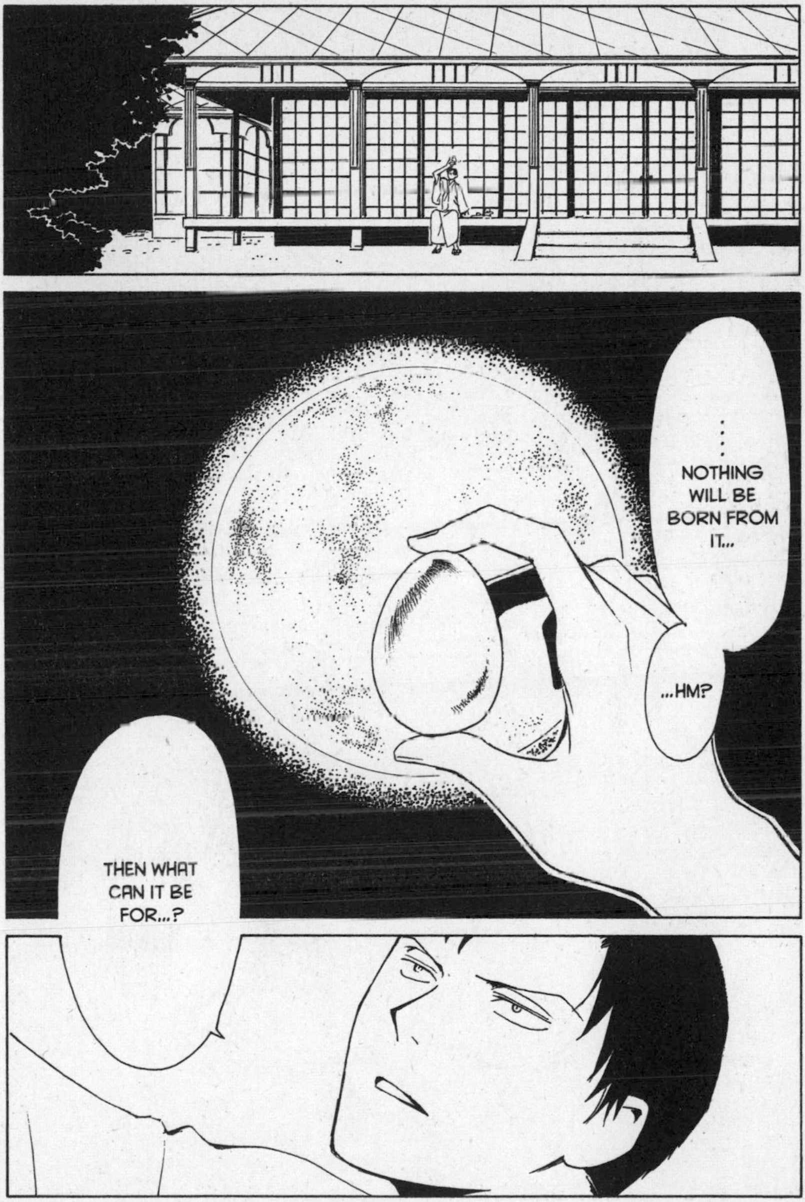
... NOTHING WILL BE BORN FROM IT...
...HM?
THEN WHAT CAN IT BE FOR...?

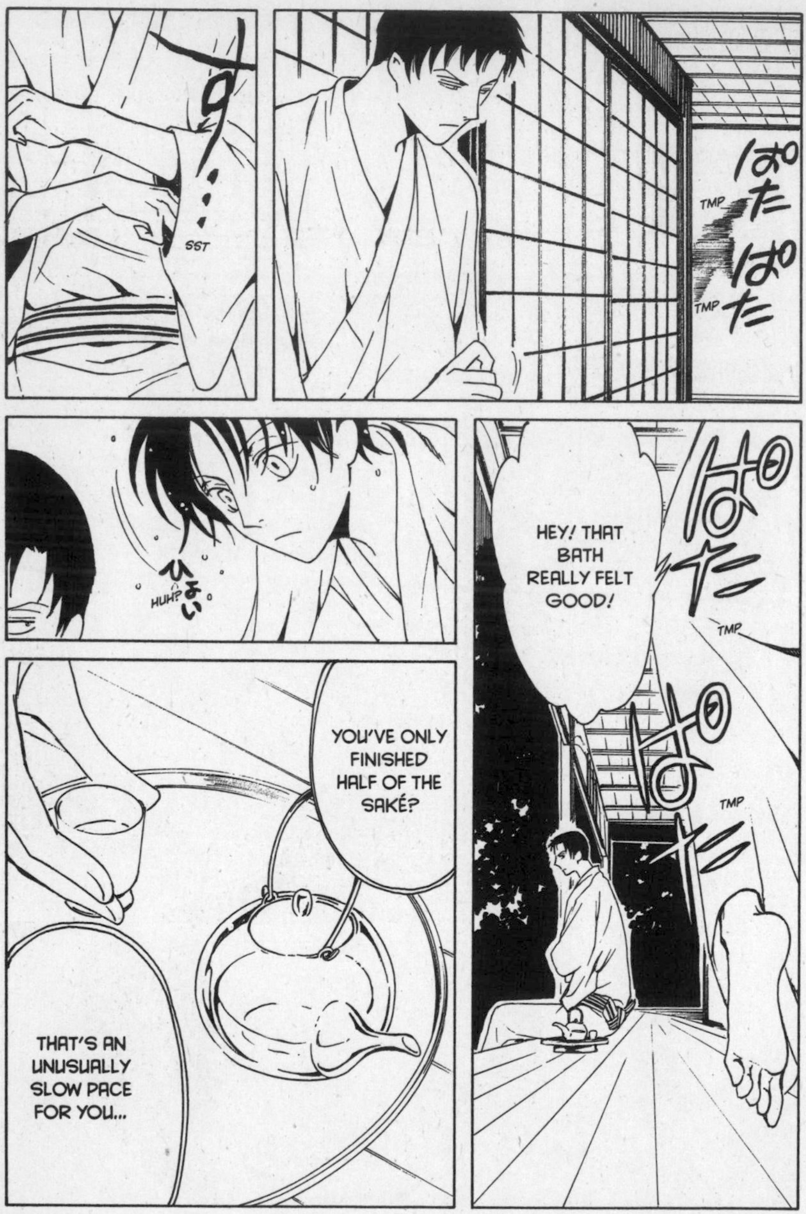
ぱたぱた
TMP
TMP
す…
SST
HEY! THAT BATH REALLY FELT GOOD!
ぱた
TMP
ぱた
TMP
ひょい
HUH?
YOU'VE ONLY FINISHED HALF OF THE SAKÉ?
THAT'S AN UNUSUALLY SLOW PACE FOR YOU...

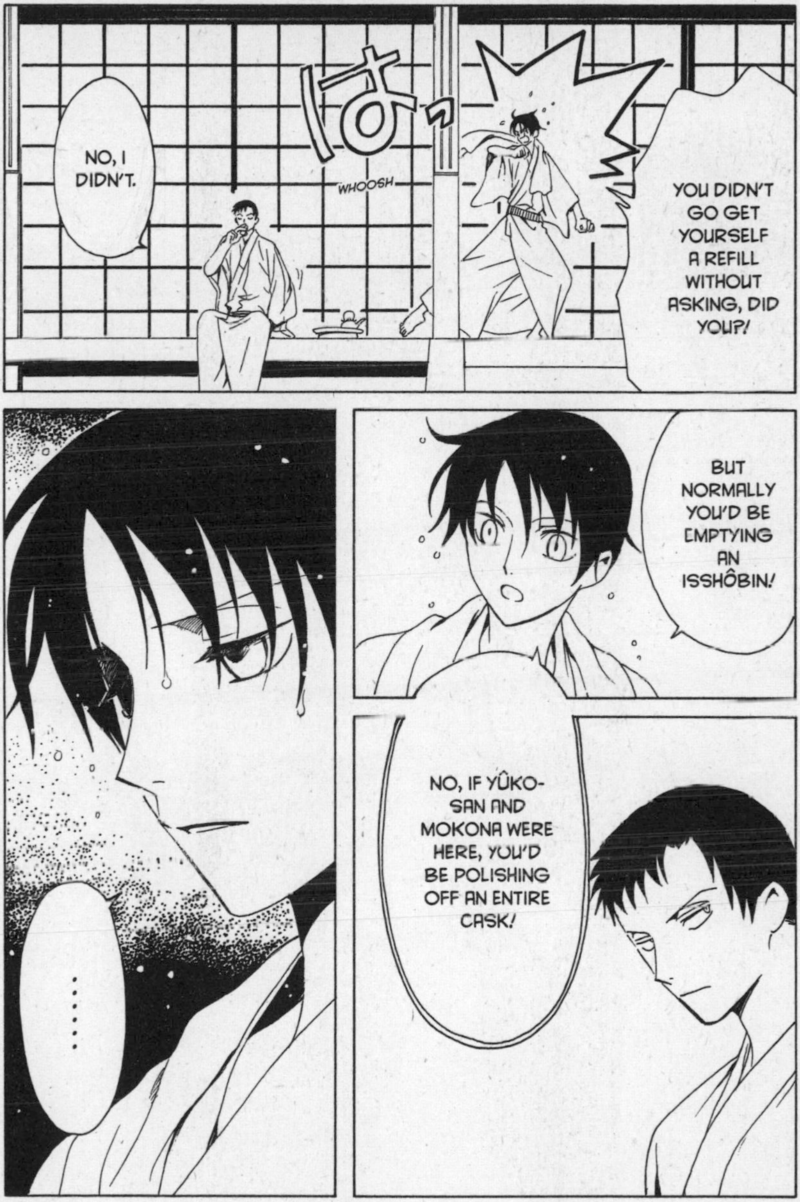
YOU DIDN'T GO GET YOURSELF A REFILL WITHOUT ASKING, DID YOU?!
はっ
WHOOSH
NO, I DIDN'T.
BUT NORMALLY YOU'D BE EMPTYING AN ISSHÔBIN!
NO, IF YÛKO-SAN AND MOKONA WERE HERE, YOU'D BE POLISHING OFF AN ENTIRE CASK!
......

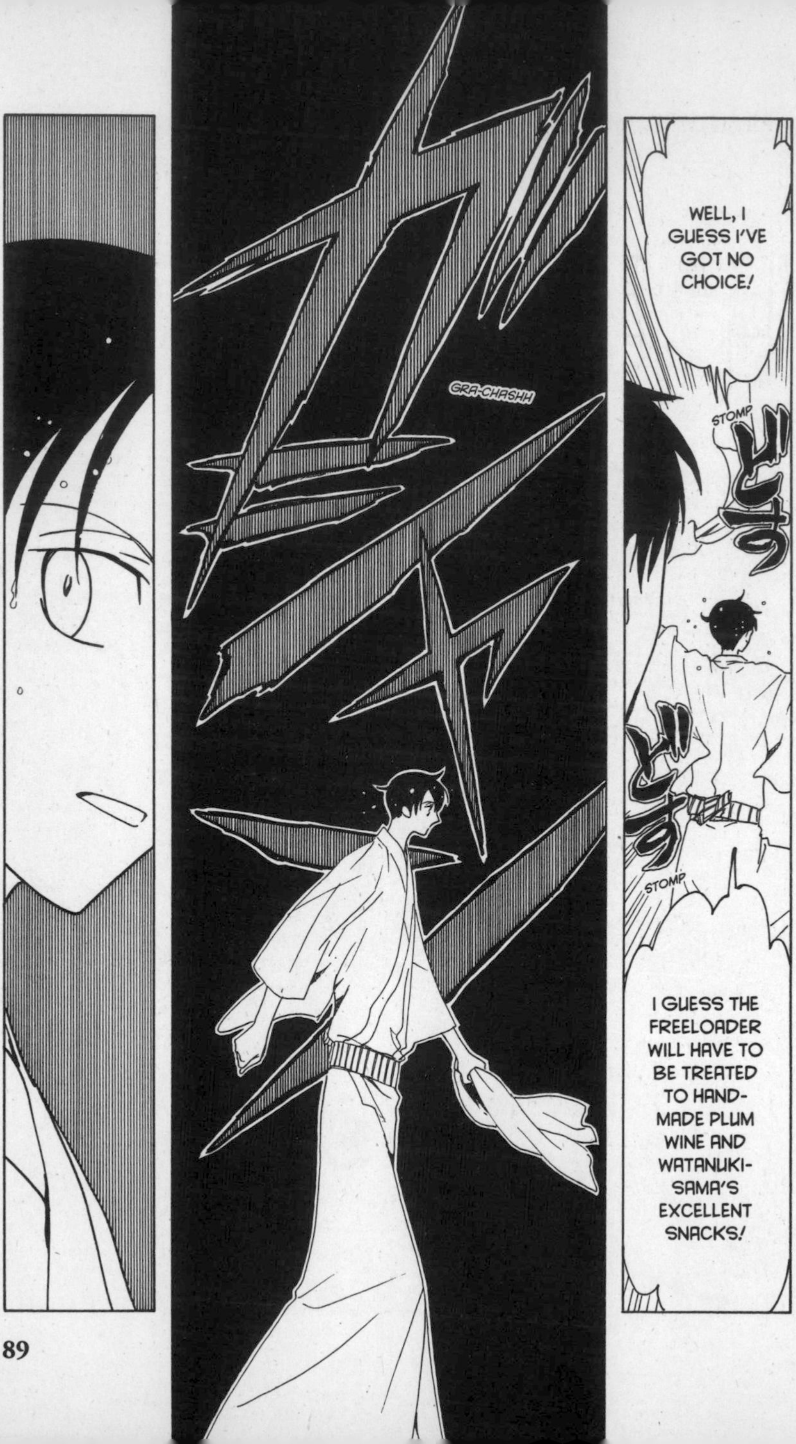
WELL, I GUESS I'VE GOT NO CHOICE!
STOMP
STOMP
I GUESS THE FREELOADER WILL HAVE TO BE TREATED TO HAND-MADE PLUM WINE AND WATANUKI-SAMA'S EXCELLENT SNACKS!
GRA-CHASHH

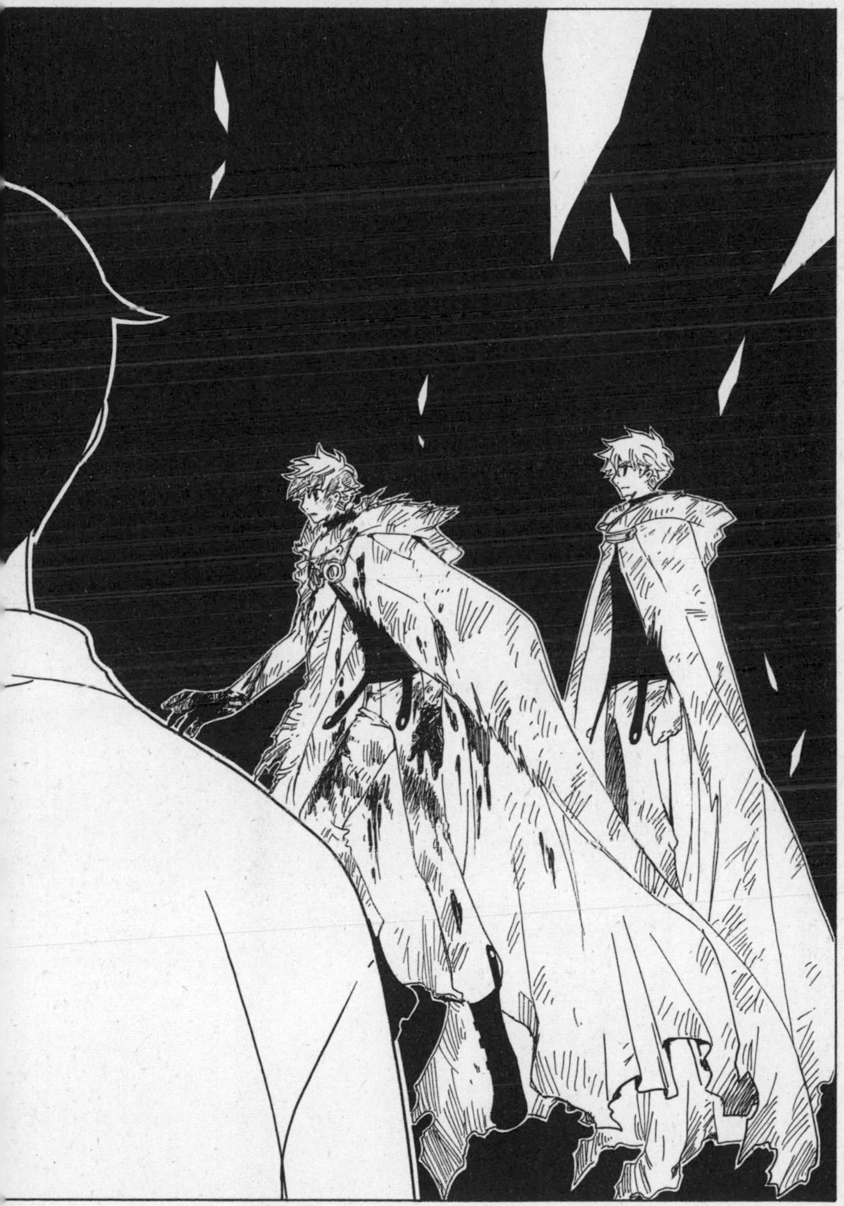

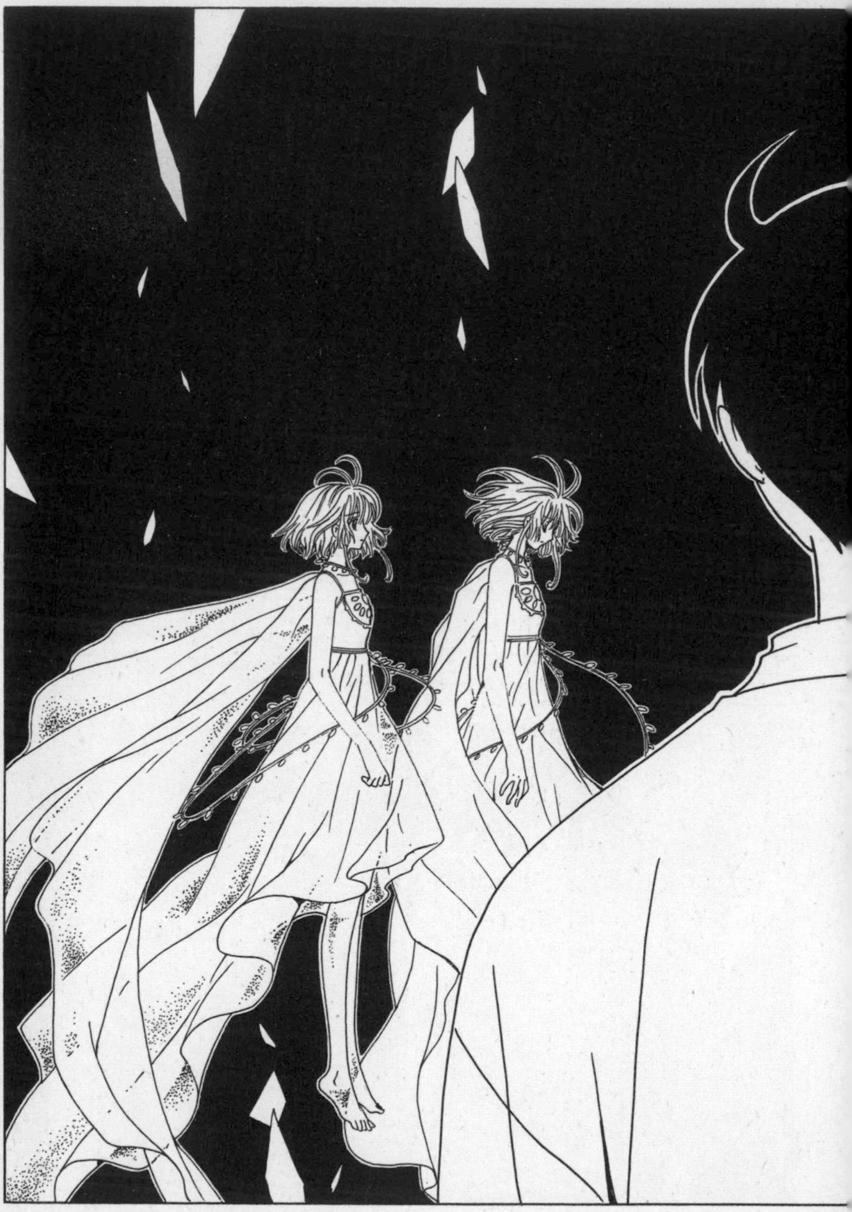

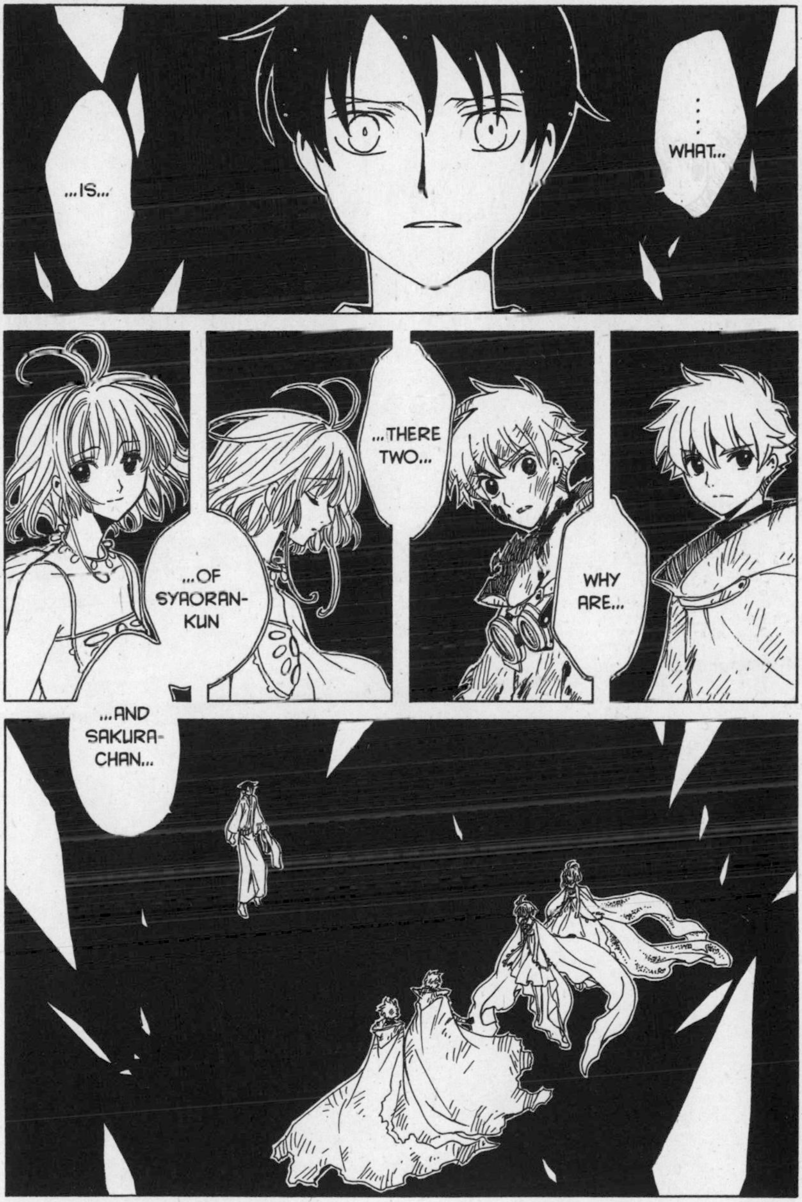
WHAT...
...IS...
WHY ARE...
...THERE TWO...
...OF SYAORAN-KUN
...AND SAKURA-CHAN...

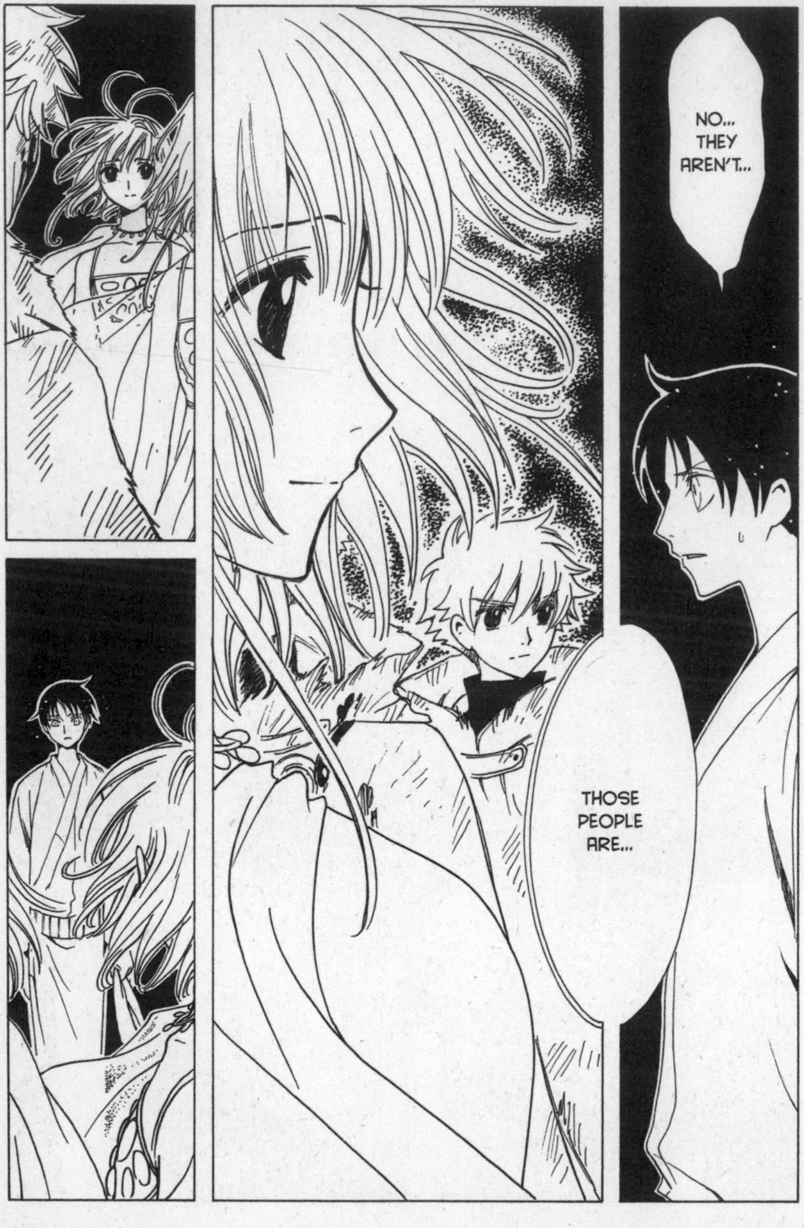
NO... THEY AREN'T...
THOSE PEOPLE ARE...

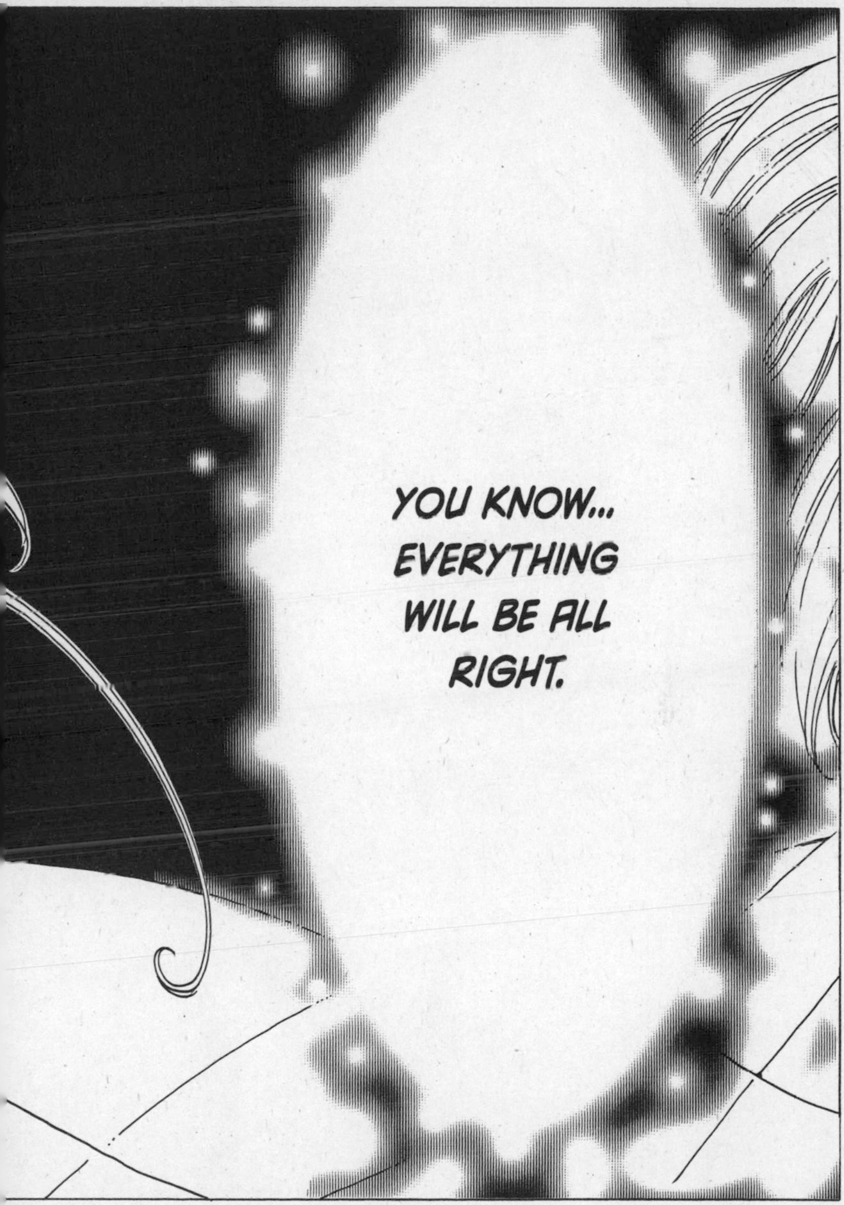
YOU KNOW... EVERYTHING WILL BE ALL RIGHT.

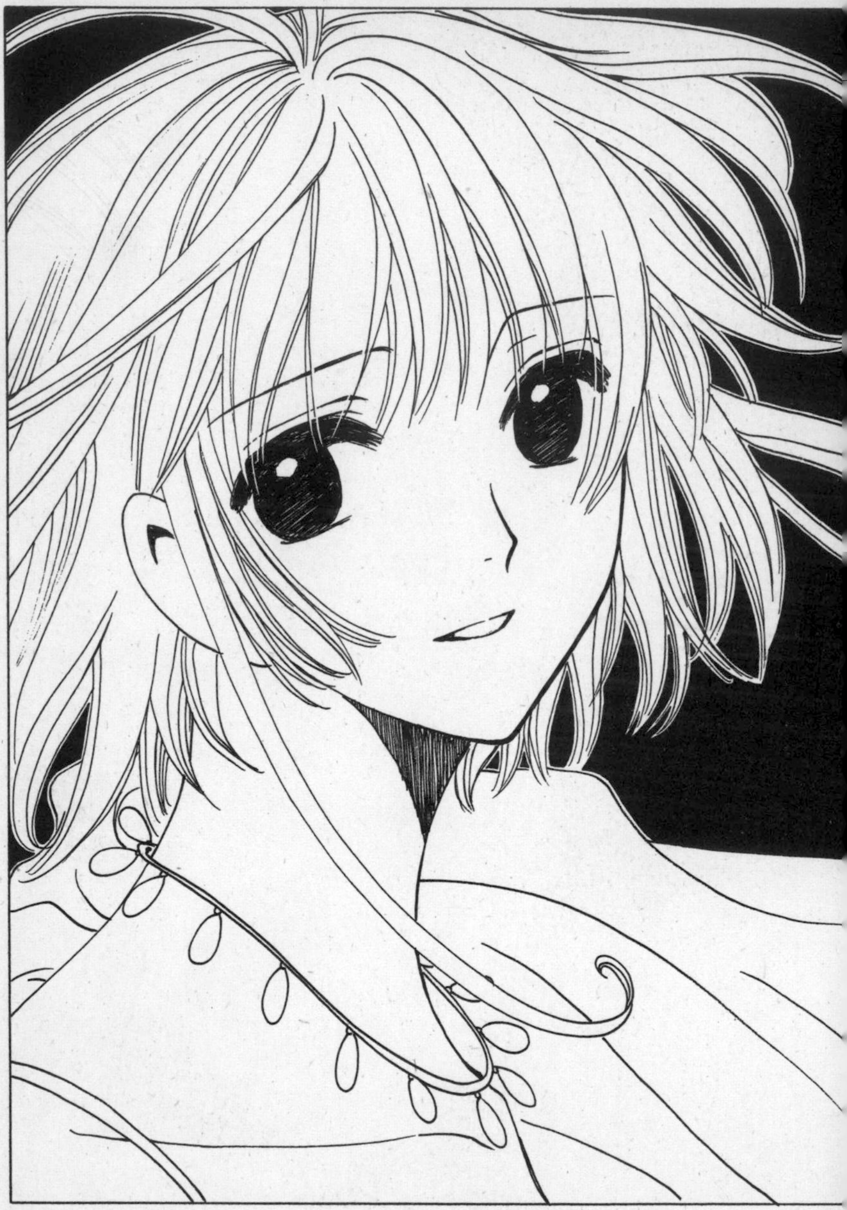

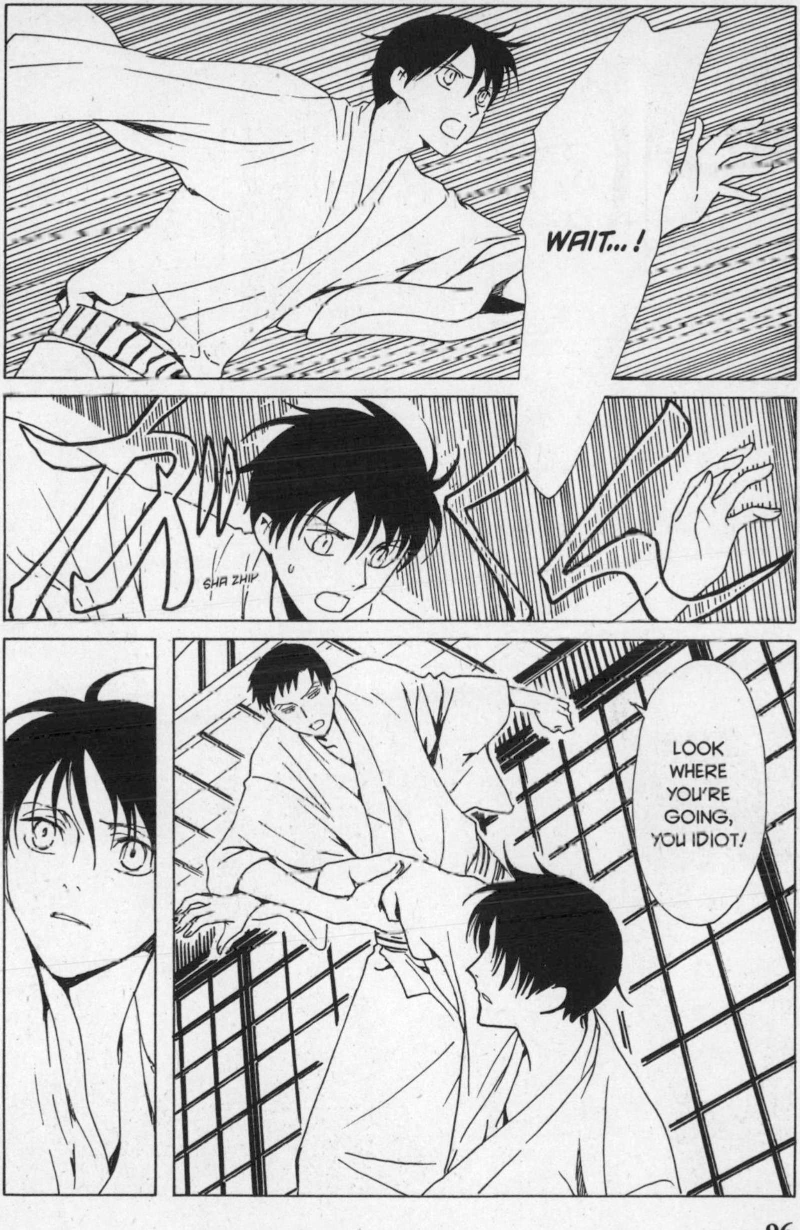
WAIT...!
SHA ZHIP
LOOK WHERE YOU'RE GOING, YOU IDIOT!

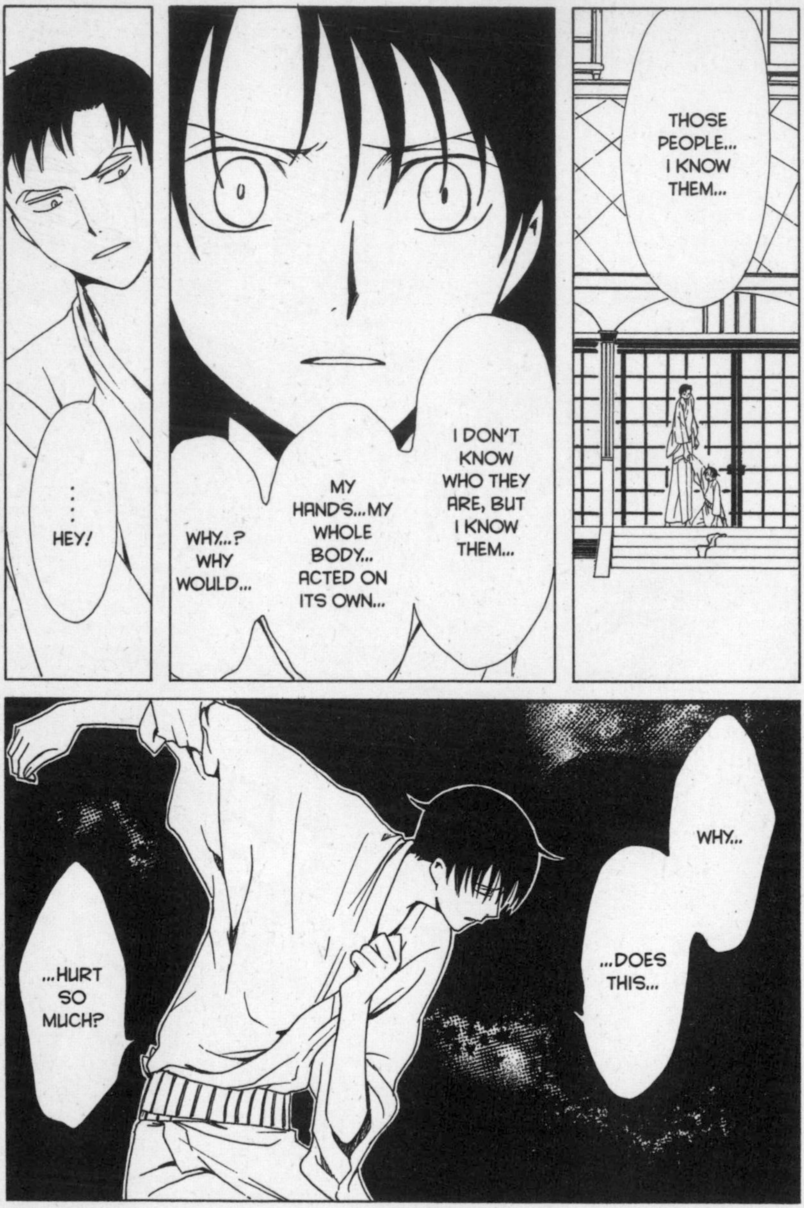
THOSE PEOPLE... I KNOW THEM...
I DON'T KNOW WHO THEY ARE, BUT I KNOW THEM...
MY HANDS...MY WHOLE BODY... ACTED ON ITS OWN...
WHY...? WHY WOULD...
...... HEY!
WHY...
...DOES THIS...
...HURT SO MUCH?

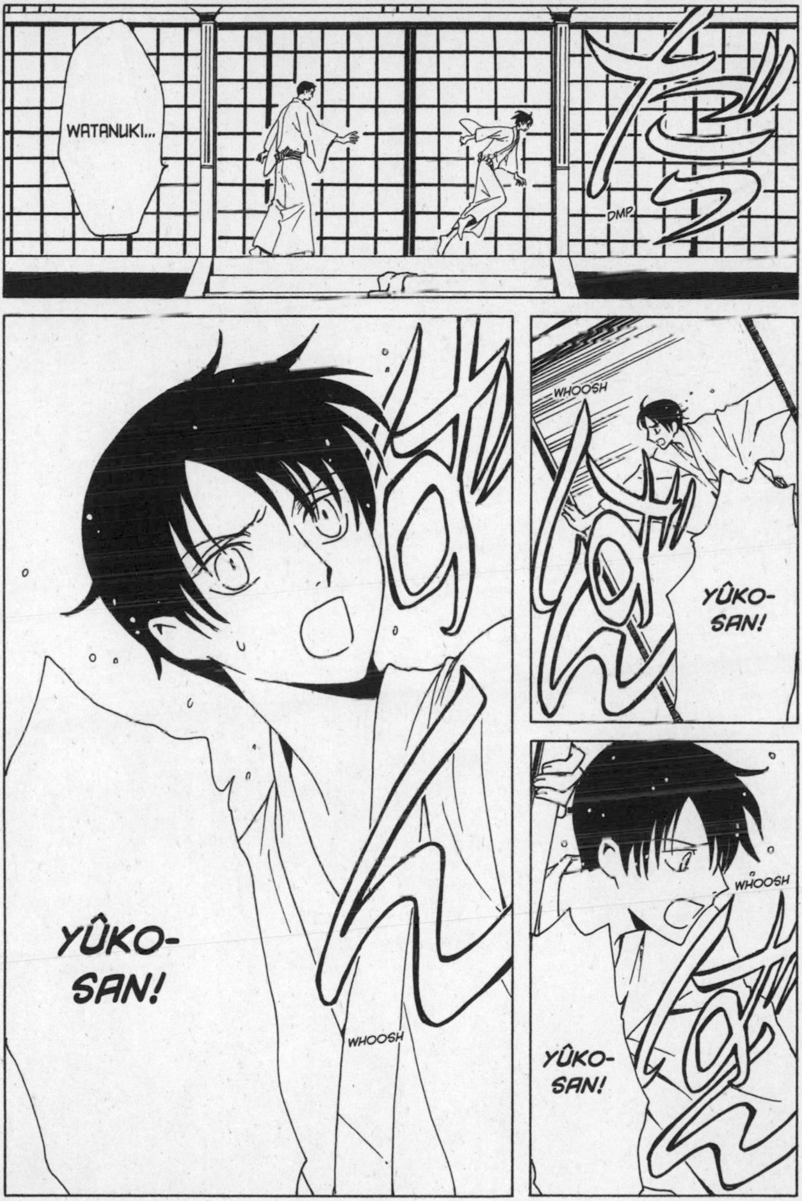
DMP
WATANUKI...
WHOOSH
YÛKO-SAN!
WHOOSH
YÛKO-SAN!
YÛKO-SAN!
WHOOSH

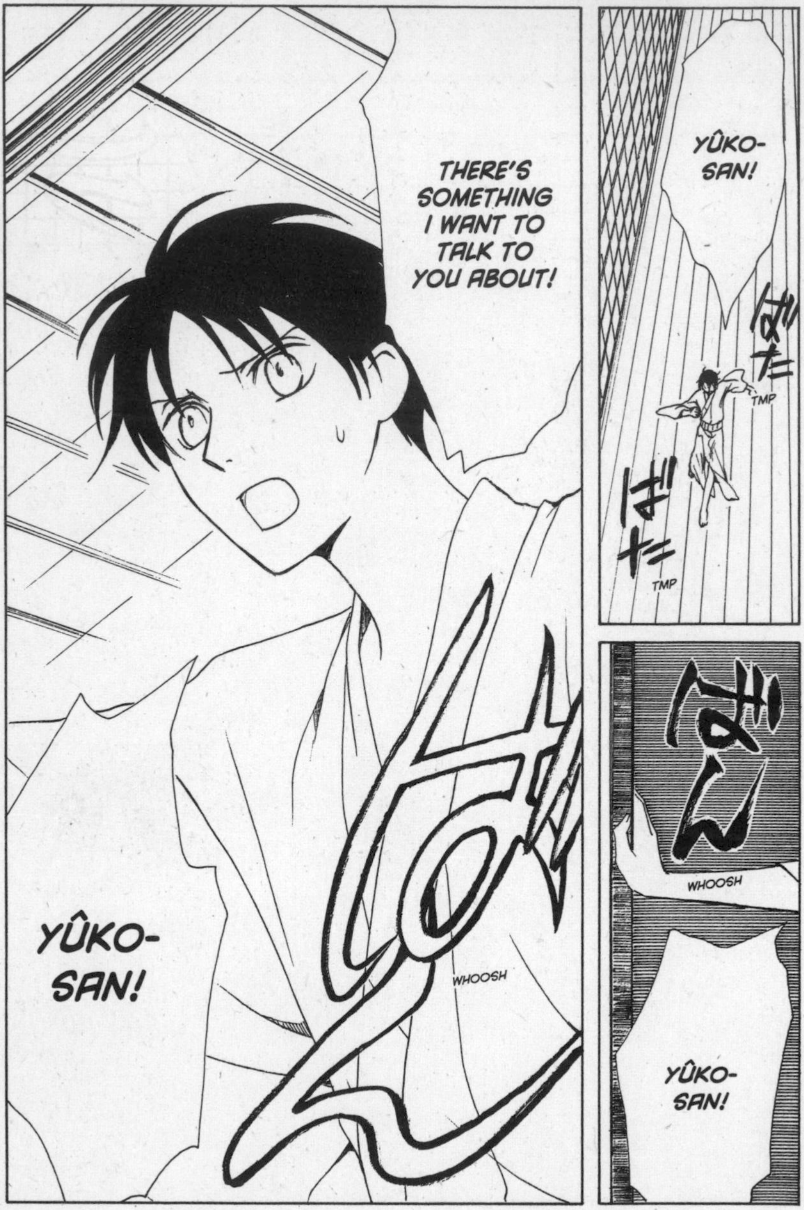
YÛKO-SAN!
TMP
TMP
WHOOSH
YÛKO-SAN!
THERE'S SOMETHING I WANT TO TALK TO YOU ABOUT!
WHOOSH
YÛKO-SAN!

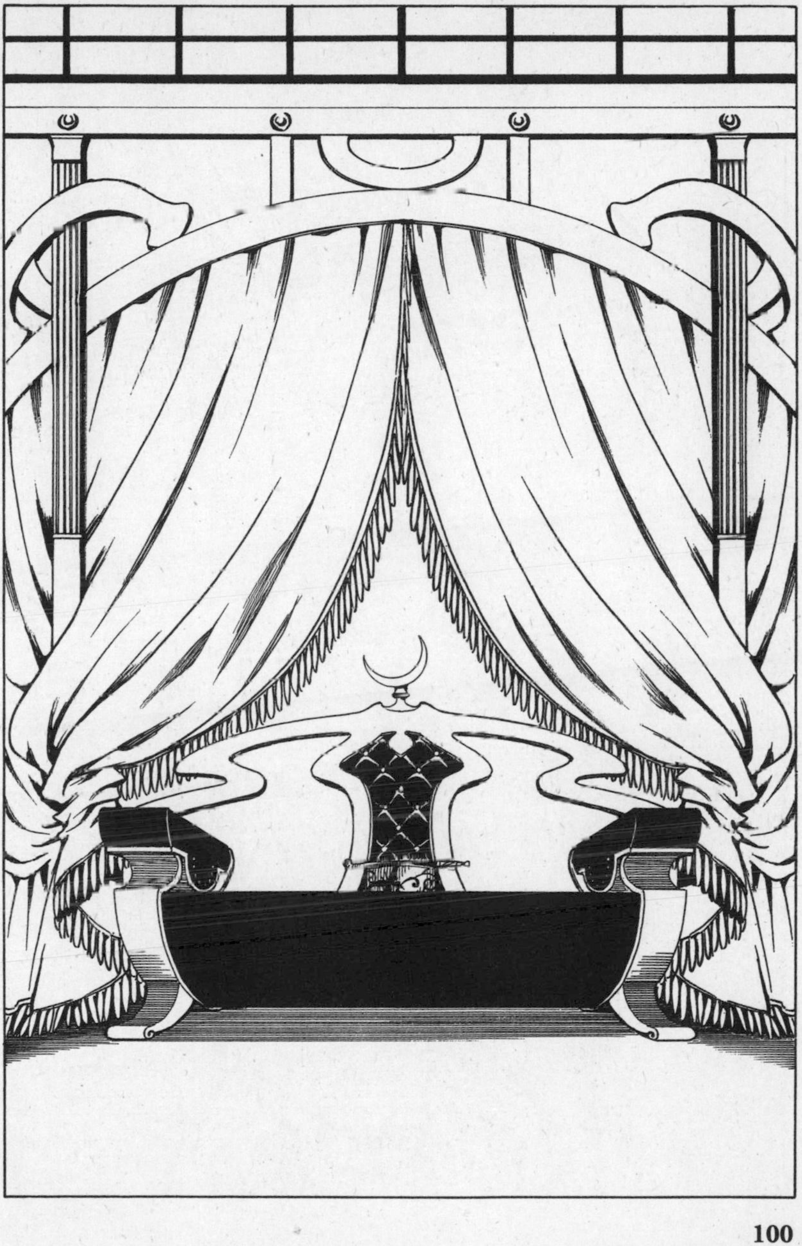

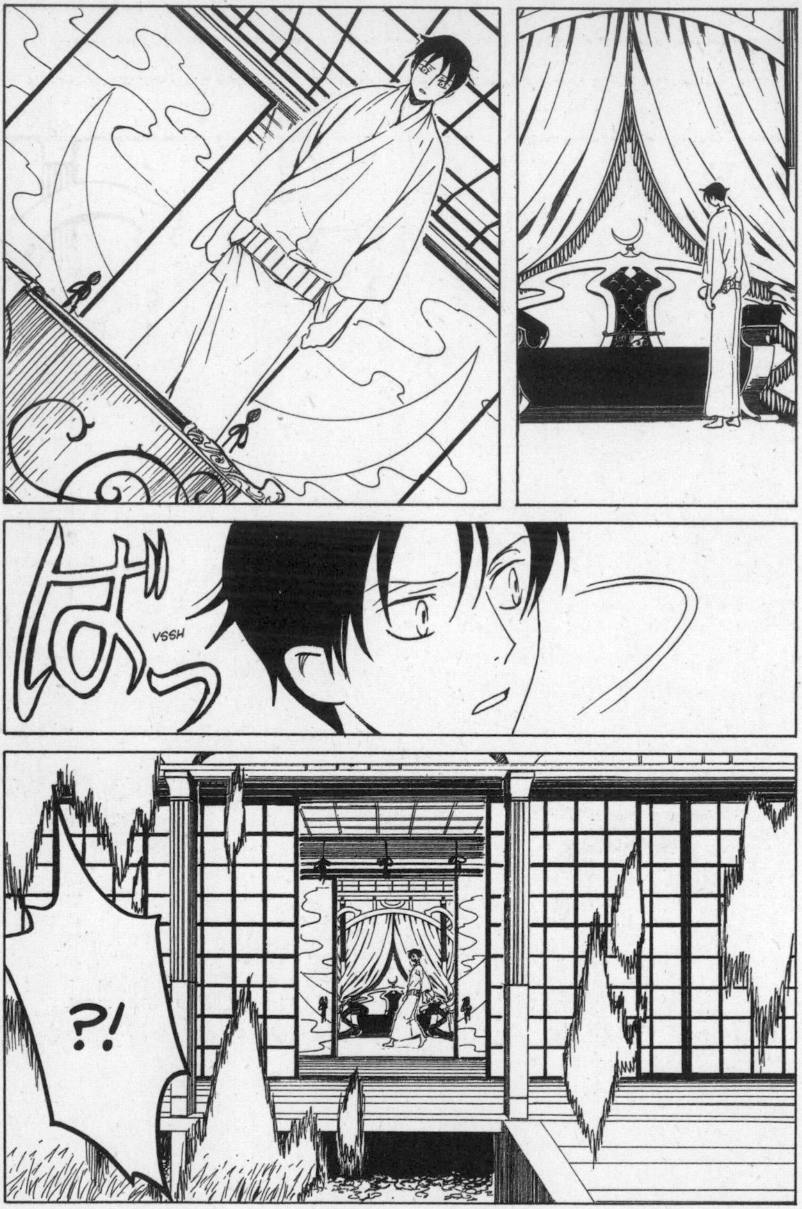
ばっ
VSSH
?!

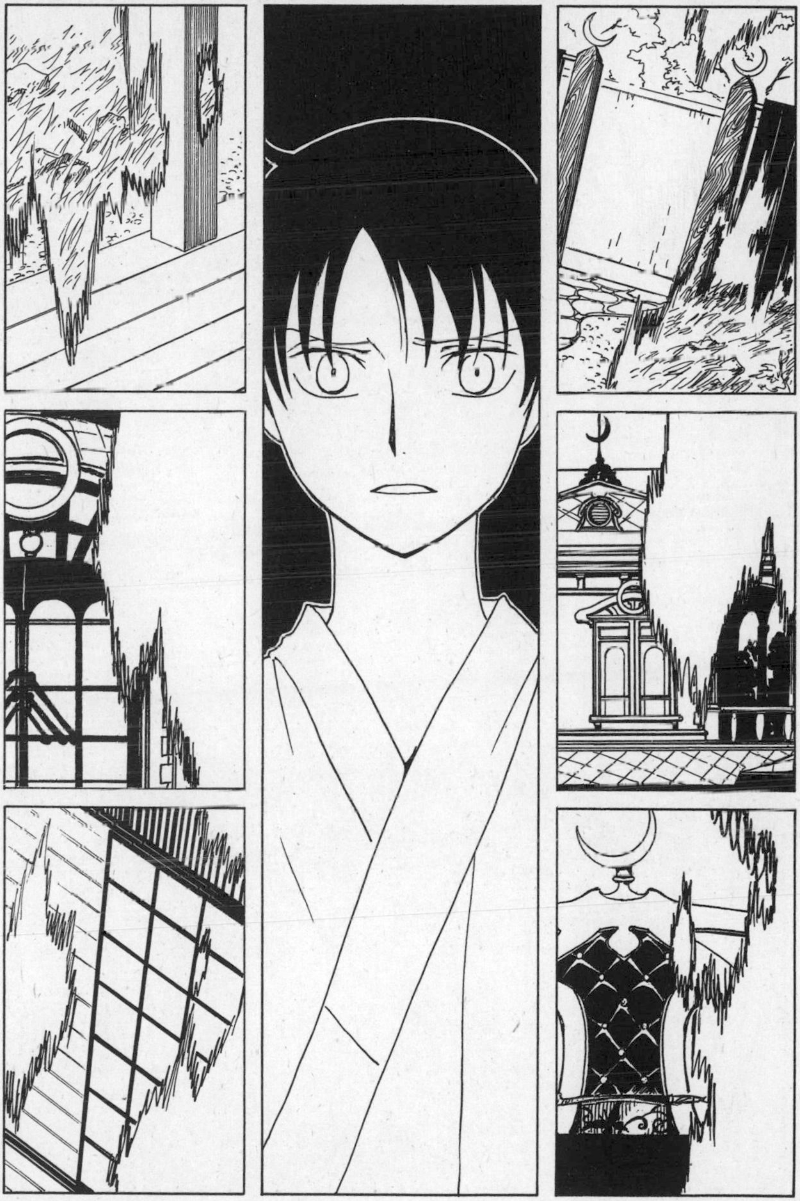

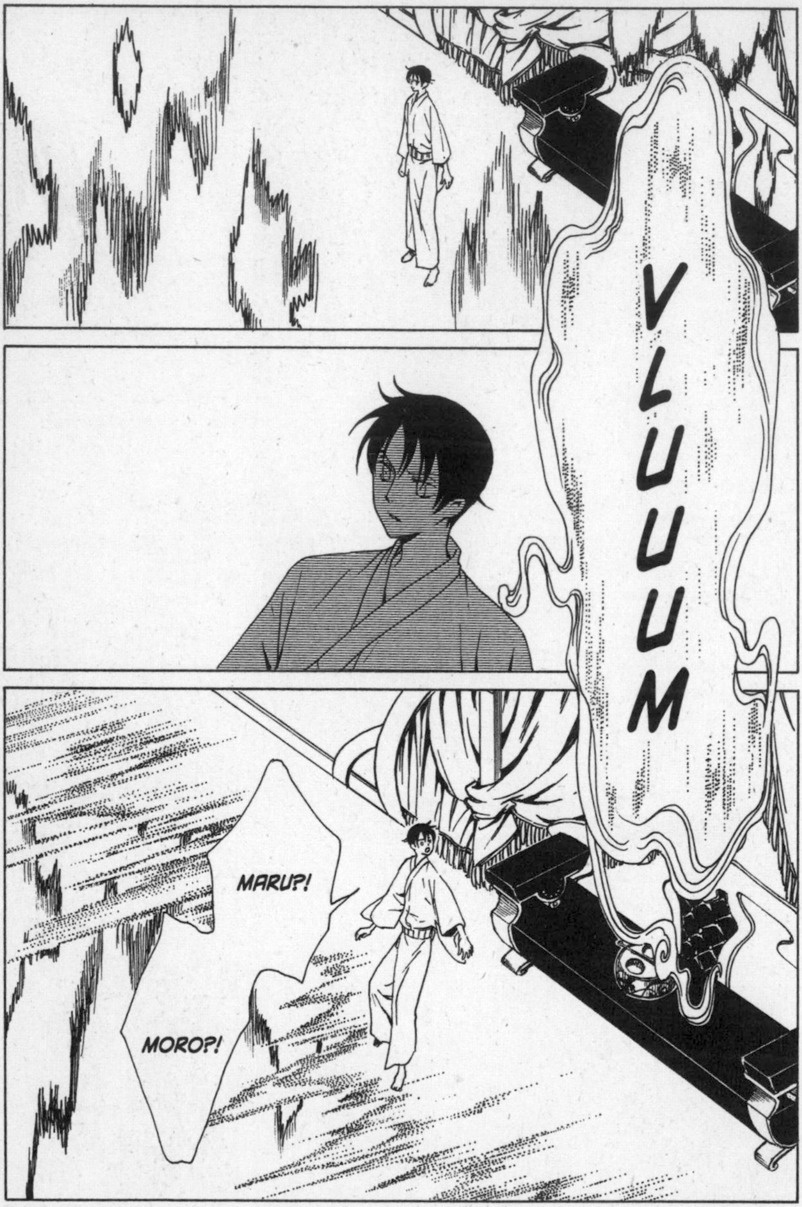
VLUUUM
MARU?!
MORO?!

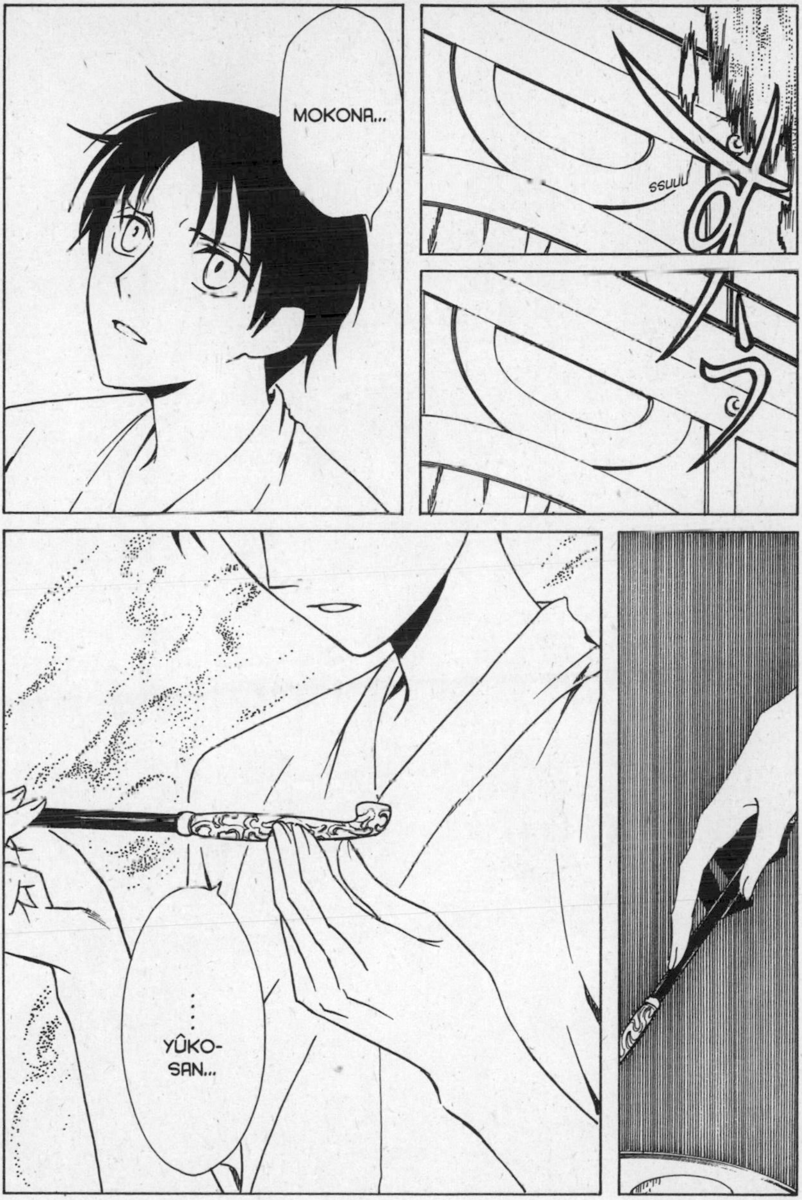
ssuuu
MOKONA...
...
YÛKO-SAN...

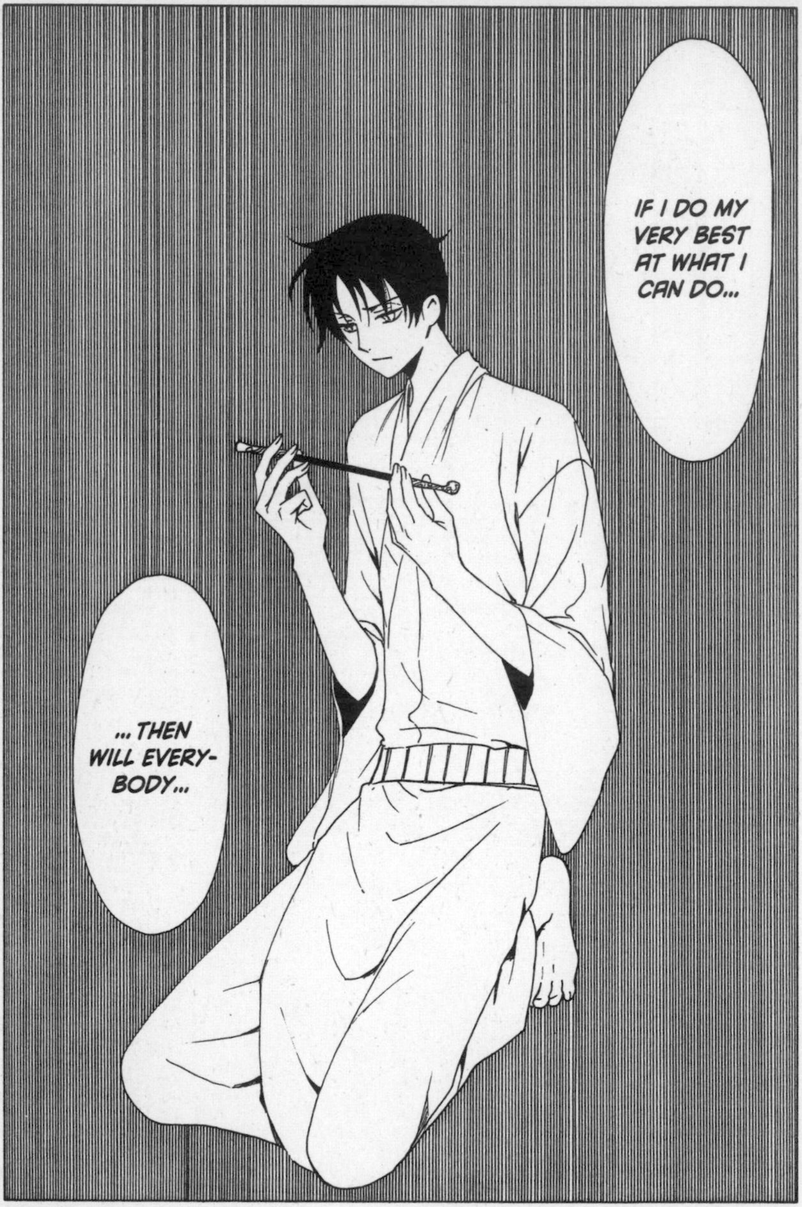
IF I DO MY VERY BEST AT WHAT I CAN DO...
...THEN WILL EVERY-BODY...

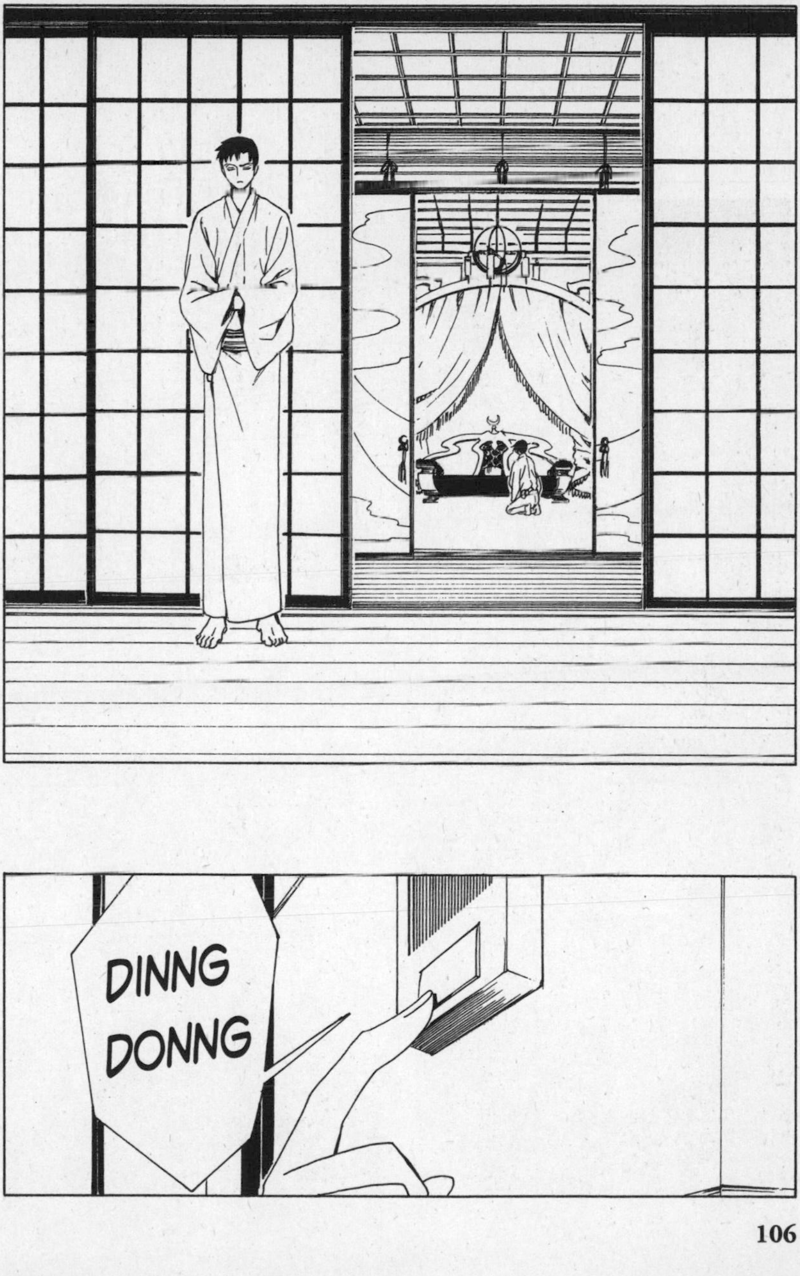
DINNG DONNG

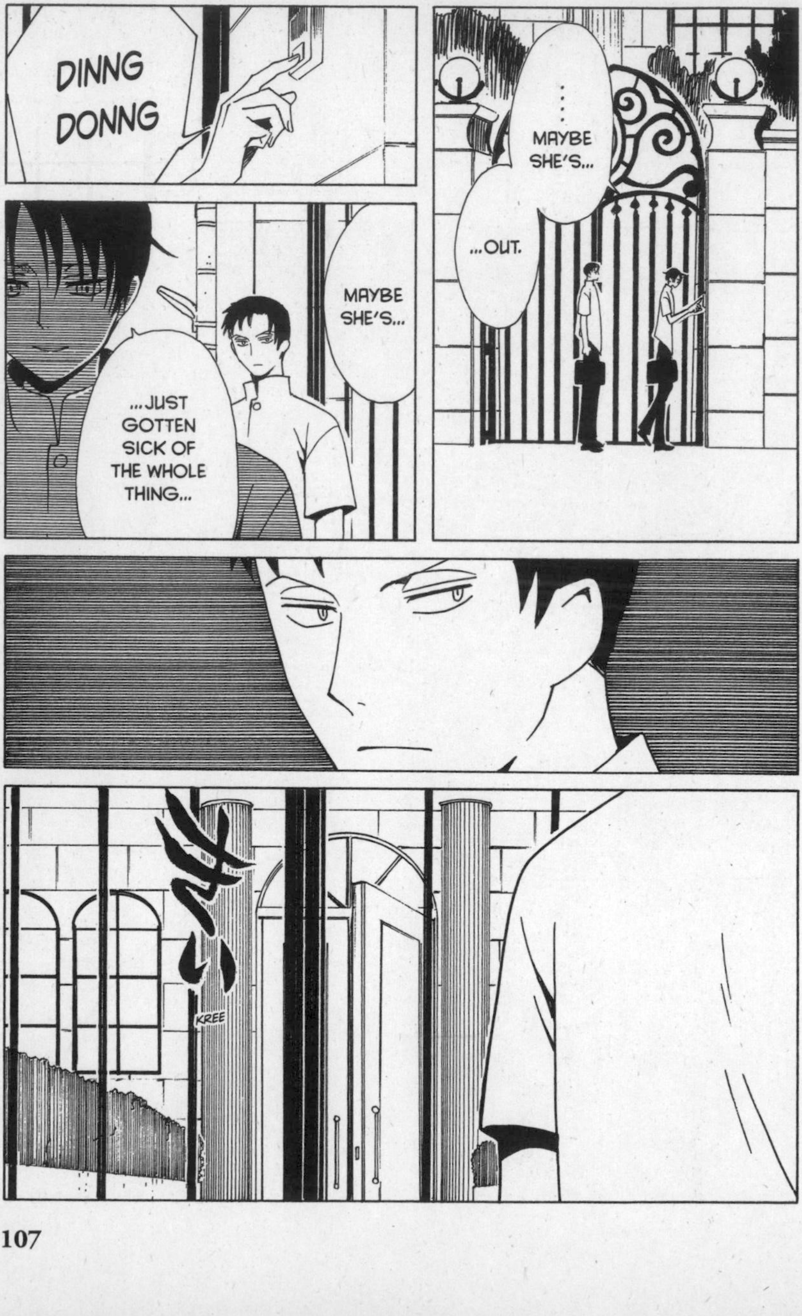

...... MAYBE SHE'S...
...OUT.
DINNG DONNG
MAYBE SHE'S...
...JUST GOTTEN SICK OF THE WHOLE THING...
KREE

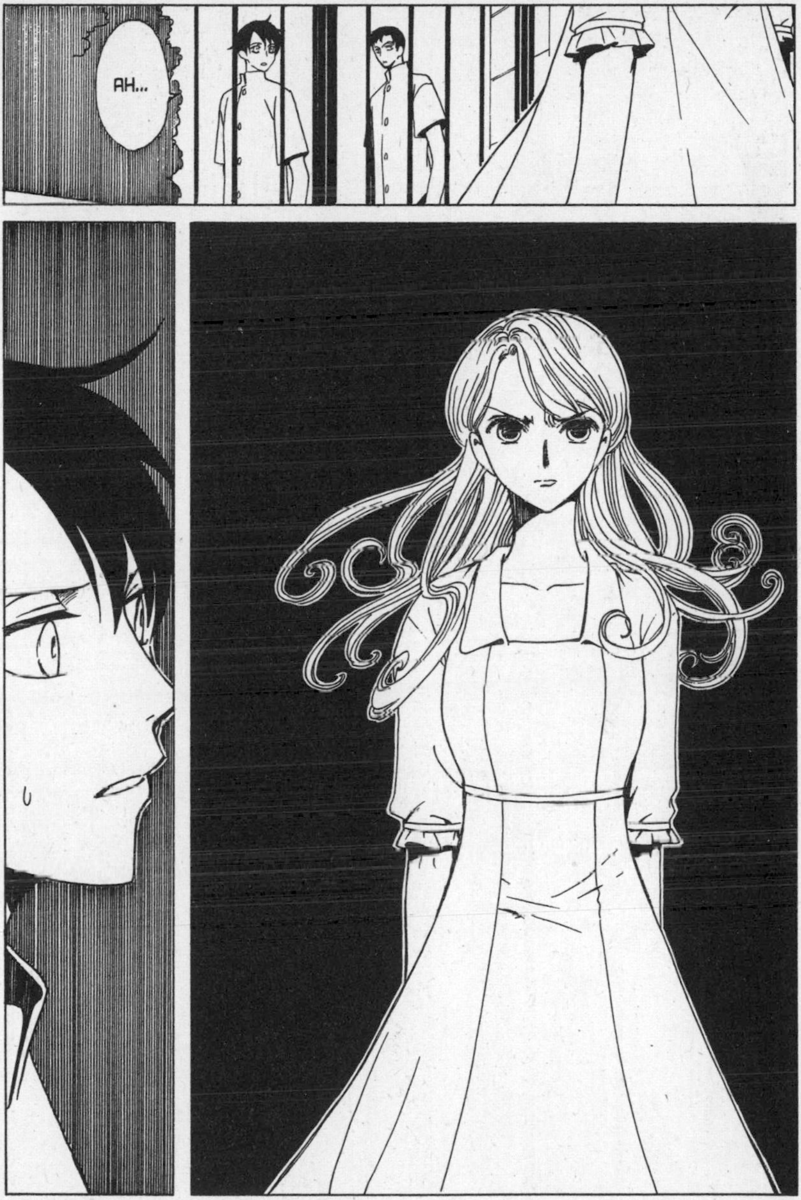
AH...

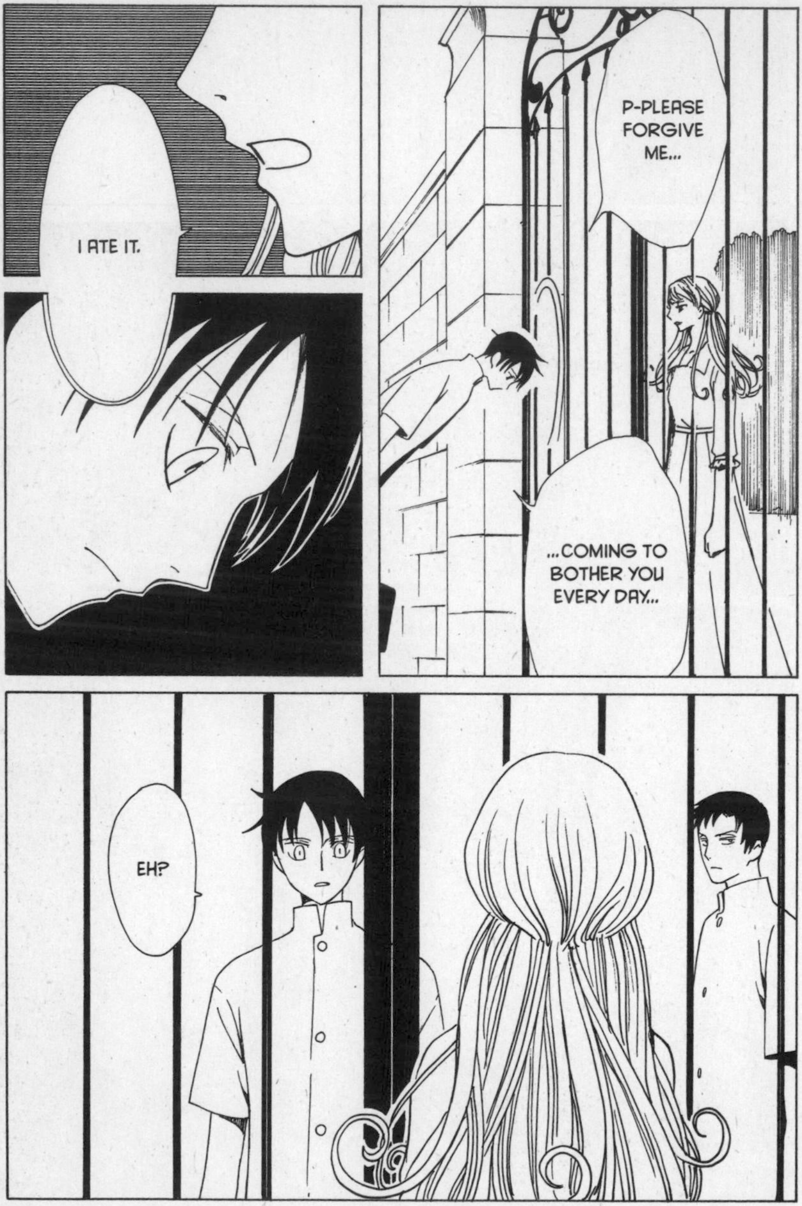
P-PLEASE FORGIVE ME...
...COMING TO BOTHER YOU EVERY DAY...
I ATE IT.
EH?

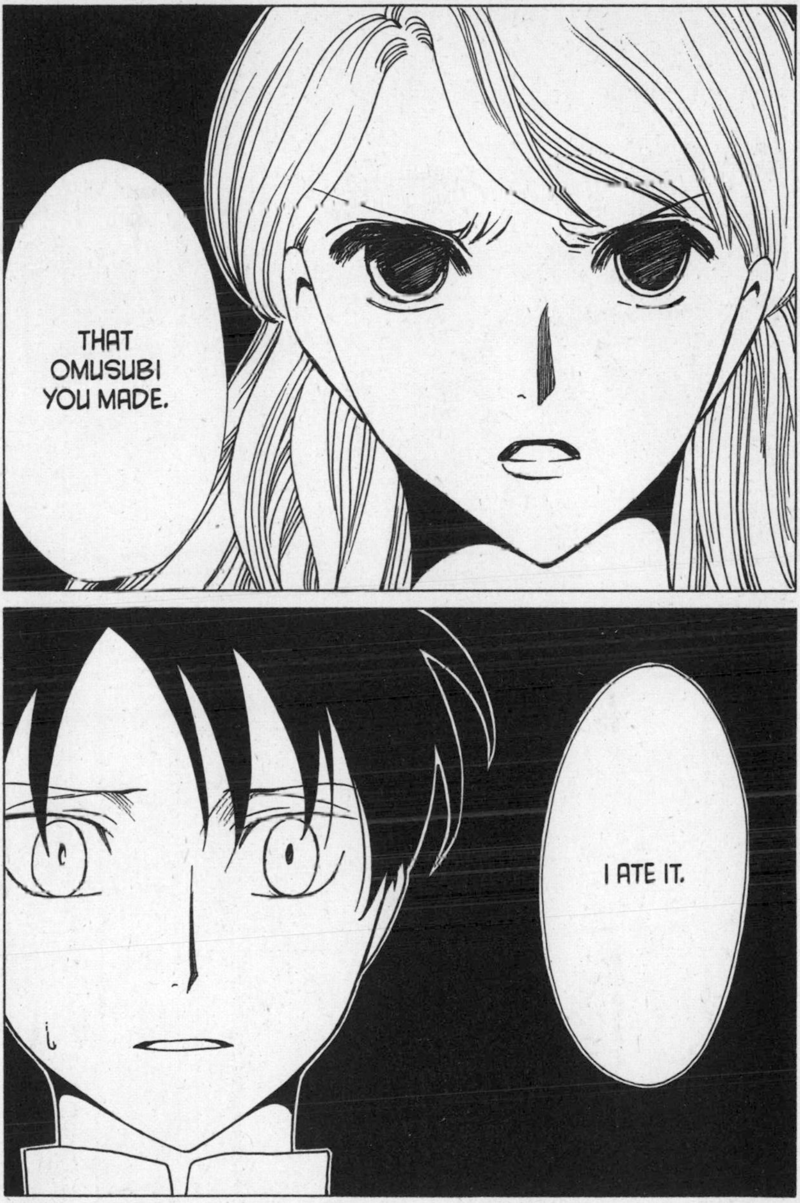
THAT OMUSUBI YOU MADE.
I ATE IT.

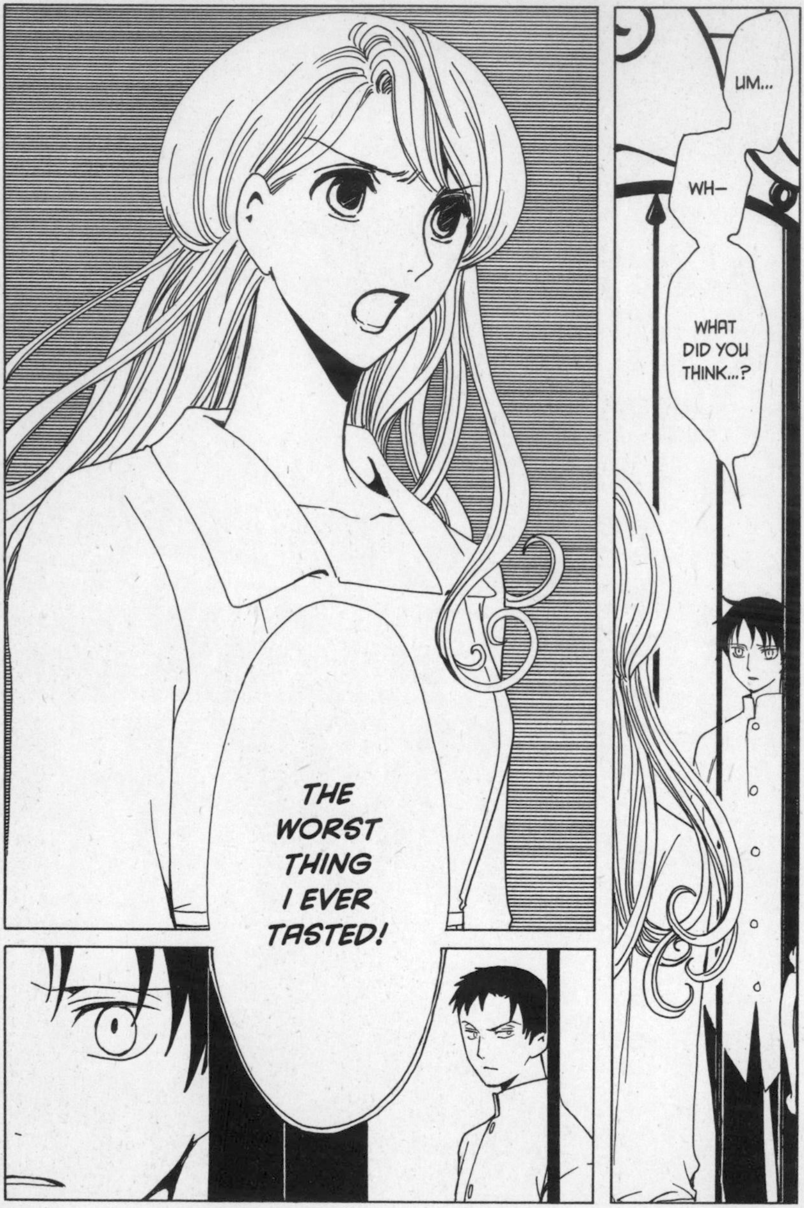
UM...
WH—
WHAT DID YOU THINK...?
THE WORST THING I EVER TASTED!

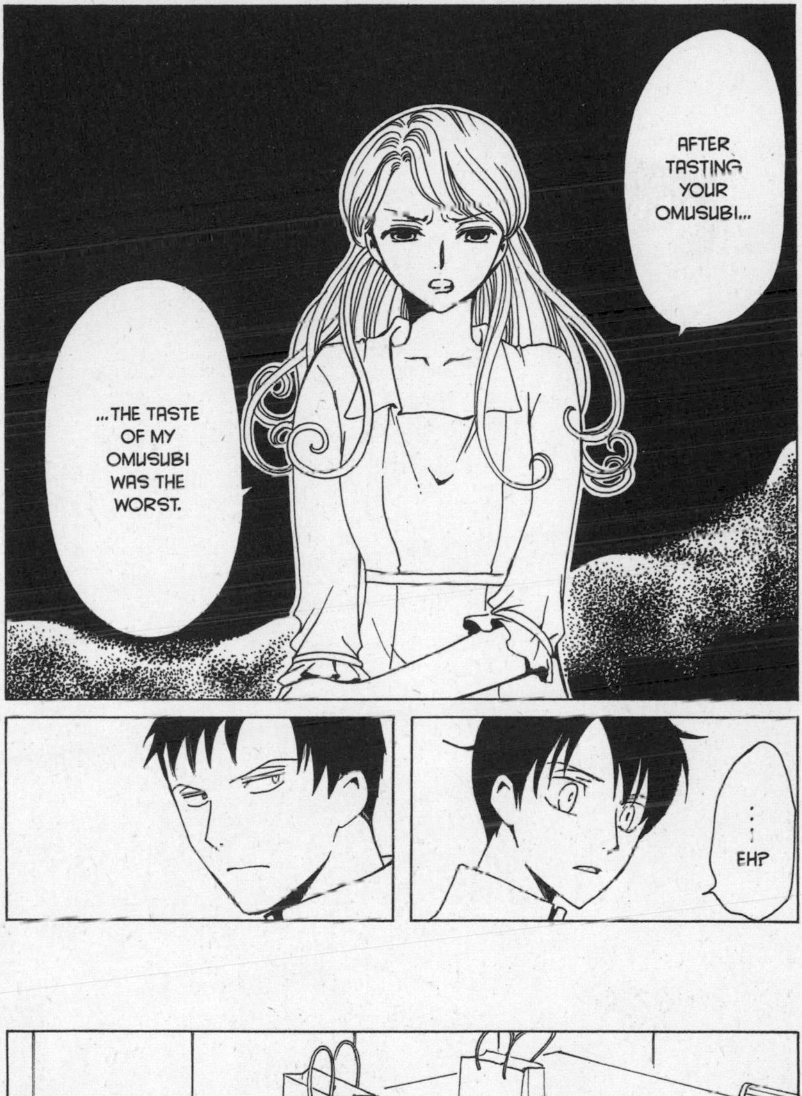
AFTER TASTING YOUR OMUSUBI...
...THE TASTE OF MY OMUSUBI WAS THE WORST.
... EH?

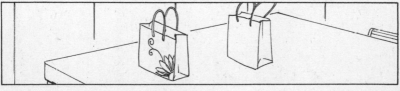

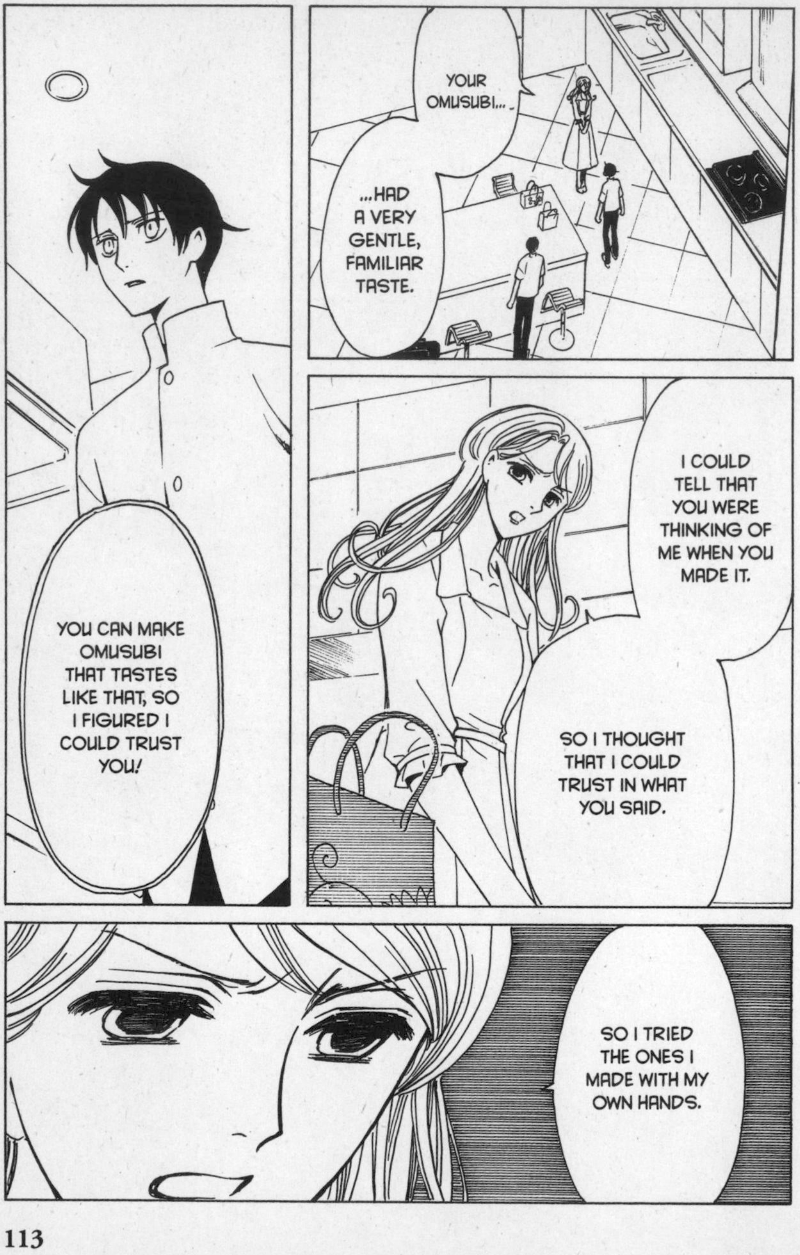
YOUR OMUSUBI...
...HAD A VERY GENTLE, FAMILIAR TASTE.
I COULD TELL THAT YOU WERE THINKING OF ME WHEN YOU MADE IT.
SO I THOUGHT THAT I COULD TRUST IN WHAT YOU SAID.
YOU CAN MAKE OMUSUBI THAT TASTES LIKE THAT, SO I FIGURED I COULD TRUST YOU!
SO I TRIED THE ONES I MADE WITH MY OWN HANDS.

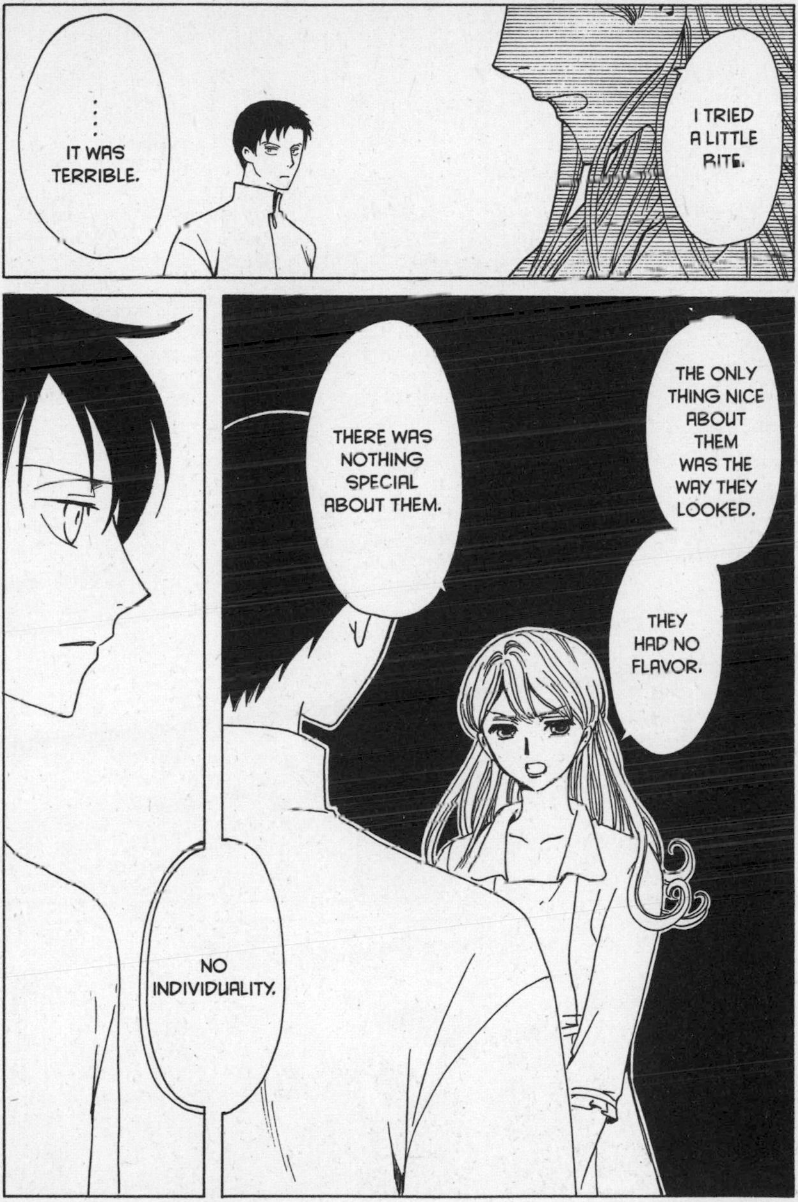
I TRIED A LITTLE BITE.
...
IT WAS TERRIBLE.
THE ONLY THING NICE ABOUT THEM WAS THE WAY THEY LOOKED.
THEY HAD NO FLAVOR.
THERE WAS NOTHING SPECIAL ABOUT THEM.
NO INDIVIDUALITY.

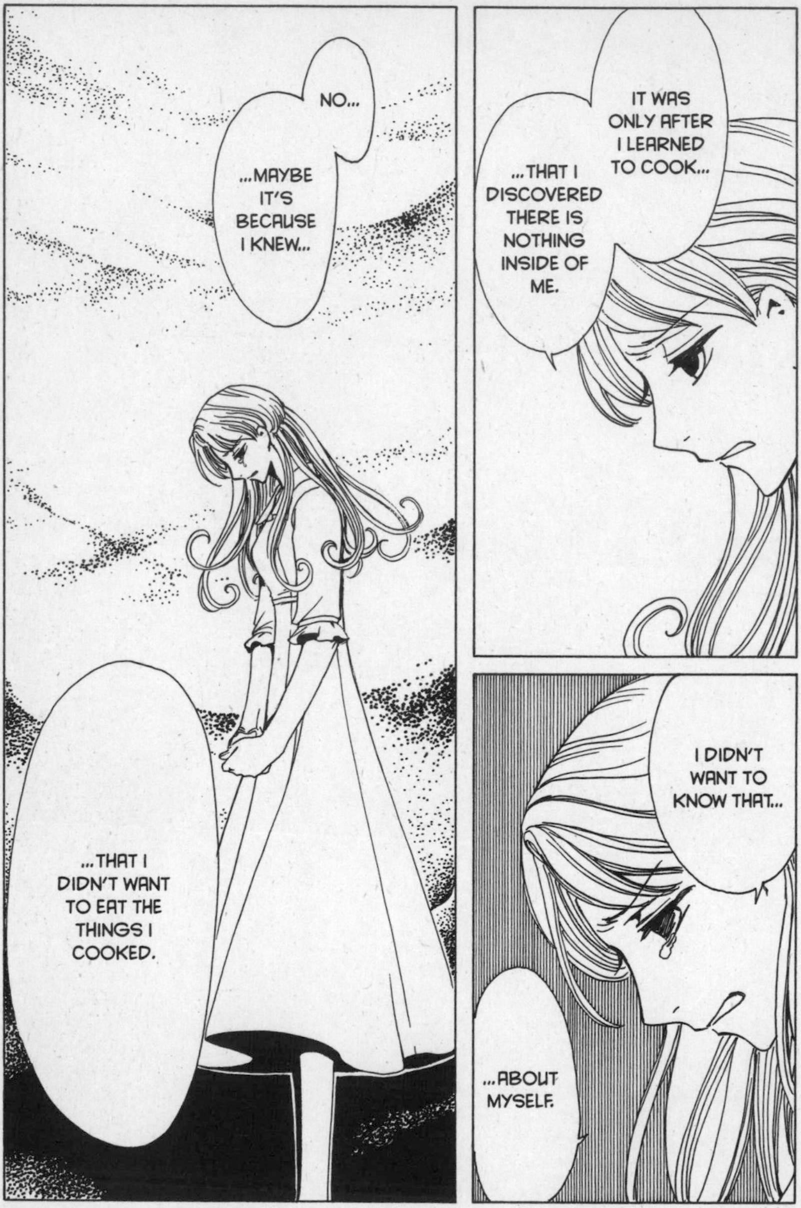
IT WAS ONLY AFTER I LEARNED TO COOK...
...THAT I DISCOVERED THERE IS NOTHING INSIDE OF ME.
I DIDN'T WANT TO KNOW THAT...
...ABOUT MYSELF.
NO...
...MAYBE IT'S BECAUSE I KNEW...
...THAT I DIDN'T WANT TO EAT THE THINGS I COOKED.

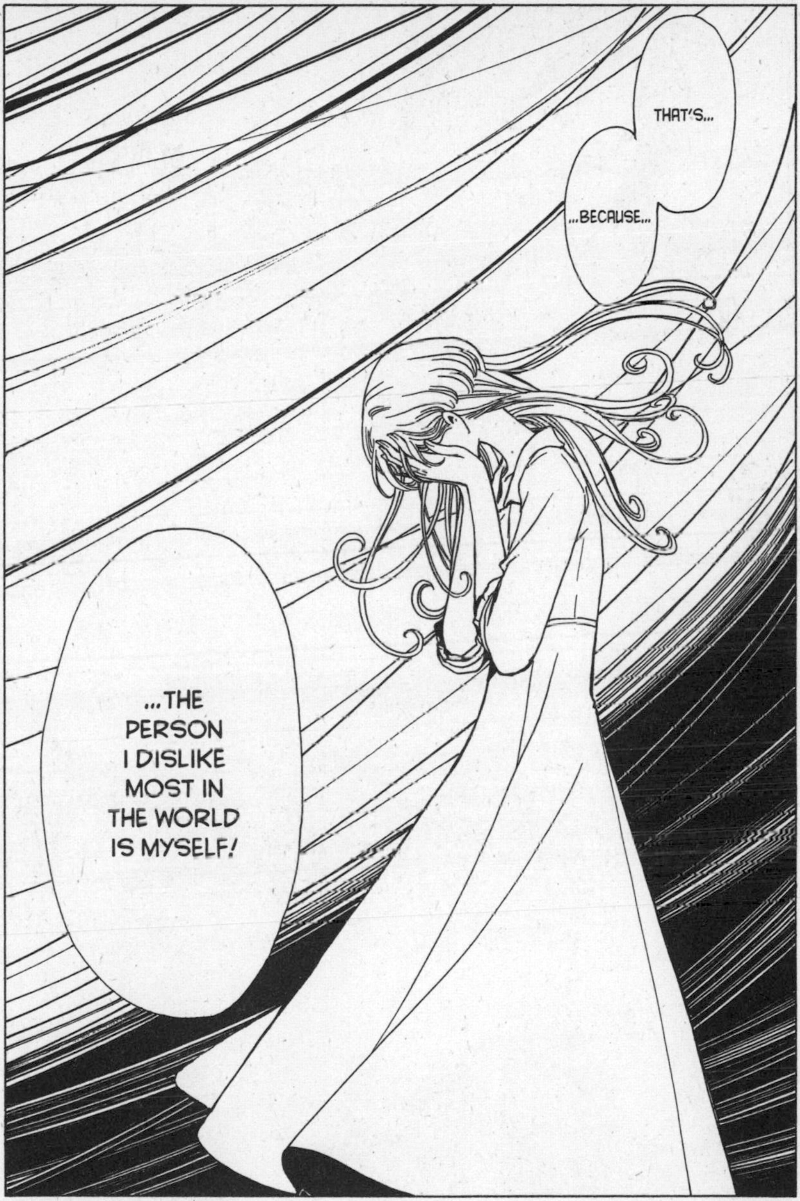
THAT'S...
...BECAUSE...
...THE PERSON I DISLIKE MOST IN THE WORLD IS MYSELF!

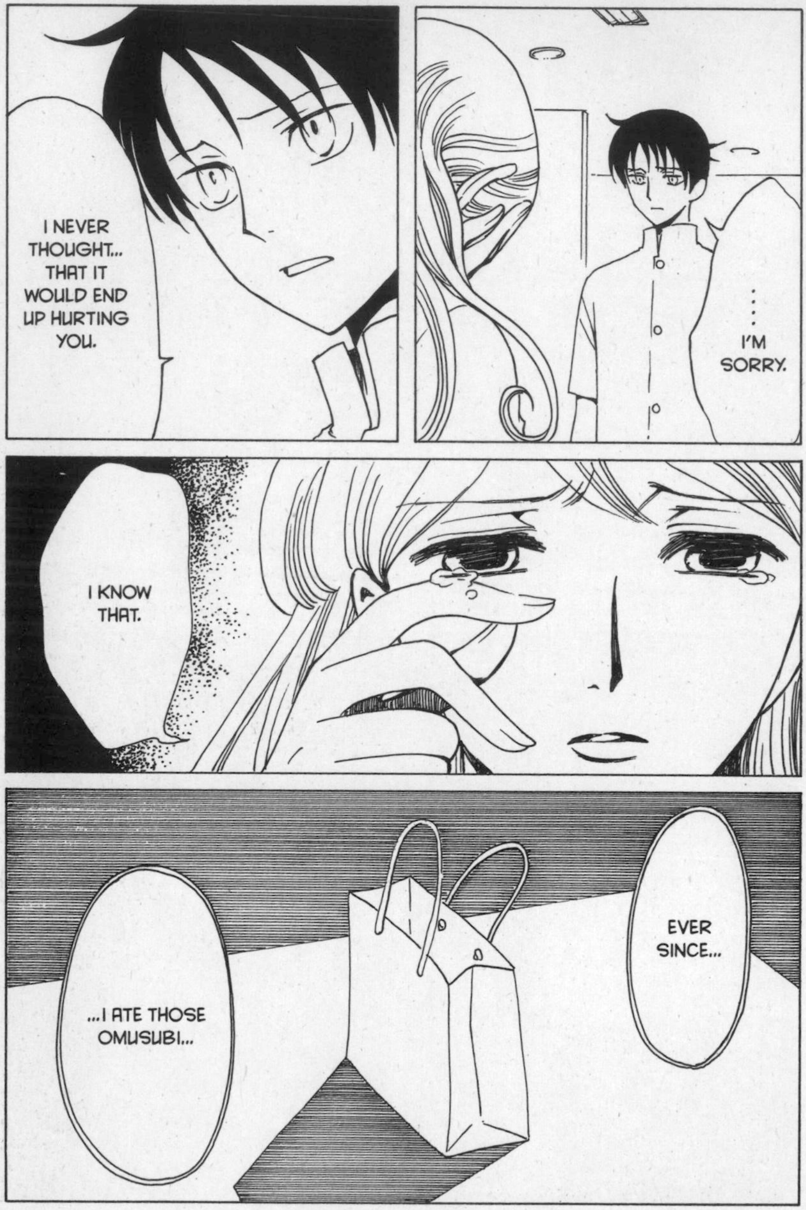

.... I'M SORRY.
I NEVER THOUGHT... THAT IT WOULD END UP HURTING YOU.
I KNOW THAT.
EVER SINCE...
...I ATE THOSE OMUSUBI...

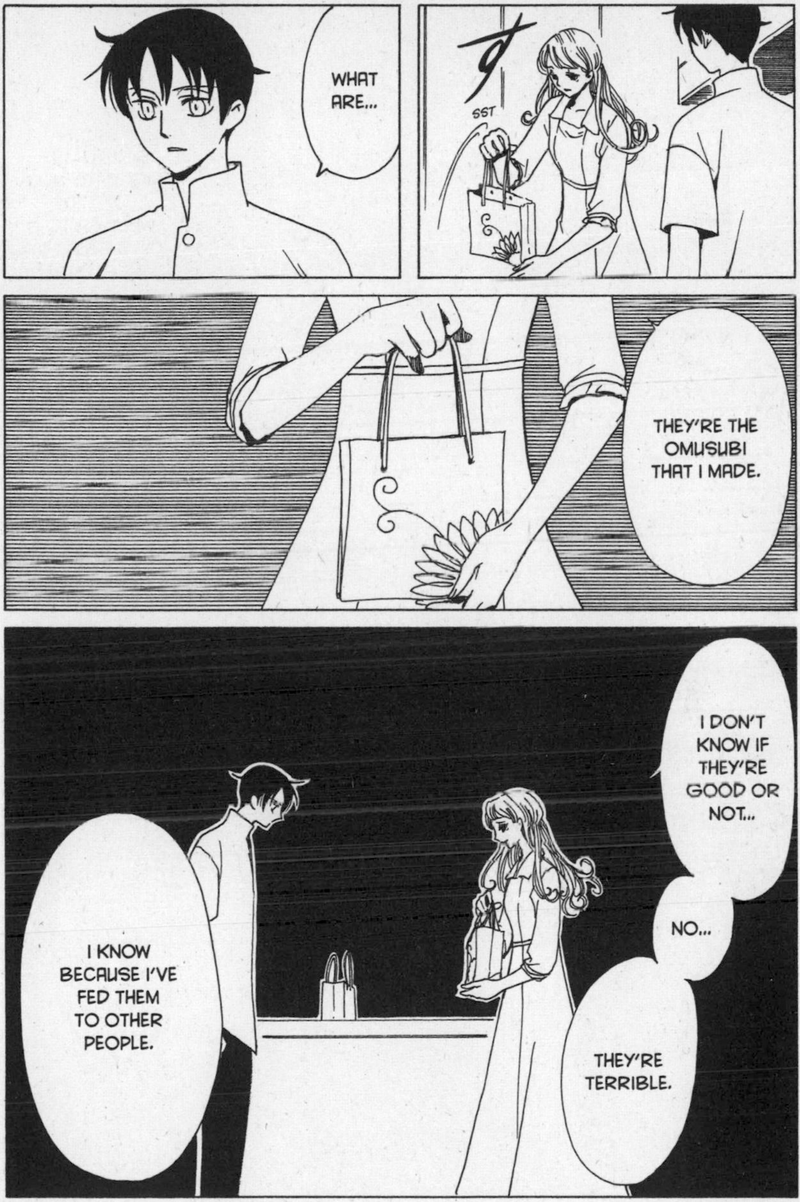
す
SST
WHAT ARE...
THEY'RE THE OMUSUBI THAT I MADE.
I DON'T KNOW IF THEY'RE GOOD OR NOT...
NO...
THEY'RE TERRIBLE.
I KNOW BECAUSE I'VE FED THEM TO OTHER PEOPLE.

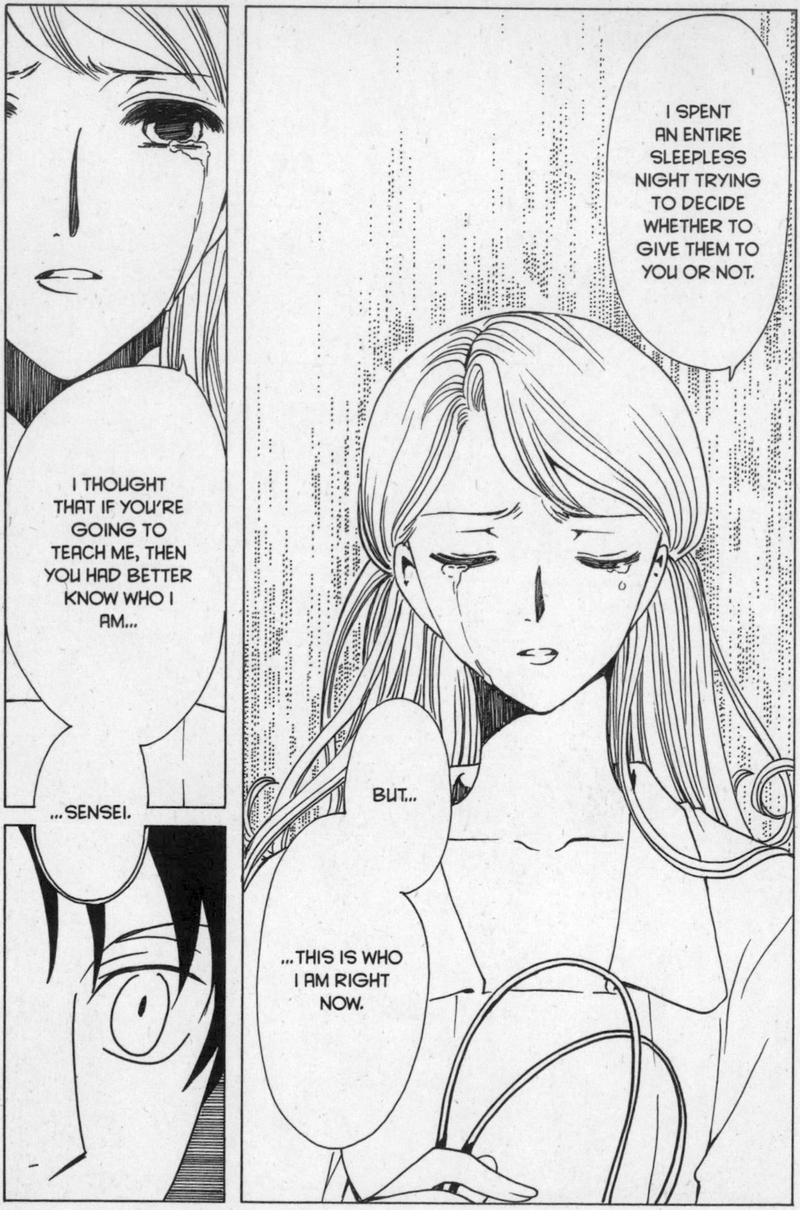

I SPENT AN ENTIRE SLEEPLESS NIGHT TRYING TO DECIDE WHETHER TO GIVE THEM TO YOU OR NOT.
BUT...
...THIS IS WHO I AM RIGHT NOW.
I THOUGHT THAT IF YOU'RE GOING TO TEACH ME, THEN YOU HAD BETTER KNOW WHO I AM...
...SENSEI.

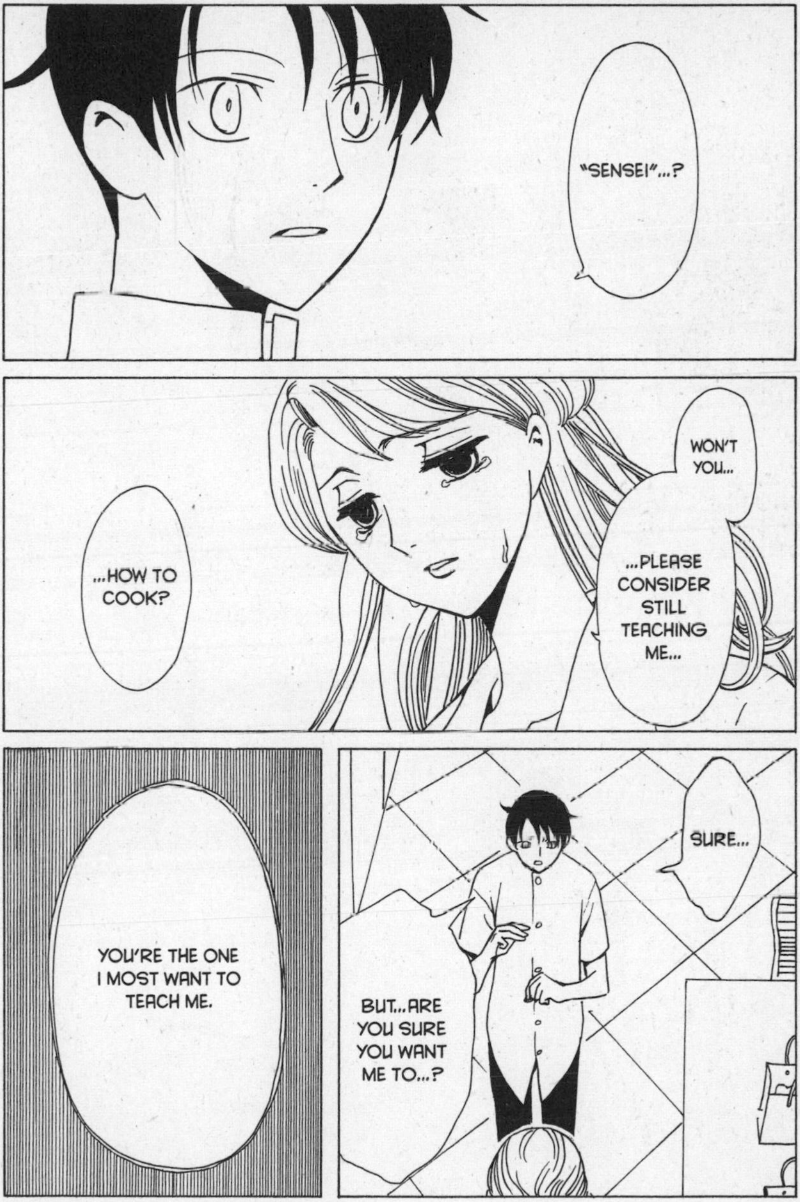
"SENSEI"...?
WON'T YOU...
...PLEASE CONSIDER STILL TEACHING ME...
...HOW TO COOK?
SURE...
BUT...ARE YOU SURE YOU WANT ME TO...?
YOU'RE THE ONE I MOST WANT TO TEACH ME.

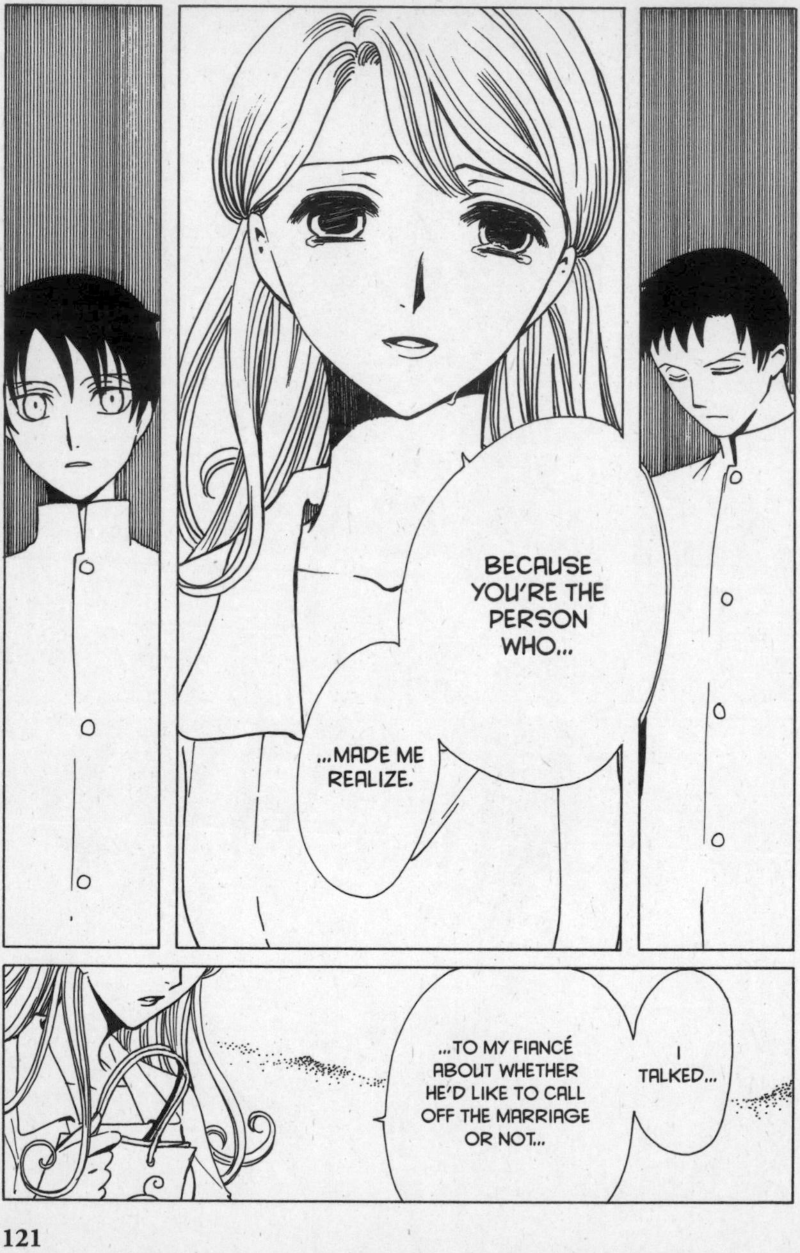
BECAUSE YOU'RE THE PERSON WHO...
...MADE ME REALIZE.
I TALKED...
...TO MY FIANCÉ ABOUT WHETHER HE'D LIKE TO CALL OFF THE MARRIAGE OR NOT...

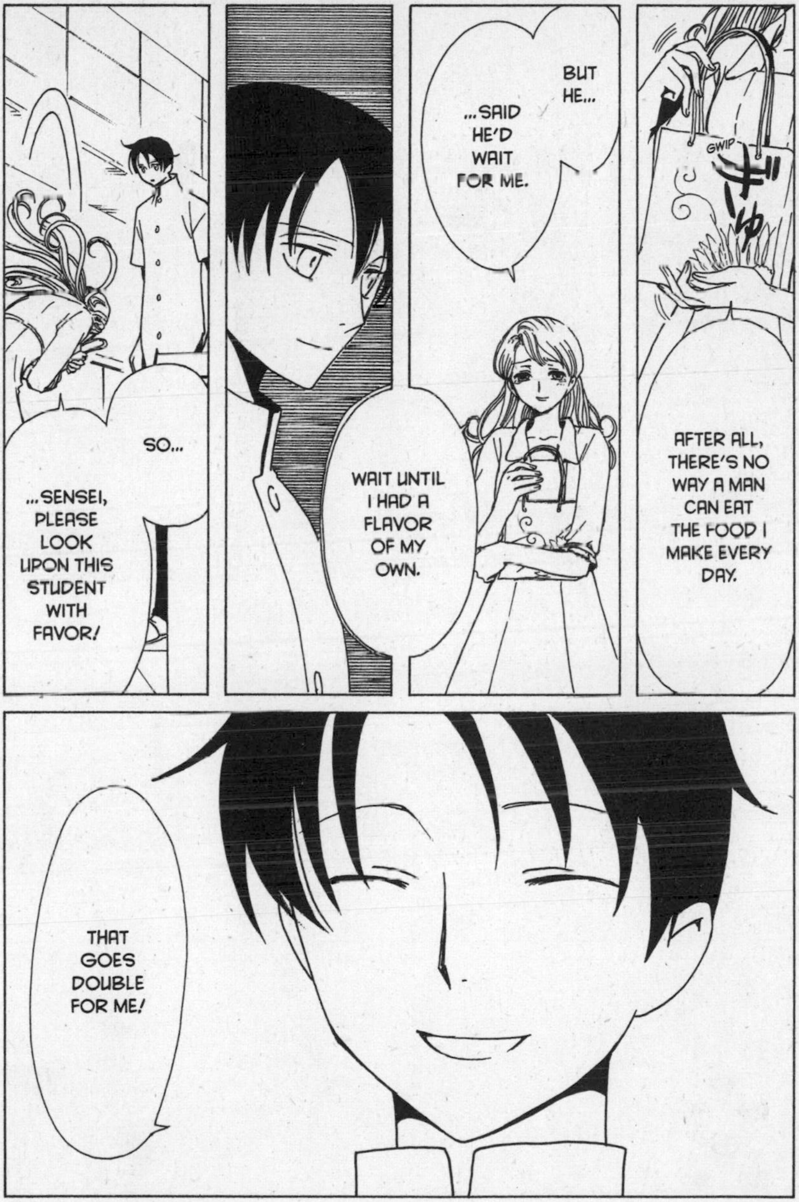
GWIP
ぎゅ
AFTER ALL, THERE'S NO WAY A MAN CAN EAT THE FOOD I MAKE EVERY DAY.
BUT HE...
...SAID HE'D WAIT FOR ME.
WAIT UNTIL I HAD A FLAVOR OF MY OWN.
SO...
...SENSEI, PLEASE LOOK UPON THIS STUDENT WITH FAVOR!
THAT GOES DOUBLE FOR ME!

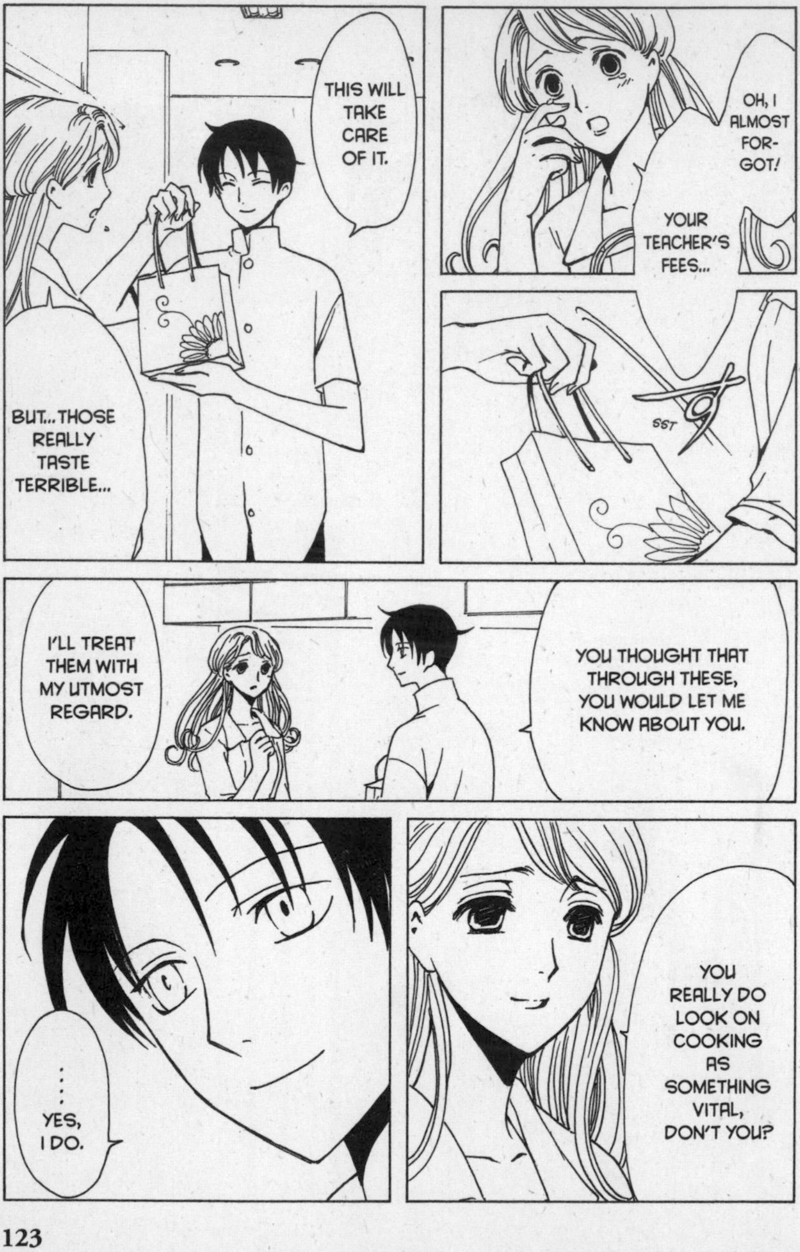
OH, I ALMOST FOR-GOT!
YOUR TEACHER'S FEES...
SST
THIS WILL TAKE CARE OF IT.
BUT... THOSE REALLY TASTE TERRIBLE...
YOU THOUGHT THAT THROUGH THESE, YOU WOULD LET ME KNOW ABOUT YOU.
I'LL TREAT THEM WITH MY UTMOST REGARD.
YOU REALLY DO LOOK ON COOKING AS SOMETHING VITAL, DON'T YOU?
.... YES, I DO.

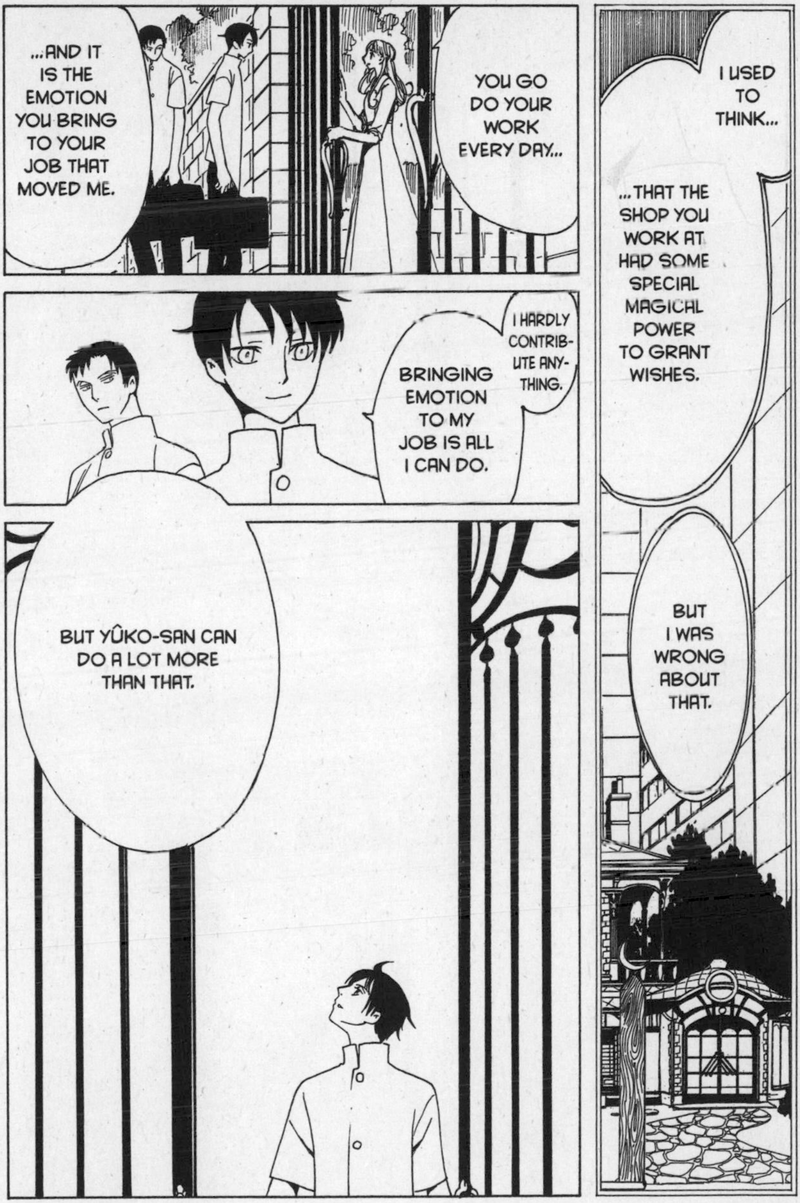
I USED TO THINK...
...THAT THE SHOP YOU WORK AT HAD SOME SPECIAL MAGICAL POWER TO GRANT WISHES.
BUT I WAS WRONG ABOUT THAT.
YOU GO DO YOUR WORK EVERY DAY...
...AND IT IS THE EMOTION YOU BRING TO YOUR JOB THAT MOVED ME.
I HARDLY CONTRIBUTE ANYTHING.
BRINGING EMOTION TO MY JOB IS ALL I CAN DO.
BUT YÛKO-SAN CAN DO A LOT MORE THAN THAT.

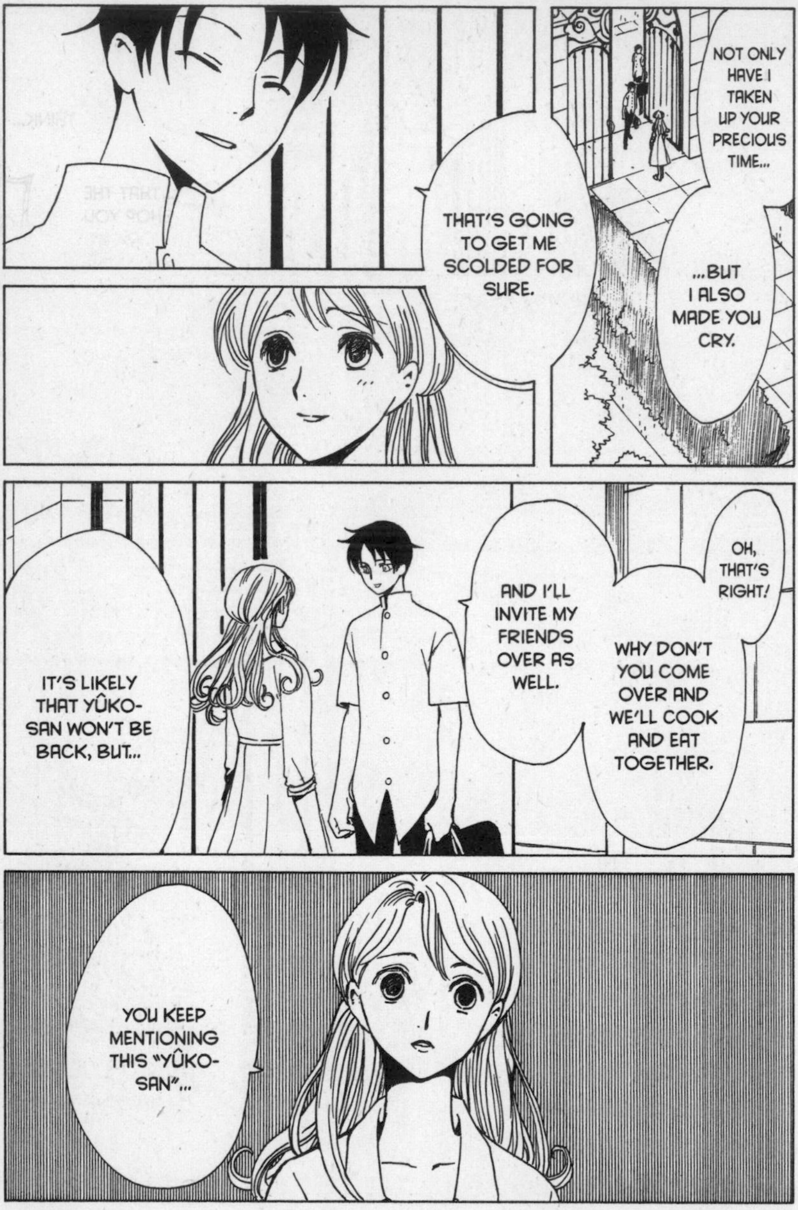
NOT ONLY HAVE I TAKEN UP YOUR PRECIOUS TIME...
...BUT I ALSO MADE YOU CRY.
THAT'S GOING TO GET ME SCOLDED FOR SURE.
OH, THAT'S RIGHT!
WHY DON'T YOU COME OVER AND WE'LL COOK AND EAT TOGETHER.
AND I'LL INVITE MY FRIENDS OVER AS WELL.
IT'S LIKELY THAT YÛKO-SAN WON'T BE BACK, BUT...
YOU KEEP MENTIONING THIS "YÛKO-SAN"...

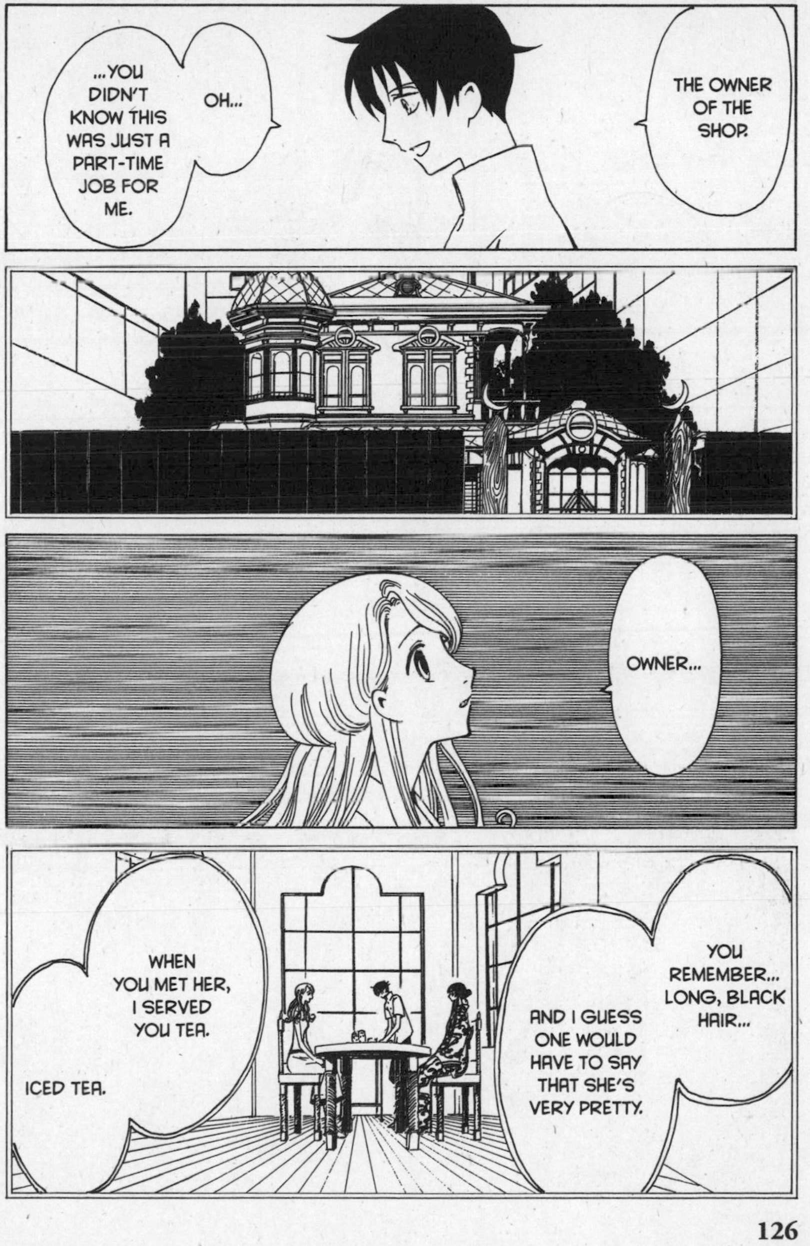
THE OWNER OF THE SHOP.
OH...
...YOU DIDN'T KNOW THIS WAS JUST A PART-TIME JOB FOR ME.
OWNER...
YOU REMEMBER... LONG, BLACK HAIR...
AND I GUESS ONE WOULD HAVE TO SAY THAT SHE'S VERY PRETTY.
WHEN YOU MET HER, I SERVED YOU TEA.
ICED TEA.

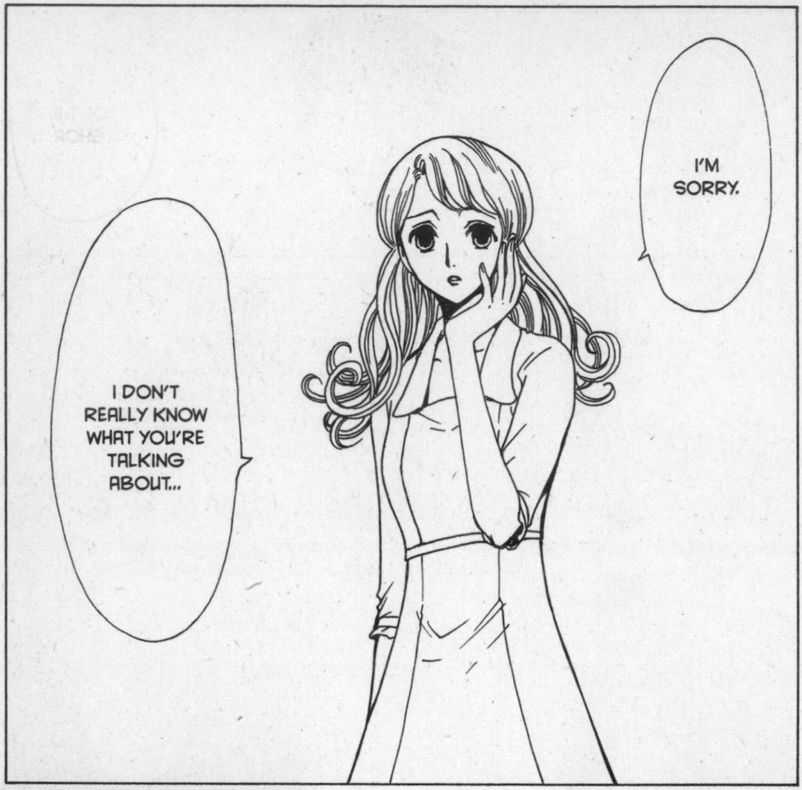
I'M SORRY.
I DON'T REALLY KNOW WHAT YOU'RE TALKING ABOUT...
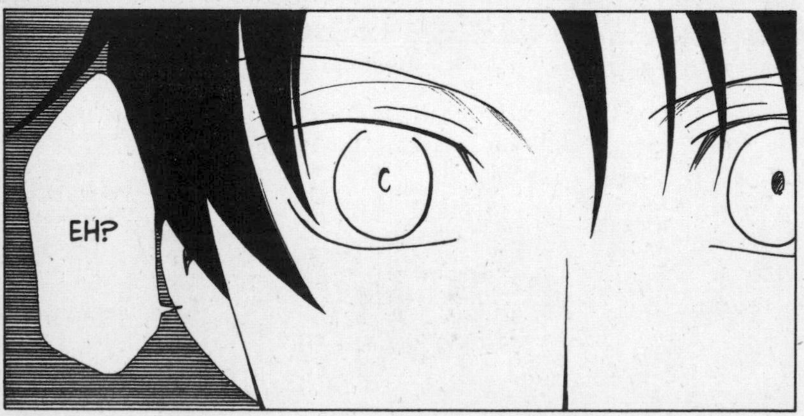
EH?

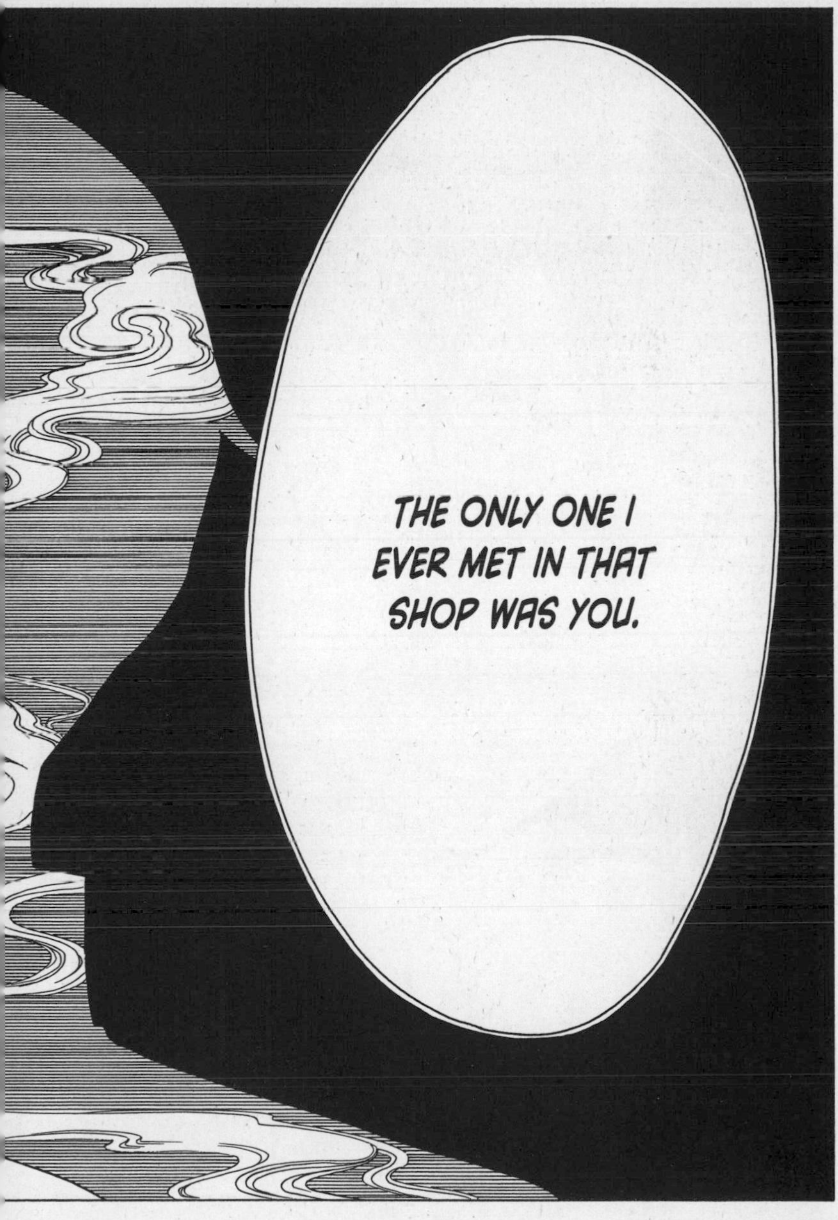
THE ONLY ONE I EVER MET IN THAT SHOP WAS YOU.

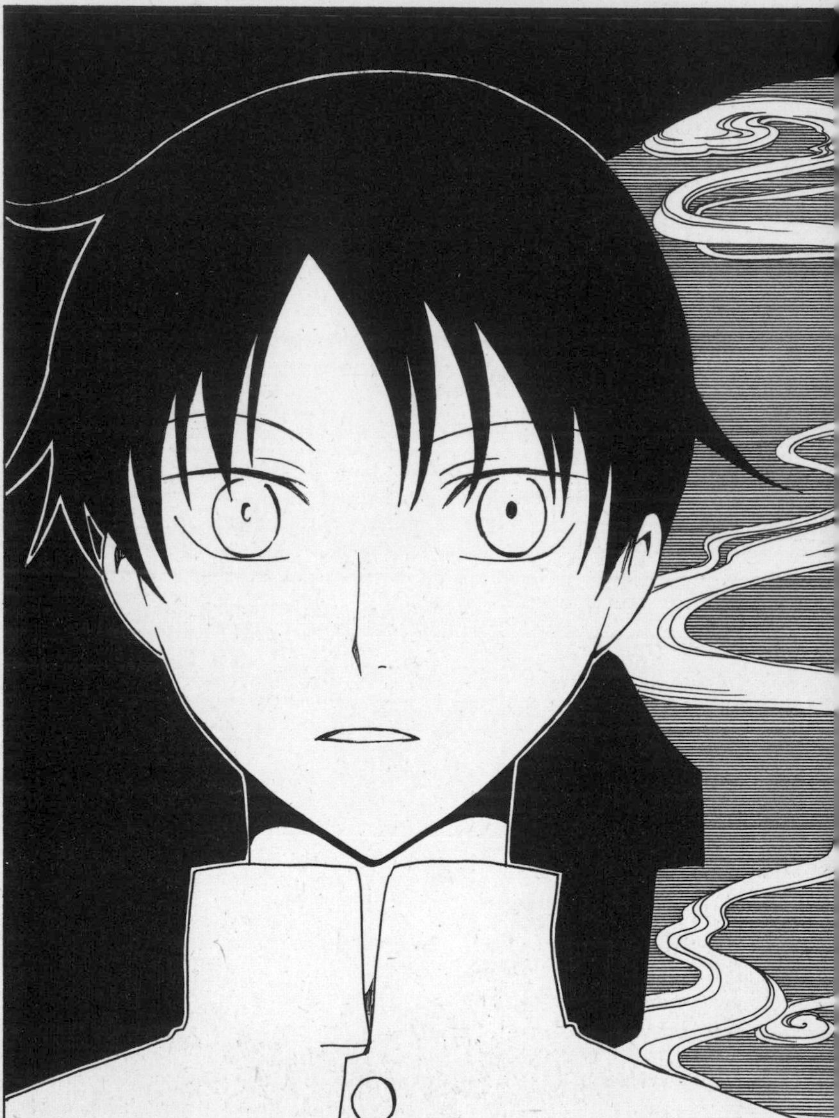

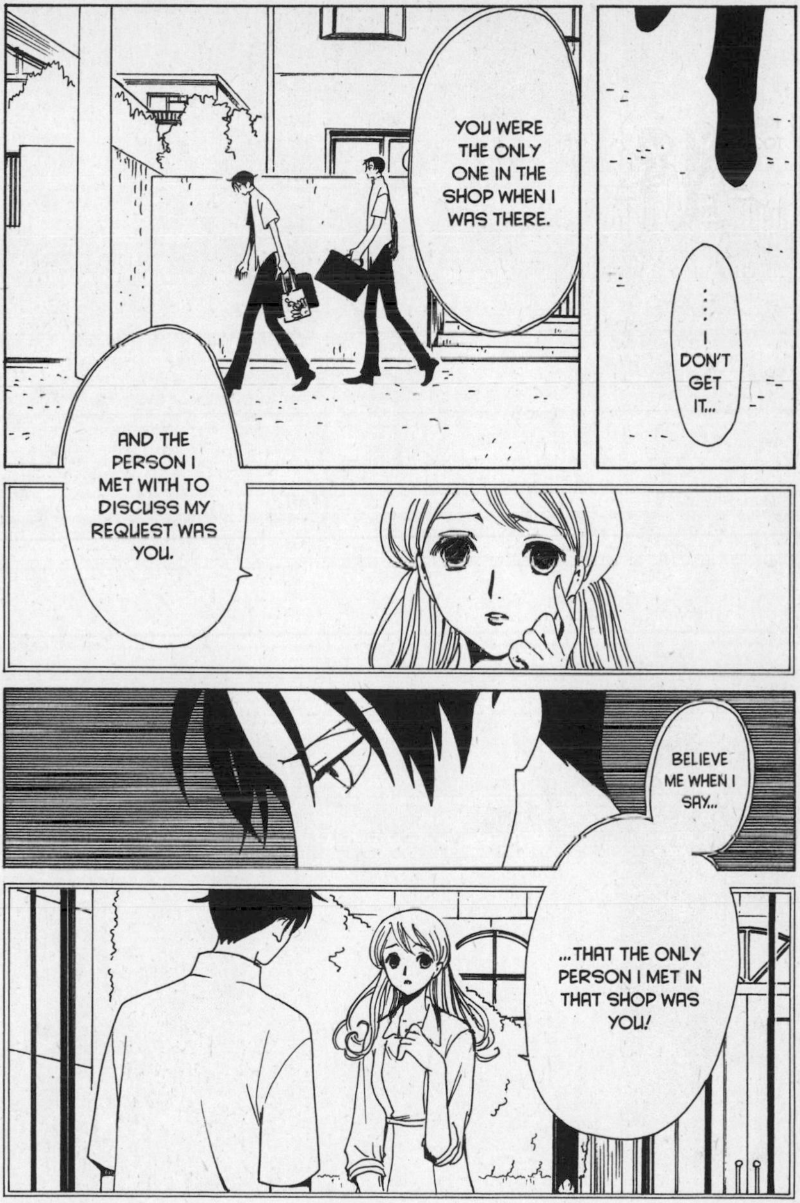
......I DON'T GET IT...
YOU WERE THE ONLY ONE IN THE SHOP WHEN I WAS THERE.
AND THE PERSON I MET WITH TO DISCUSS MY REQUEST WAS YOU.
BELIEVE ME WHEN I SAY...
...THAT THE ONLY PERSON I MET IN THAT SHOP WAS YOU!

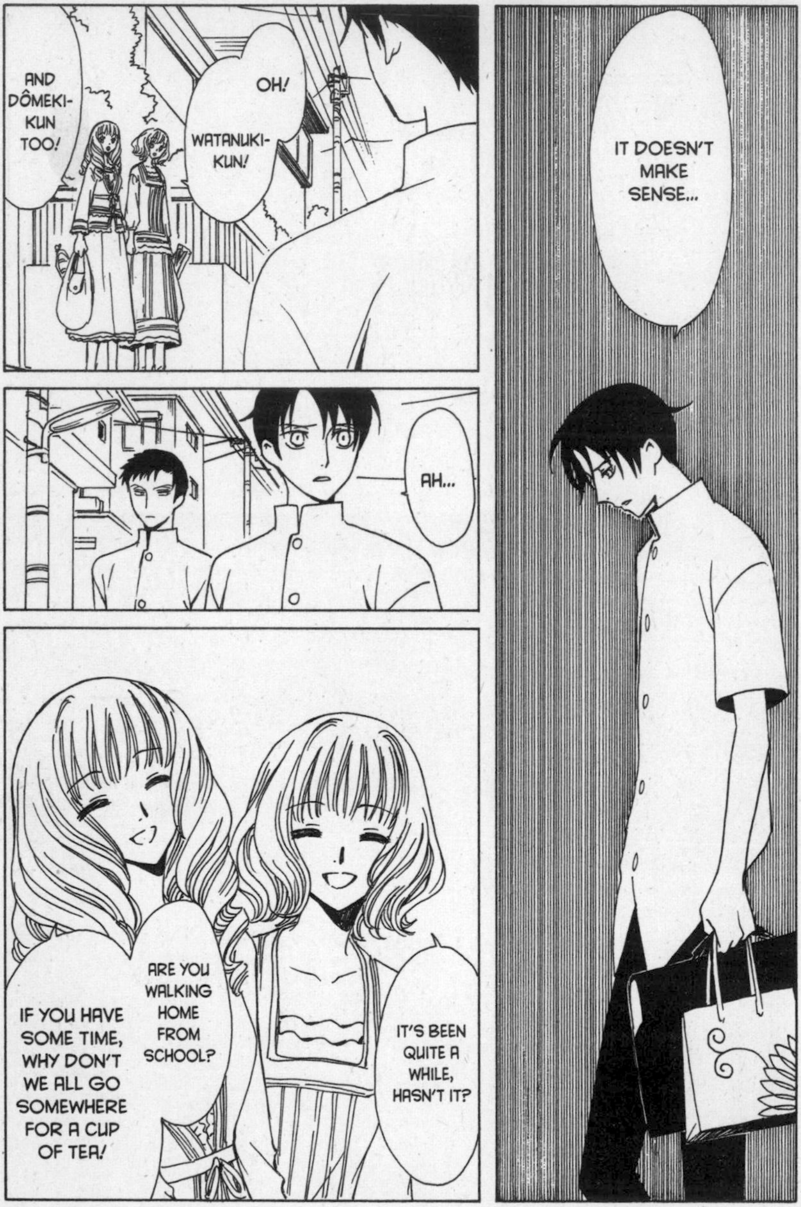
IT DOESN'T MAKE SENSE...
OH!
WATANUKI-KUN!
AND DÔMEKI-KUN TOO!
AH...
IT'S BEEN QUITE A WHILE, HASN'T IT?
ARE YOU WALKING HOME FROM SCHOOL?
IF YOU HAVE SOME TIME, WHY DON'T WE ALL GO SOMEWHERE FOR A CUP OF TEA!

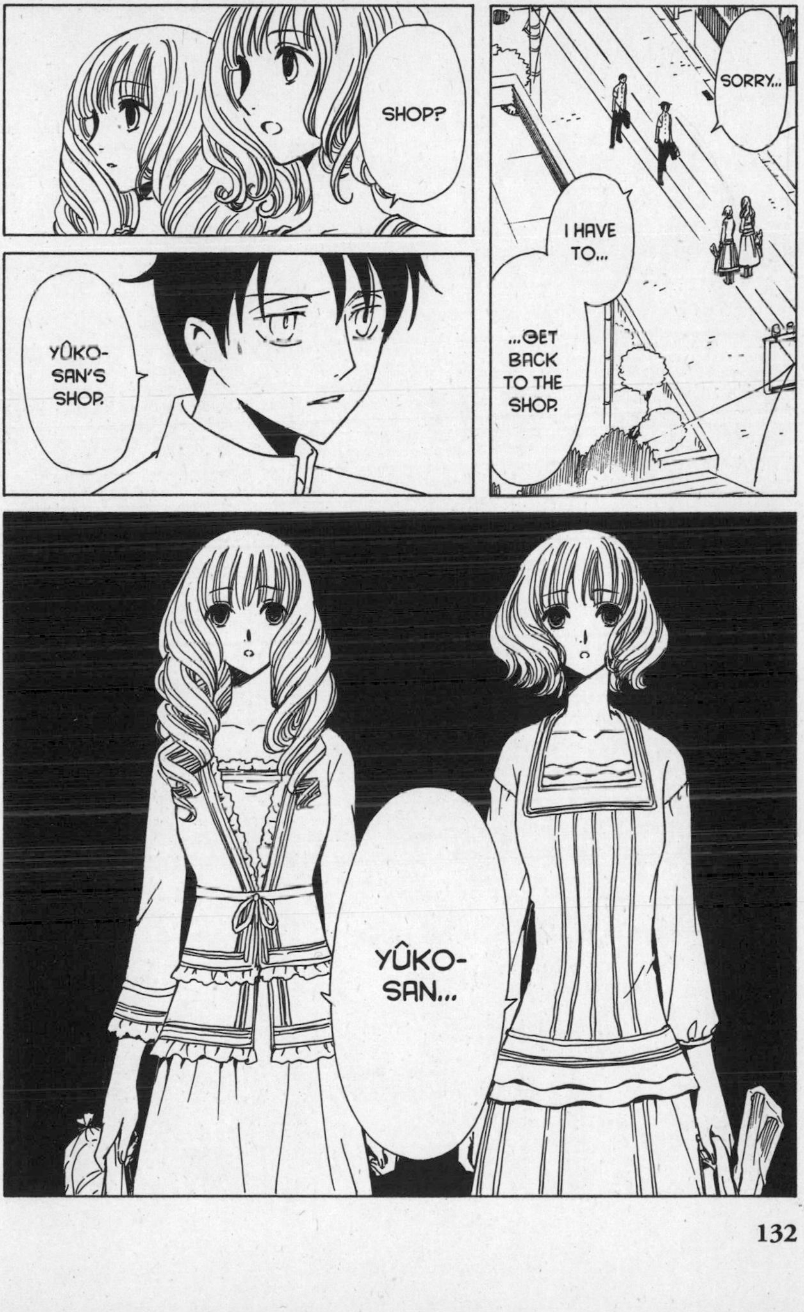
SORRY...
I HAVE TO...
...GET BACK TO THE SHOP.
SHOP?
YÛKO-SAN'S SHOP.
YÛKO-SAN...

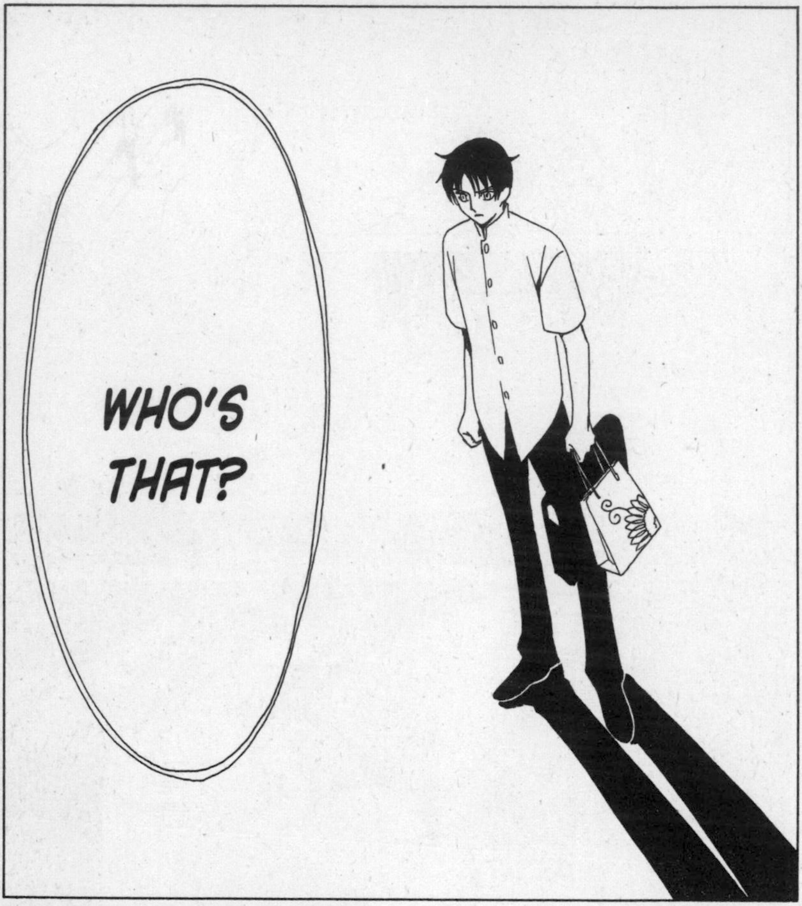
WHO'S THAT?
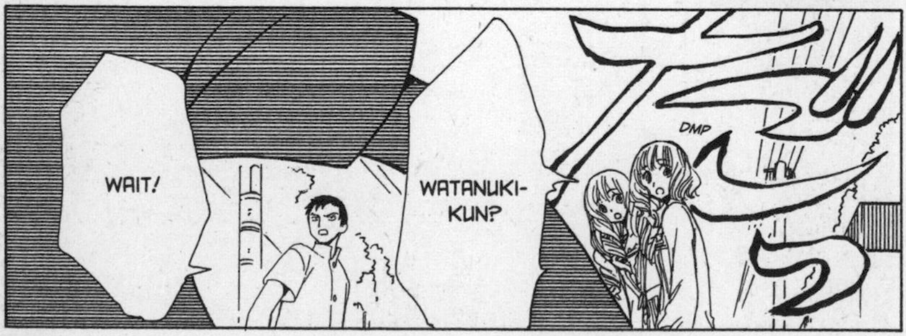
DMP
WATANUKI-KUN?
WAIT!

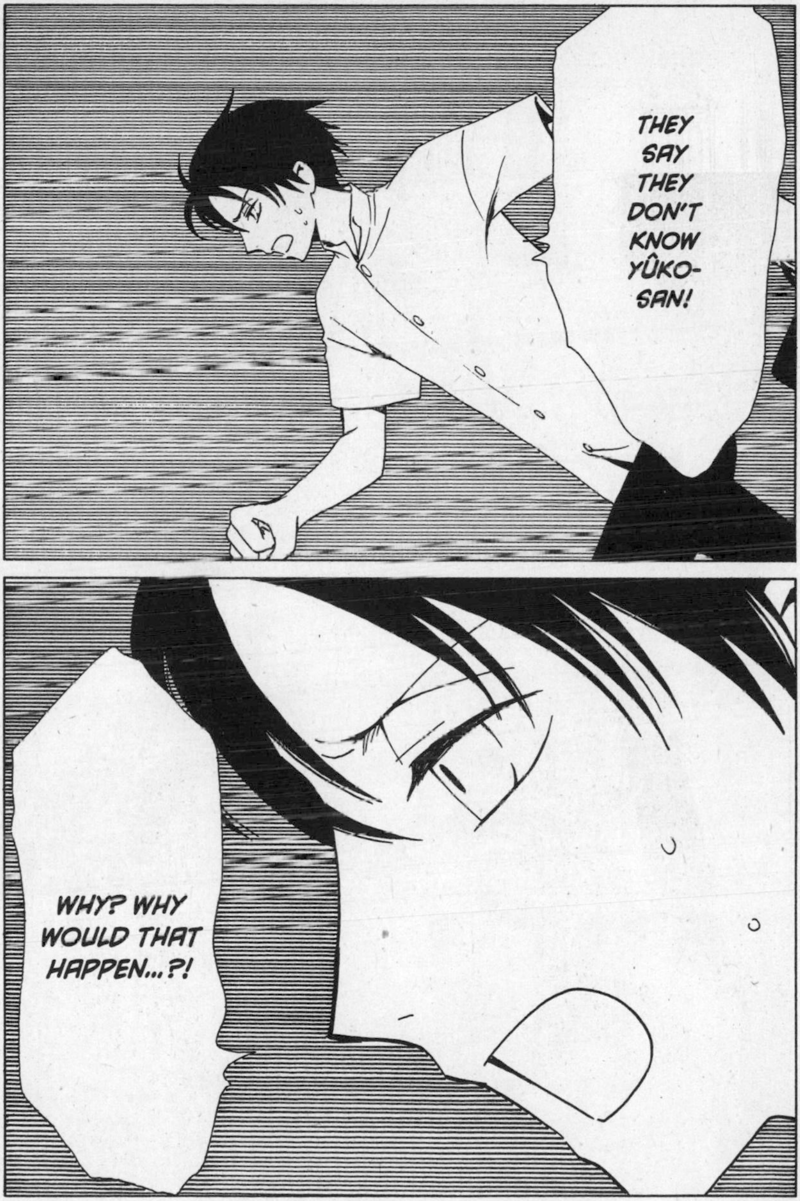
THEY SAY THEY DON'T KNOW YÛKO-SAN!
WHY? WHY WOULD THAT HAPPEN...?!

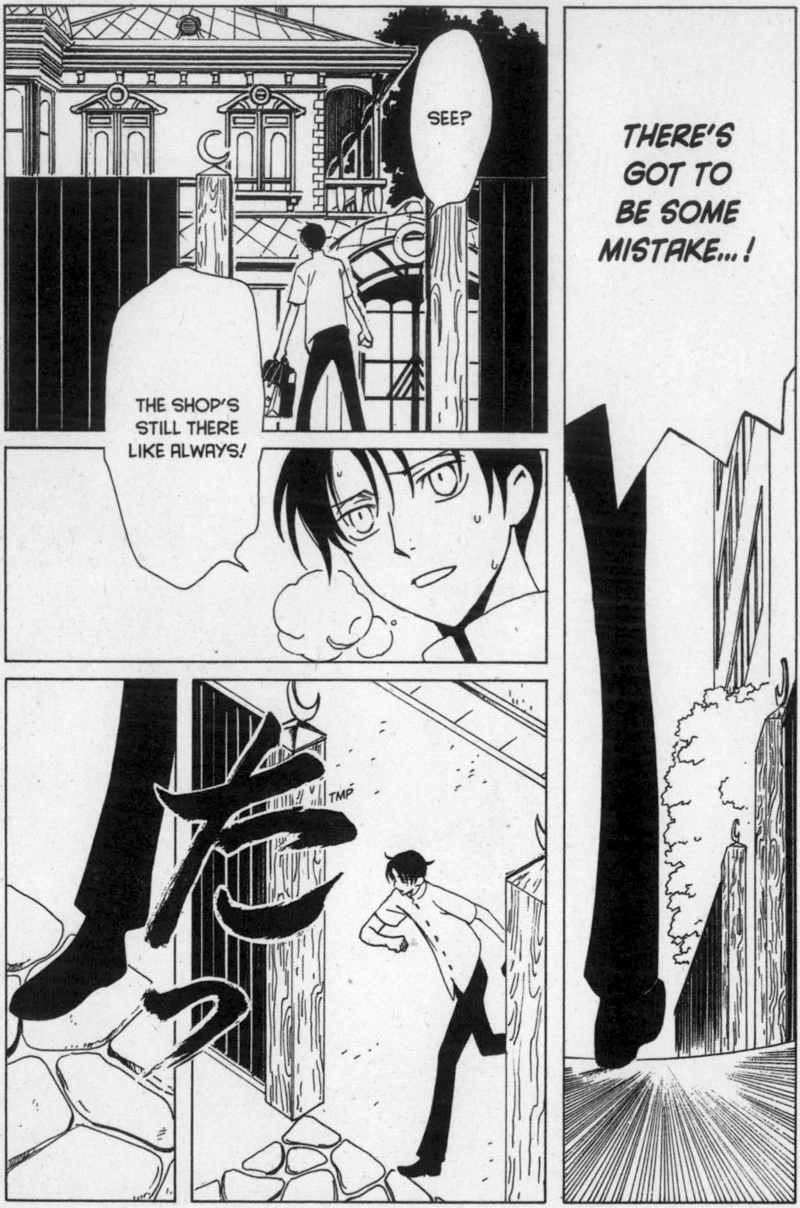
THERE'S GOT TO BE SOME MISTAKE...!
SEE?
THE SHOP'S STILL THERE LIKE ALWAYS!
TMP
たっ

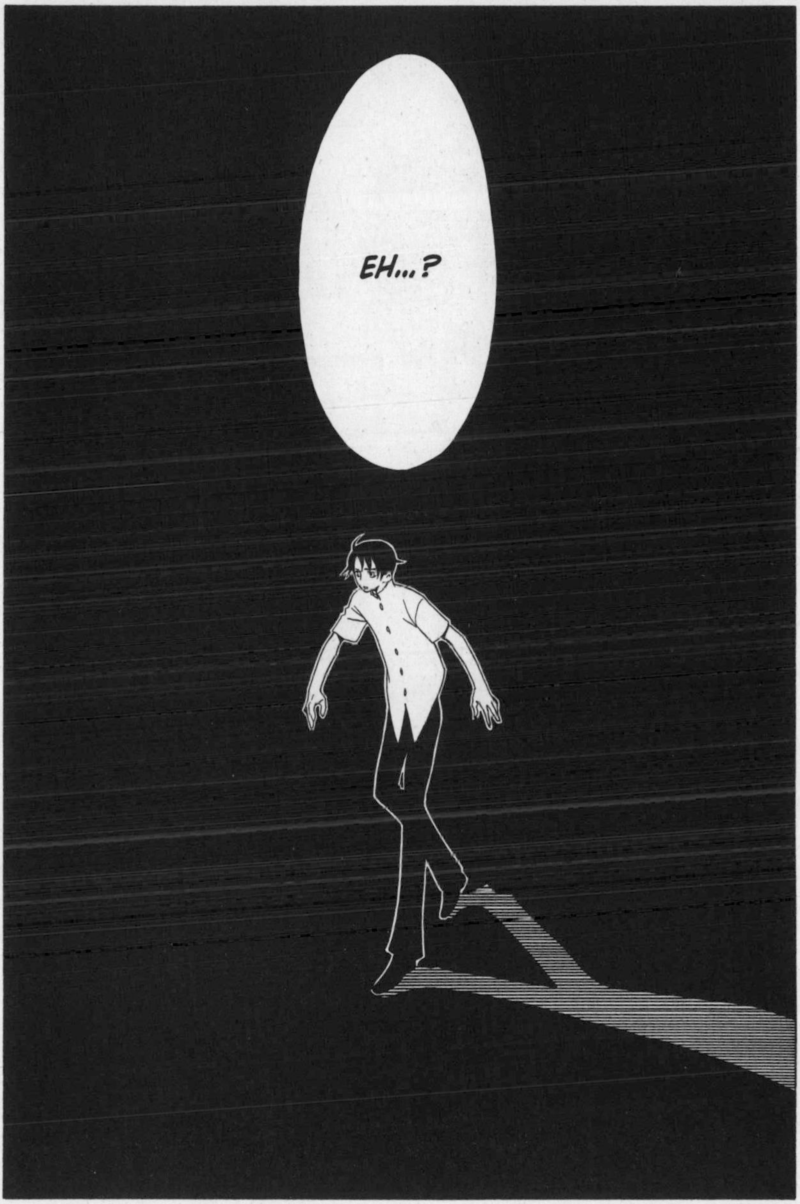
EH...?

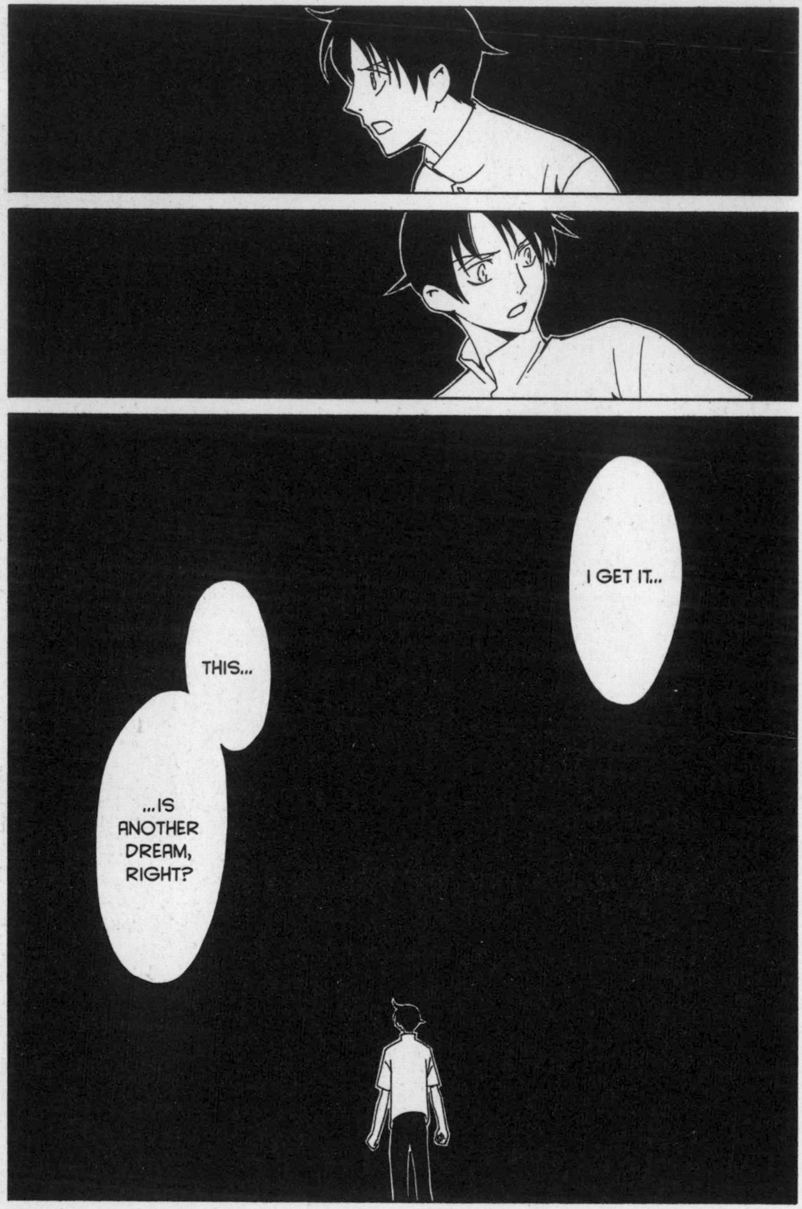
I GET IT...
THIS...
...IS ANOTHER DREAM, RIGHT?

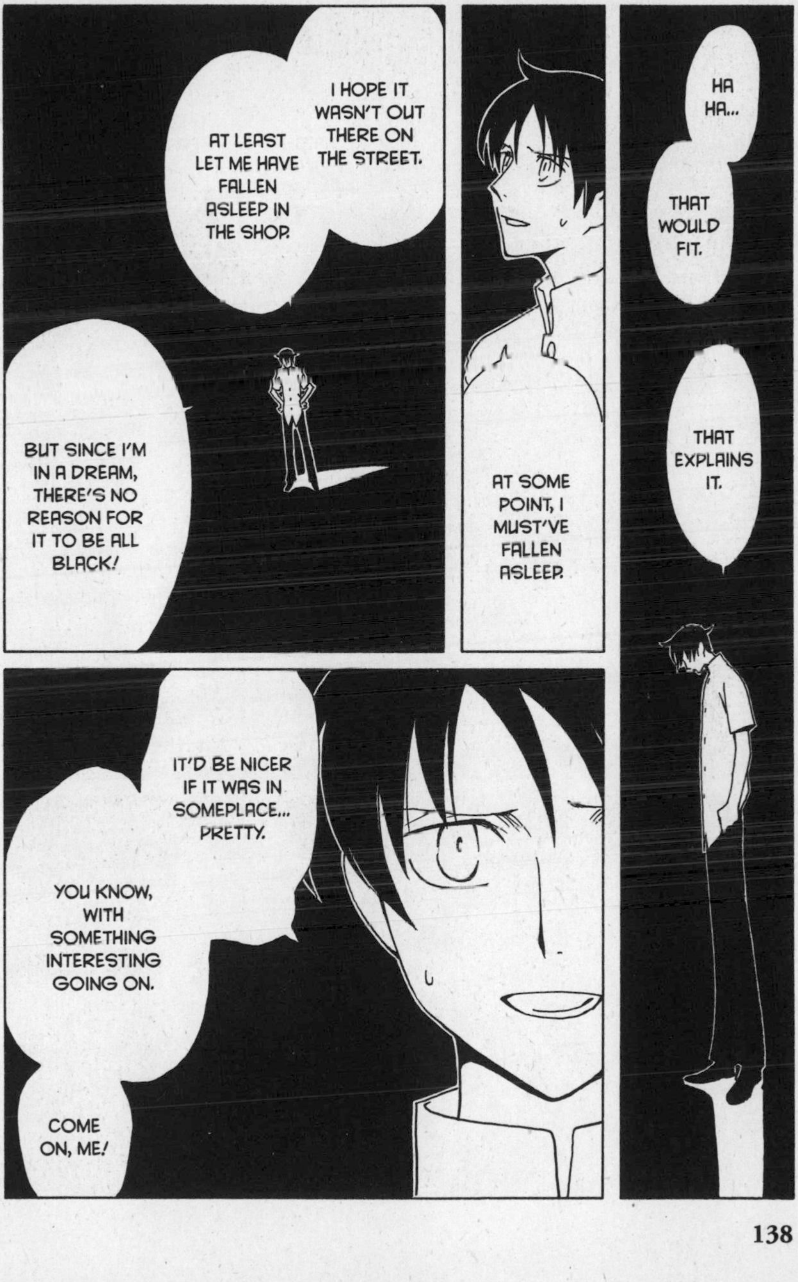
HA HA...
THAT WOULD FIT.
THAT EXPLAINS IT.
AT SOME POINT, I MUST'VE FALLEN ASLEEP.
I HOPE IT WASN'T OUT THERE ON THE STREET.
AT LEAST LET ME HAVE FALLEN ASLEEP IN THE SHOP.
BUT SINCE I'M IN A DREAM, THERE'S NO REASON FOR IT TO BE ALL BLACK!
IT'D BE NICER IF IT WAS IN SOMEPLACE... PRETTY.
YOU KNOW, WITH SOMETHING INTERESTING GOING ON.
COME ON, ME!

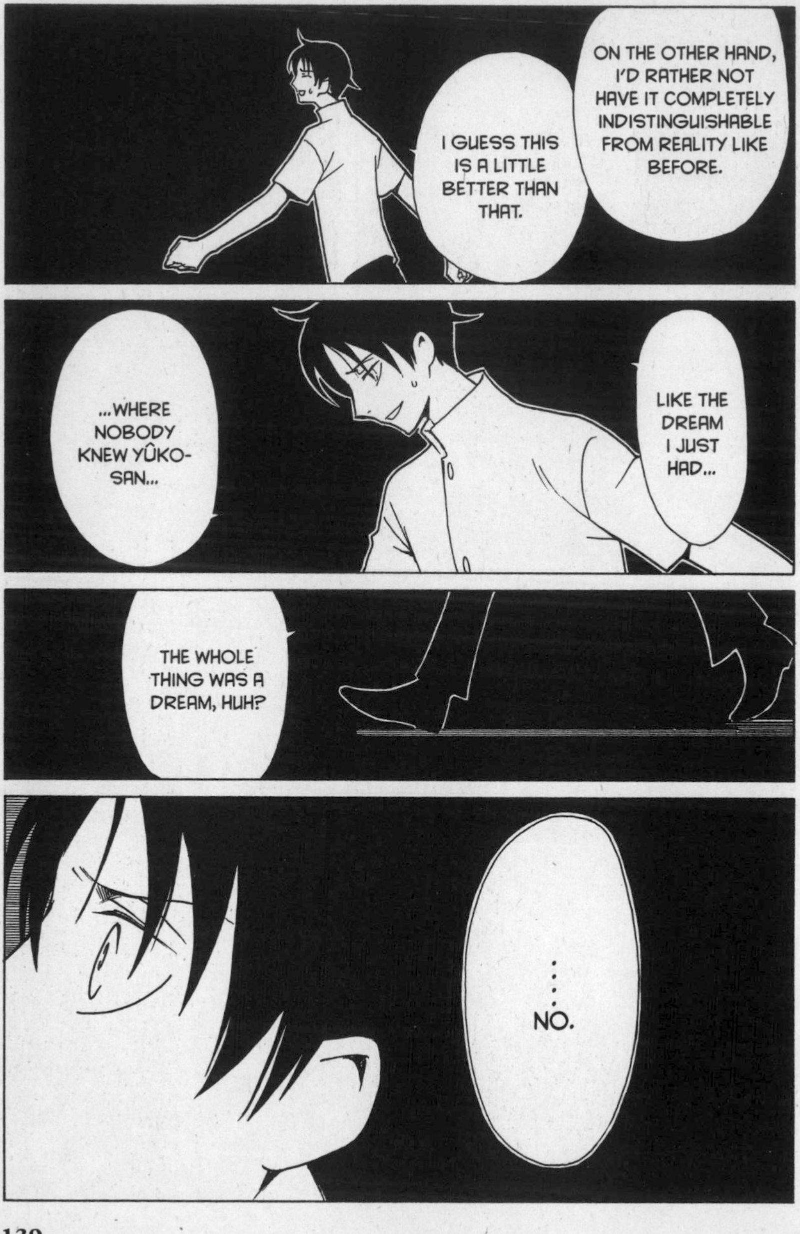
ON THE OTHER HAND, I'D RATHER NOT HAVE IT COMPLETELY INDISTINGUISHABLE FROM REALITY LIKE BEFORE.
I GUESS THIS IS A LITTLE BETTER THAN THAT.
LIKE THE DREAM I JUST HAD...
...WHERE NOBODY KNEW YÛKO-SAN...
THE WHOLE THING WAS A DREAM, HUH?
....NO.

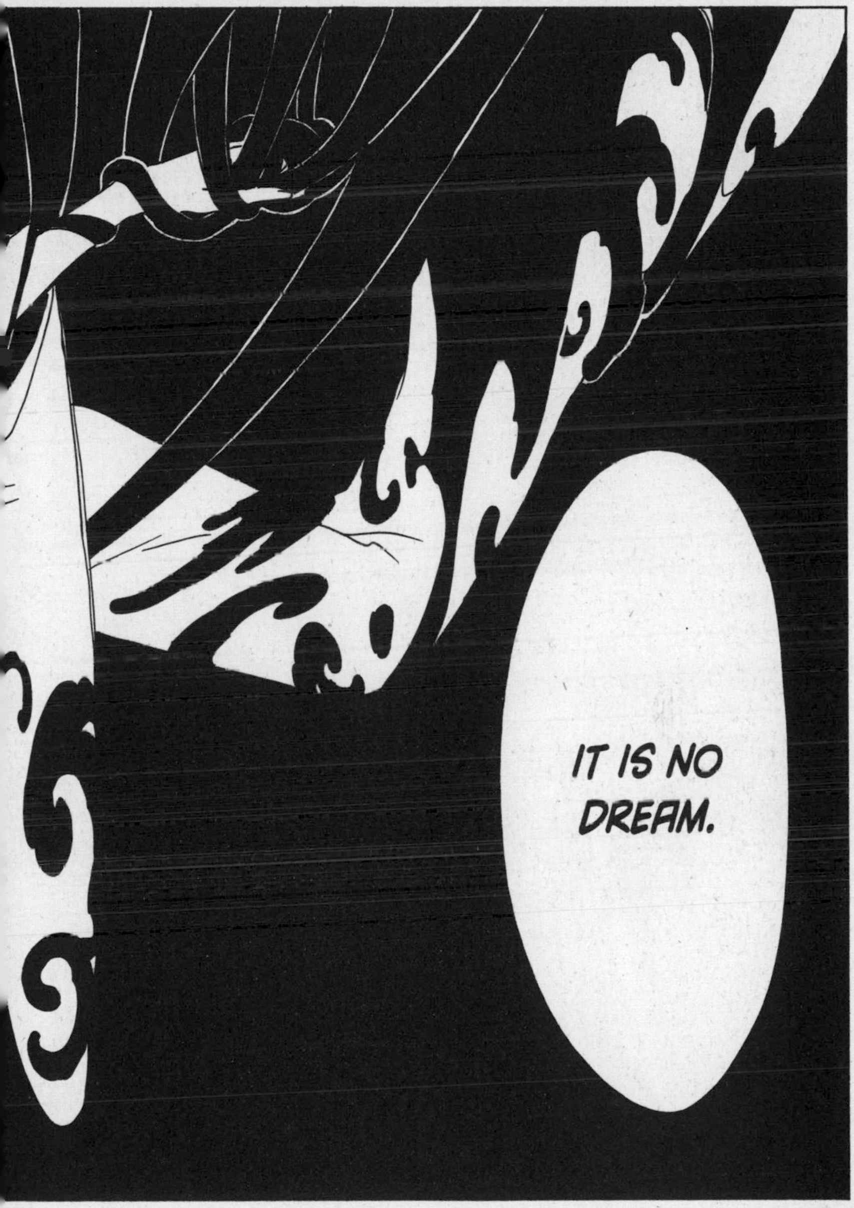
IT IS NO DREAM.

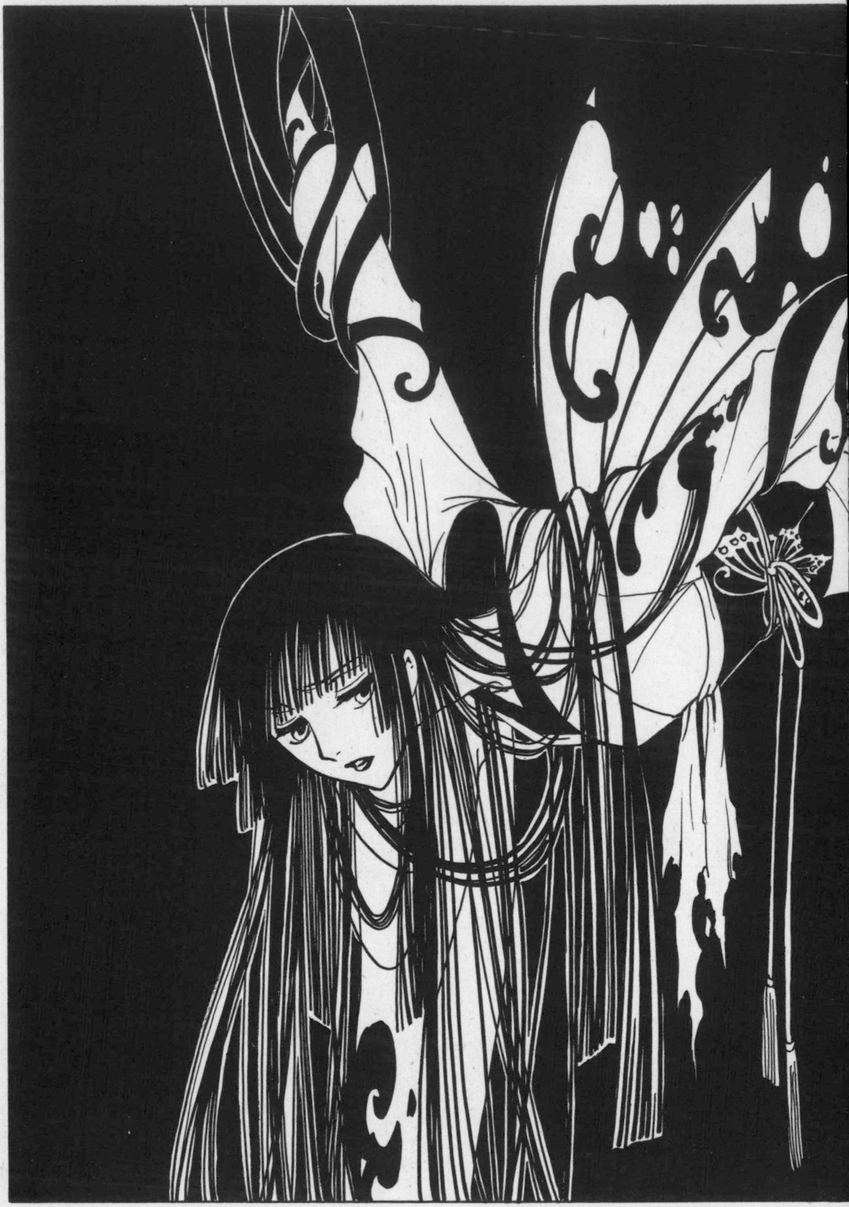

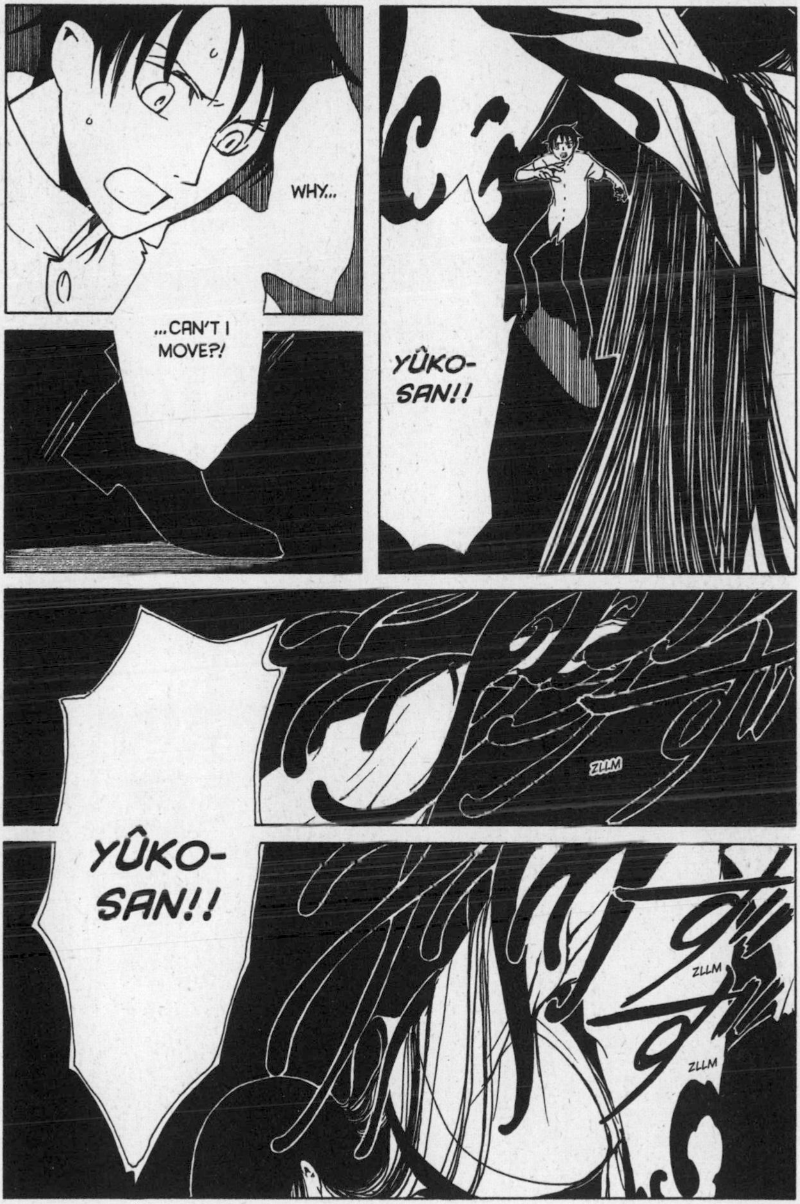
YÛKO-SAN!!
WHY...
...CAN'T I MOVE?!
ZLLM
YÛKO-SAN!!
ZLLM
ZLLM

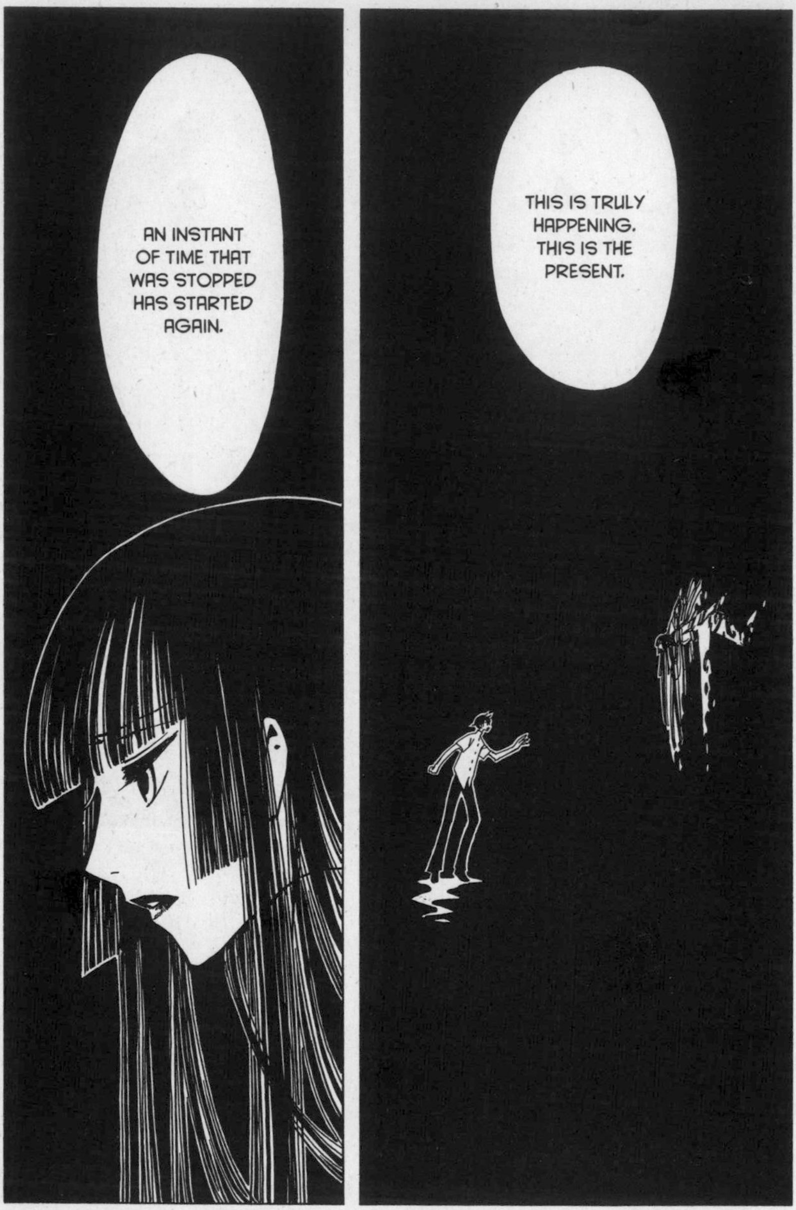
THIS IS TRULY HAPPENING. THIS IS THE PRESENT.
AN INSTANT OF TIME THAT WAS STOPPED HAS STARTED AGAIN.

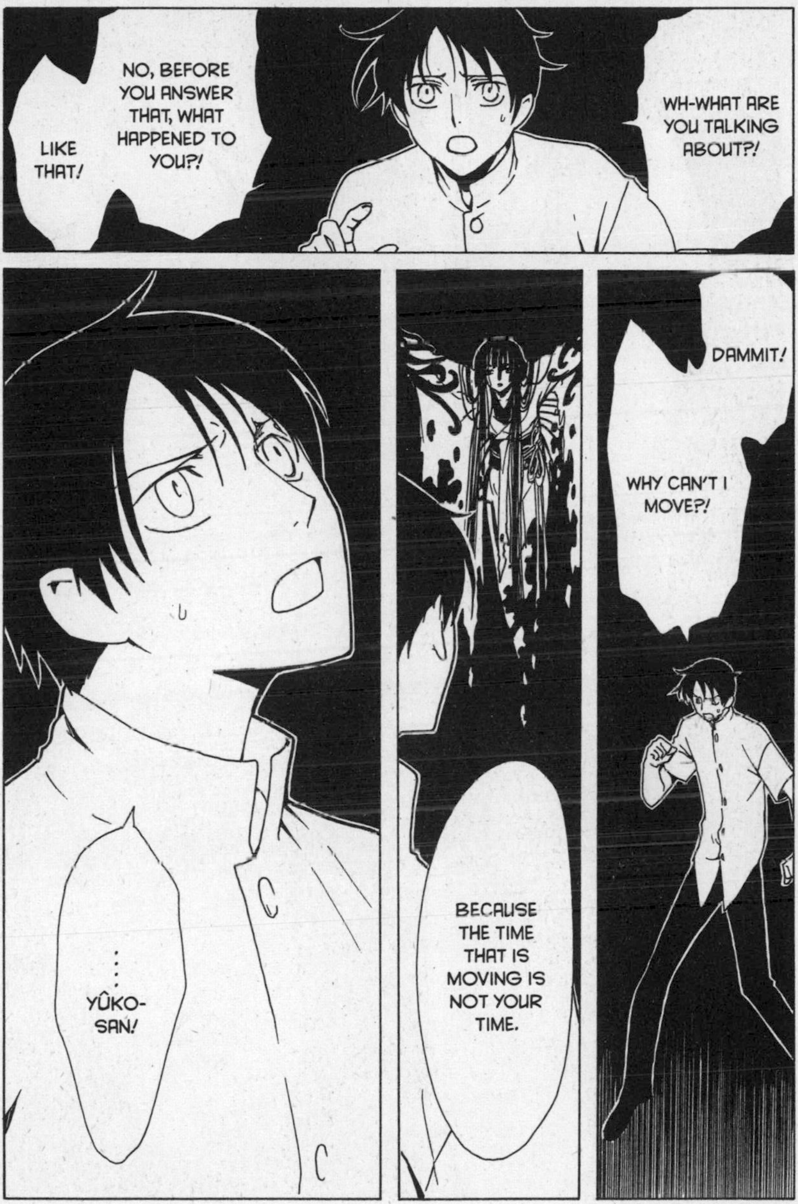
WH-WHAT ARE YOU TALKING ABOUT?!
NO, BEFORE YOU ANSWER THAT, WHAT HAPPENED TO YOU?!
LIKE THAT!
DAMMIT!
WHY CAN'T I MOVE?!
BECAUSE THE TIME THAT IS MOVING IS NOT YOUR TIME.
... YÛKO-SAN!

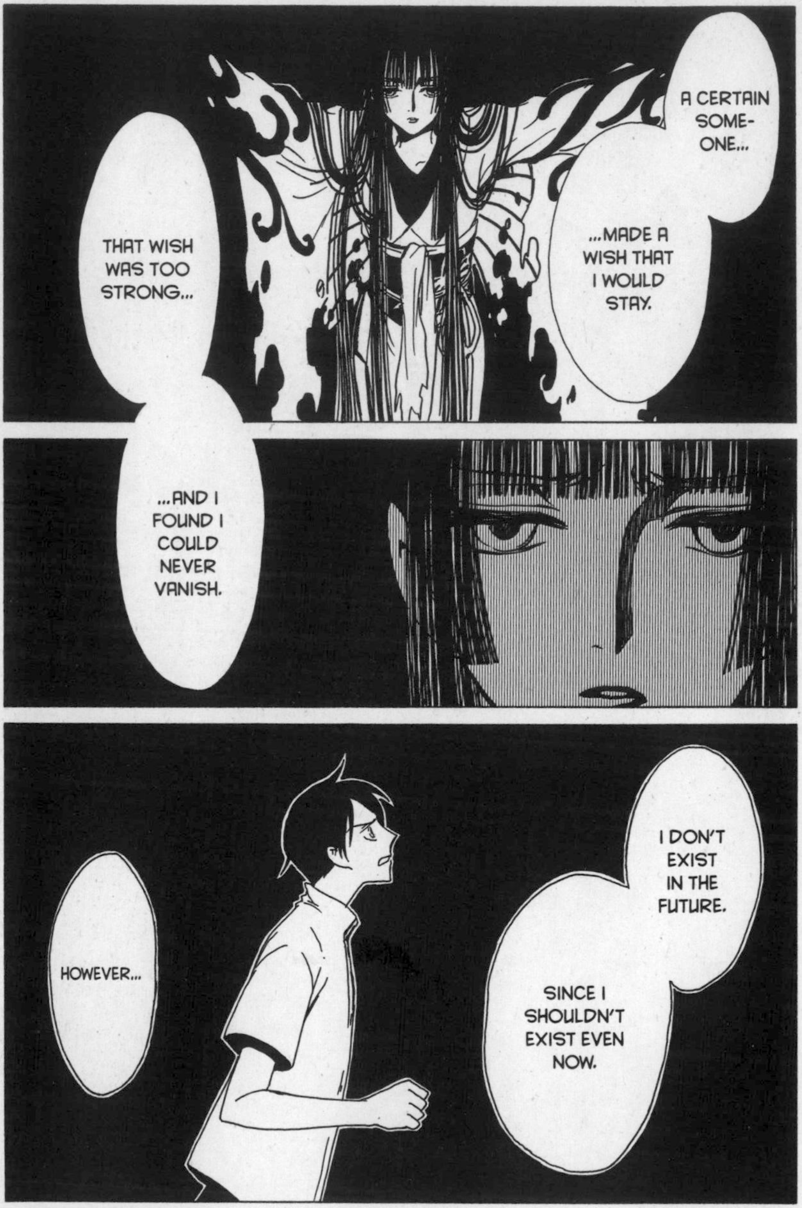
A CERTAIN SOME-ONE...
...MADE A WISH THAT I WOULD STAY.
THAT WISH WAS TOO STRONG...
...AND I FOUND I COULD NEVER VANISH.
I DON'T EXIST IN THE FUTURE.
SINCE I SHOULDN'T EXIST EVEN NOW.
HOWEVER...

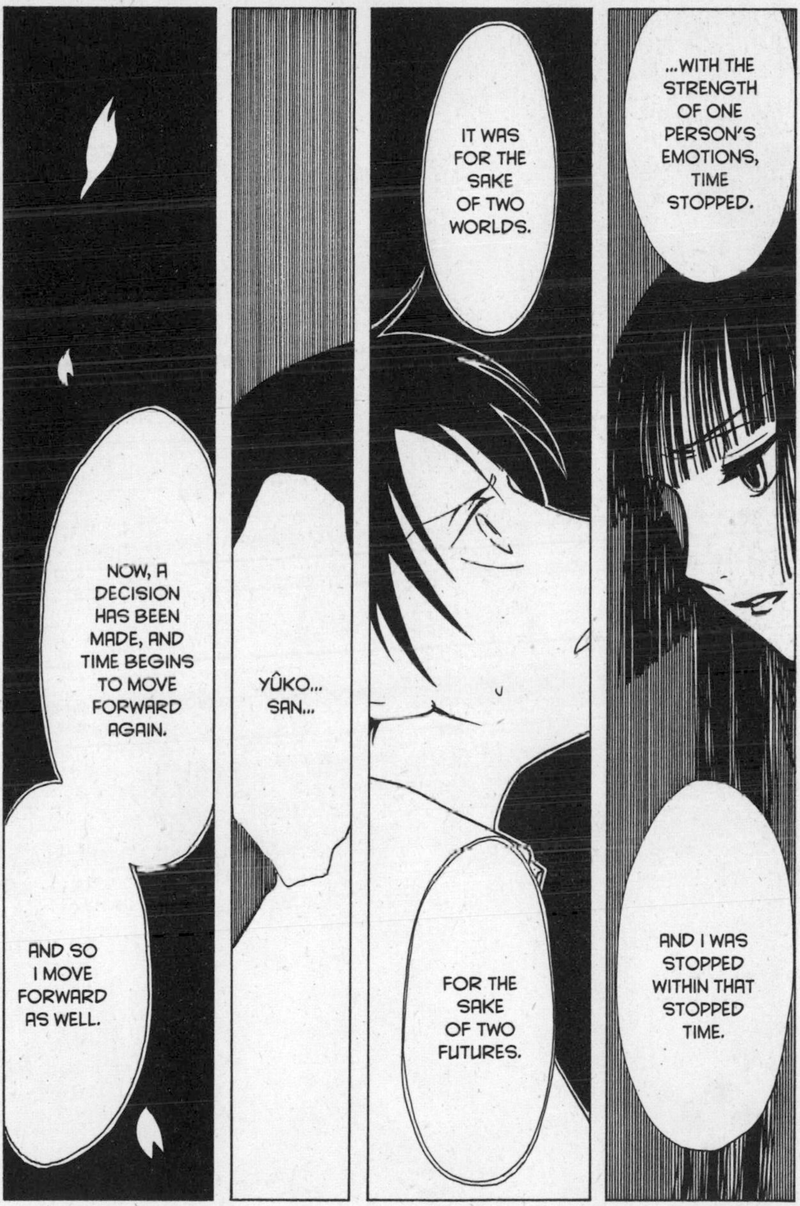
...WITH THE STRENGTH OF ONE PERSON'S EMOTIONS, TIME STOPPED.
AND I WAS STOPPED WITHIN THAT STOPPED TIME.
IT WAS FOR THE SAKE OF TWO WORLDS.
FOR THE SAKE OF TWO FUTURES.
YÛKO... SAN...
NOW, A DECISION HAS BEEN MADE, AND TIME BEGINS TO MOVE FORWARD AGAIN.
AND SO I MOVE FORWARD AS WELL.

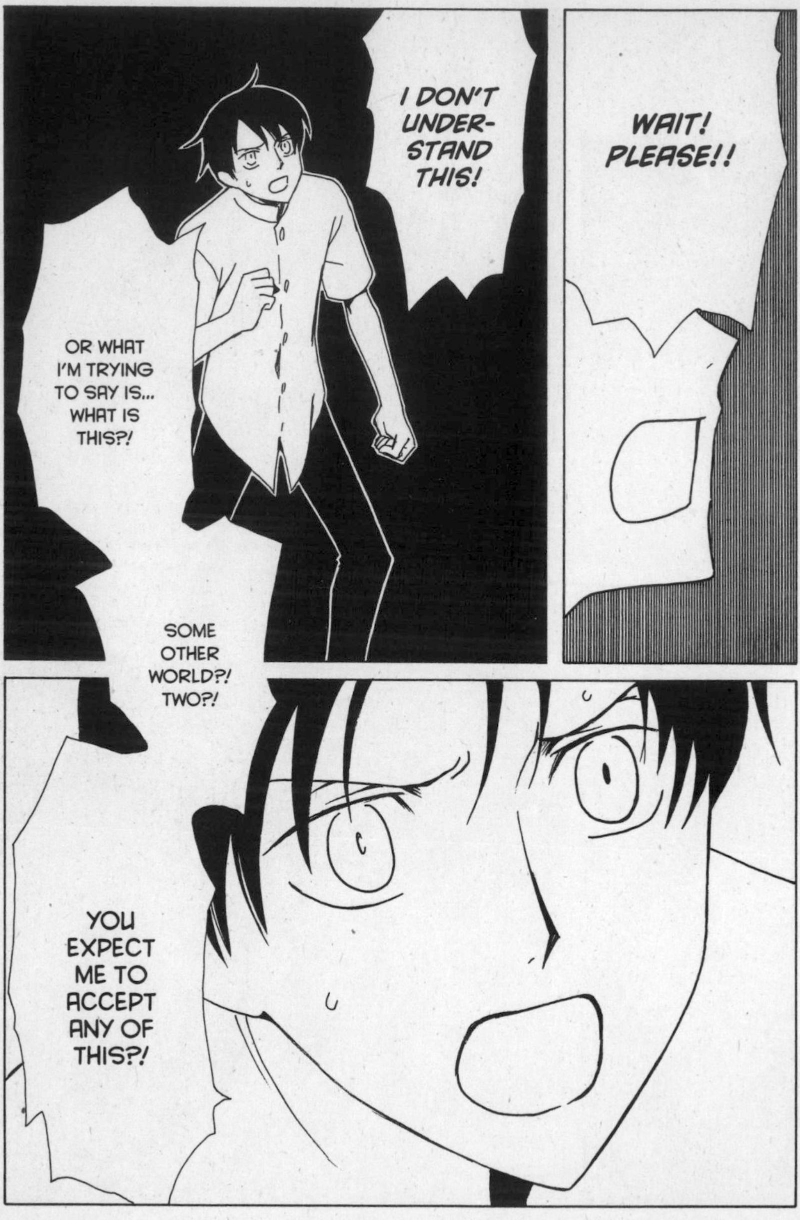
WAIT! PLEASE!!
I DON'T UNDER-STAND THIS!
OR WHAT I'M TRYING TO SAY IS... WHAT IS THIS?!
SOME OTHER WORLD?! TWO?!
YOU EXPECT ME TO ACCEPT ANY OF THIS?!

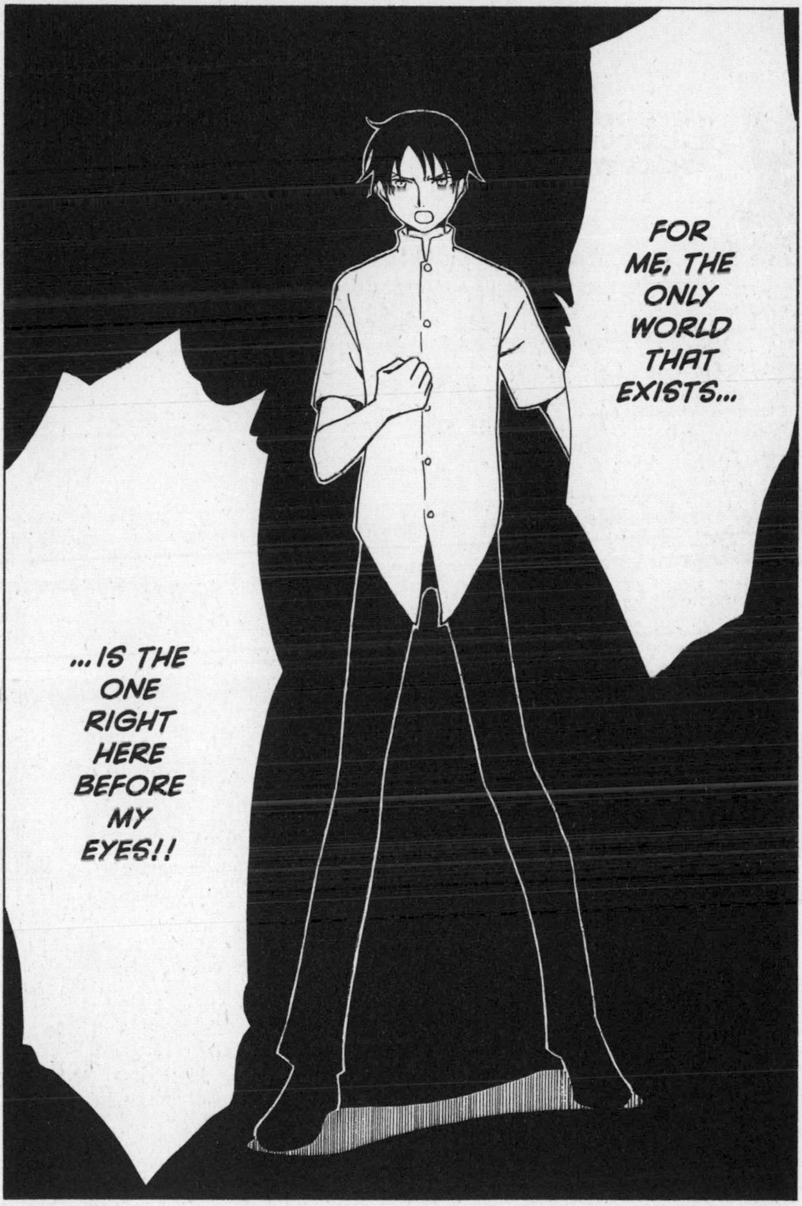
FOR ME, THE ONLY WORLD THAT EXISTS...
...IS THE ONE RIGHT HERE BEFORE MY EYES!!

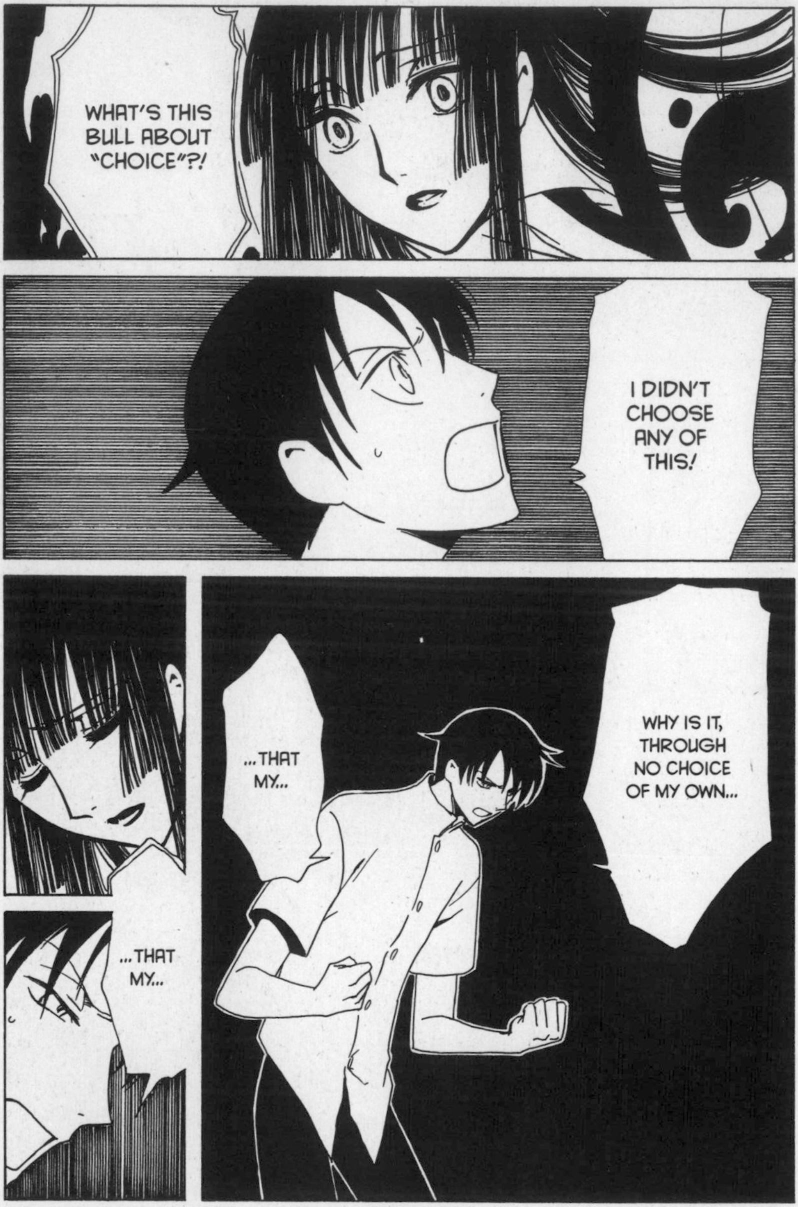
WHAT'S THIS BULL ABOUT "CHOICE"?!
I DIDN'T CHOOSE ANY OF THIS!
WHY IS IT, THROUGH NO CHOICE OF MY OWN...
...THAT MY...
...THAT MY...

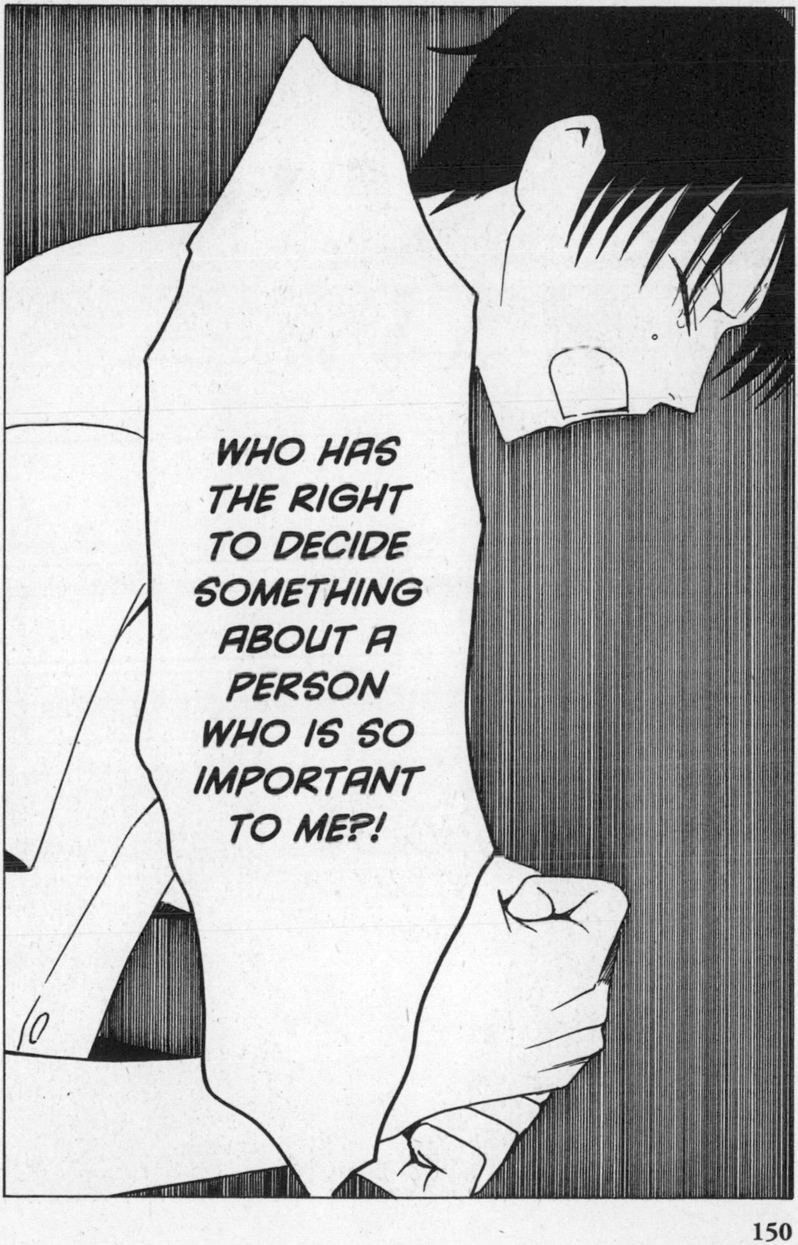
WHO HAS THE RIGHT TO DECIDE SOMETHING ABOUT A PERSON WHO IS SO IMPORTANT TO ME?!

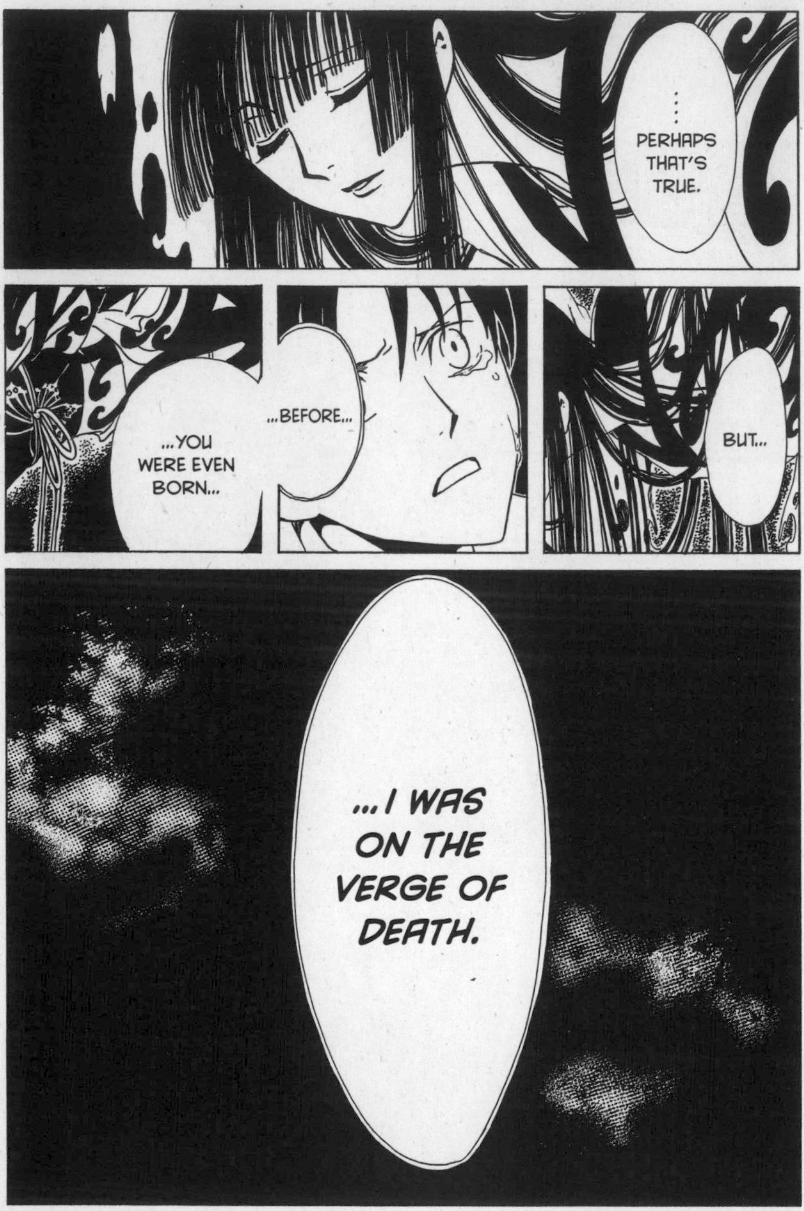
....
PERHAPS THAT'S TRUE.
BUT...
...BEFORE...
...YOU WERE EVEN BORN...
...I WAS ON THE VERGE OF DEATH.

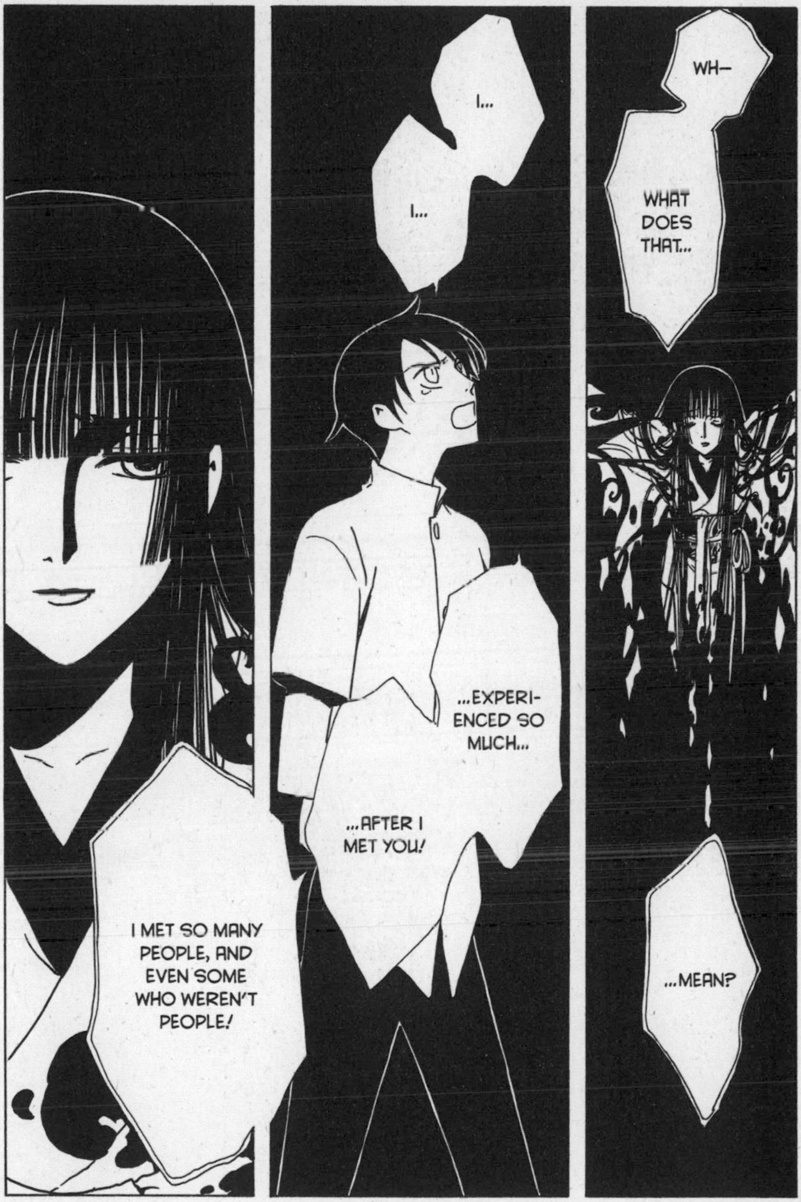
WH—
WHAT DOES THAT...
...MEAN?
I...
I...
...EXPERI-ENCED SO MUCH...
...AFTER I MET YOU!
I MET SO MANY PEOPLE, AND EVEN SOME WHO WEREN'T PEOPLE!

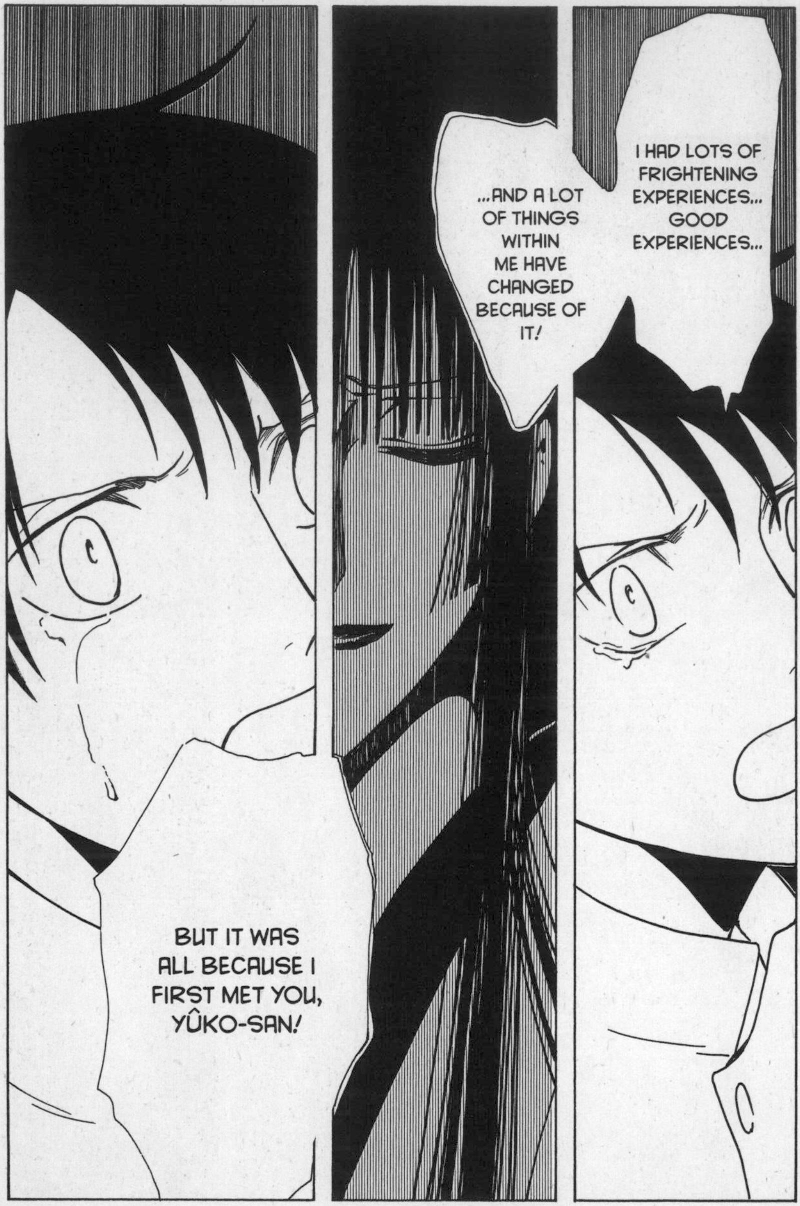
I HAD LOTS OF FRIGHTENING EXPERIENCES... GOOD EXPERIENCES...
...AND A LOT OF THINGS WITHIN ME HAVE CHANGED BECAUSE OF IT!
BUT IT WAS ALL BECAUSE I FIRST MET YOU, YÛKO-SAN!

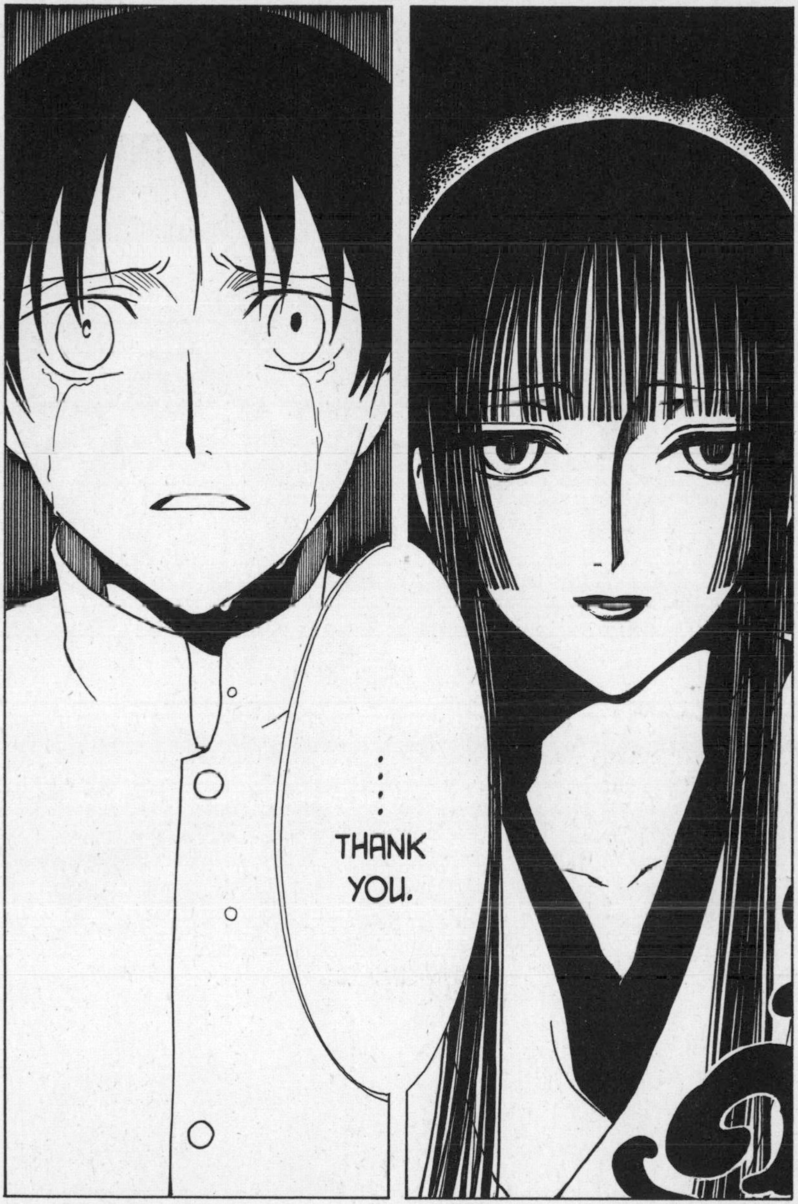

....THANK YOU.

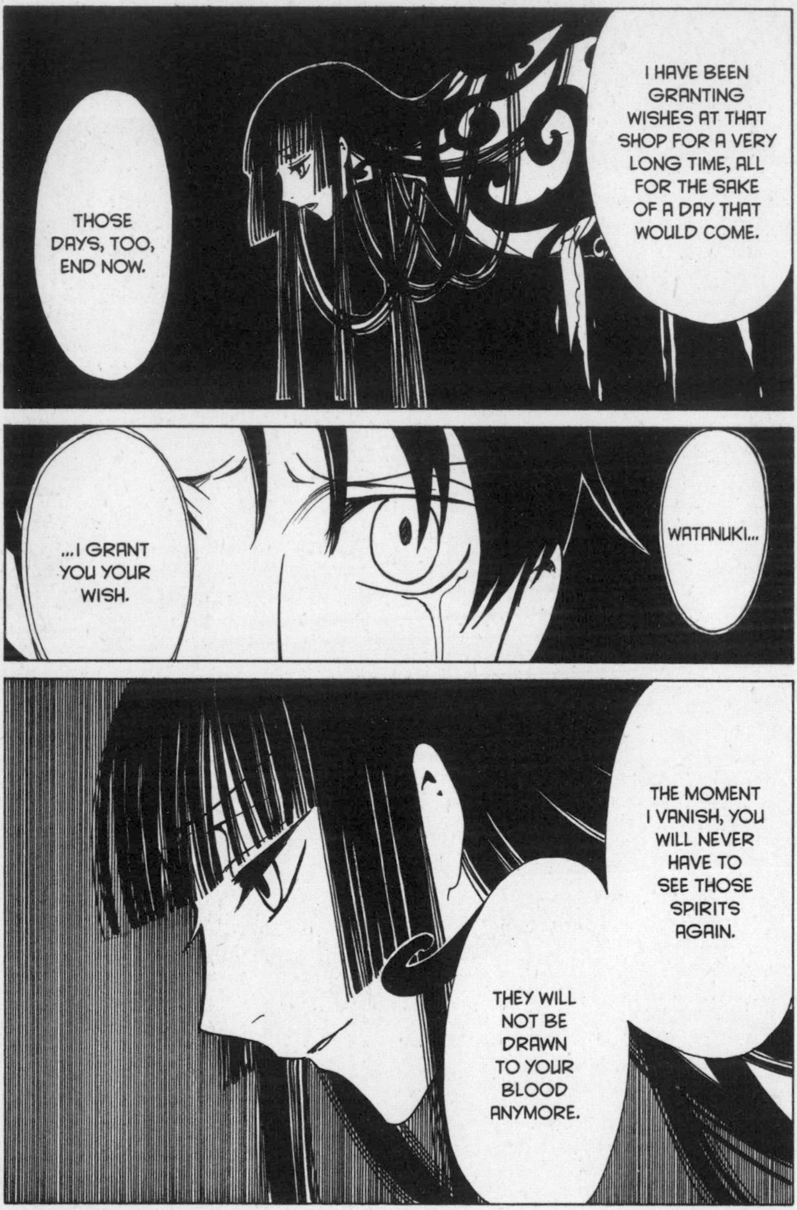
I HAVE BEEN GRANTING WISHES AT THAT SHOP FOR A VERY LONG TIME, ALL FOR THE SAKE OF A DAY THAT WOULD COME.
THOSE DAYS, TOO, END NOW.
WATANUKI...
...I GRANT YOU YOUR WISH.
THE MOMENT I VANISH, YOU WILL NEVER HAVE TO SEE THOSE SPIRITS AGAIN.
THEY WILL NOT BE DRAWN TO YOUR BLOOD ANYMORE.

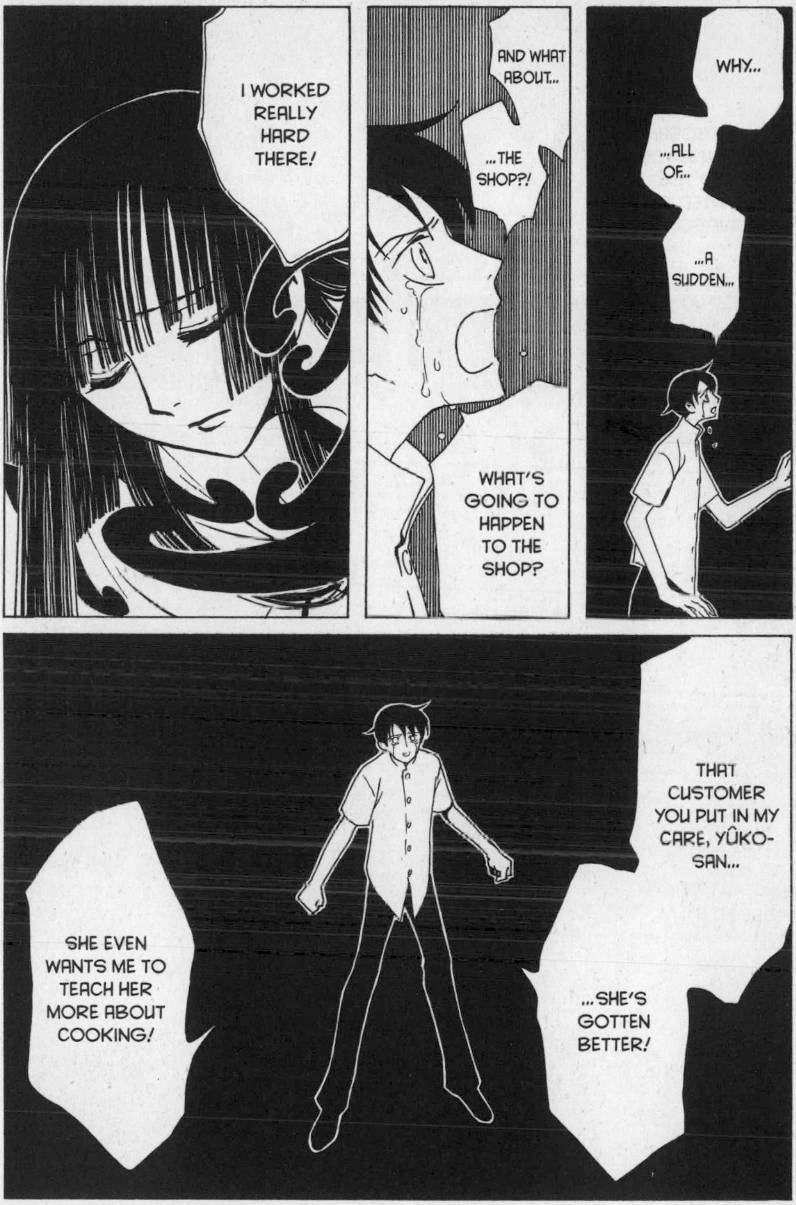
WHY...
...ALL OF...
...A SUDDEN...
AND WHAT ABOUT...
...THE SHOP?!
WHAT'S GOING TO HAPPEN TO THE SHOP?
I WORKED REALLY HARD THERE!
THAT CUSTOMER YOU PUT IN MY CARE, YÛKO-SAN...
...SHE'S GOTTEN BETTER!
SHE EVEN WANTS ME TO TEACH HER MORE ABOUT COOKING!

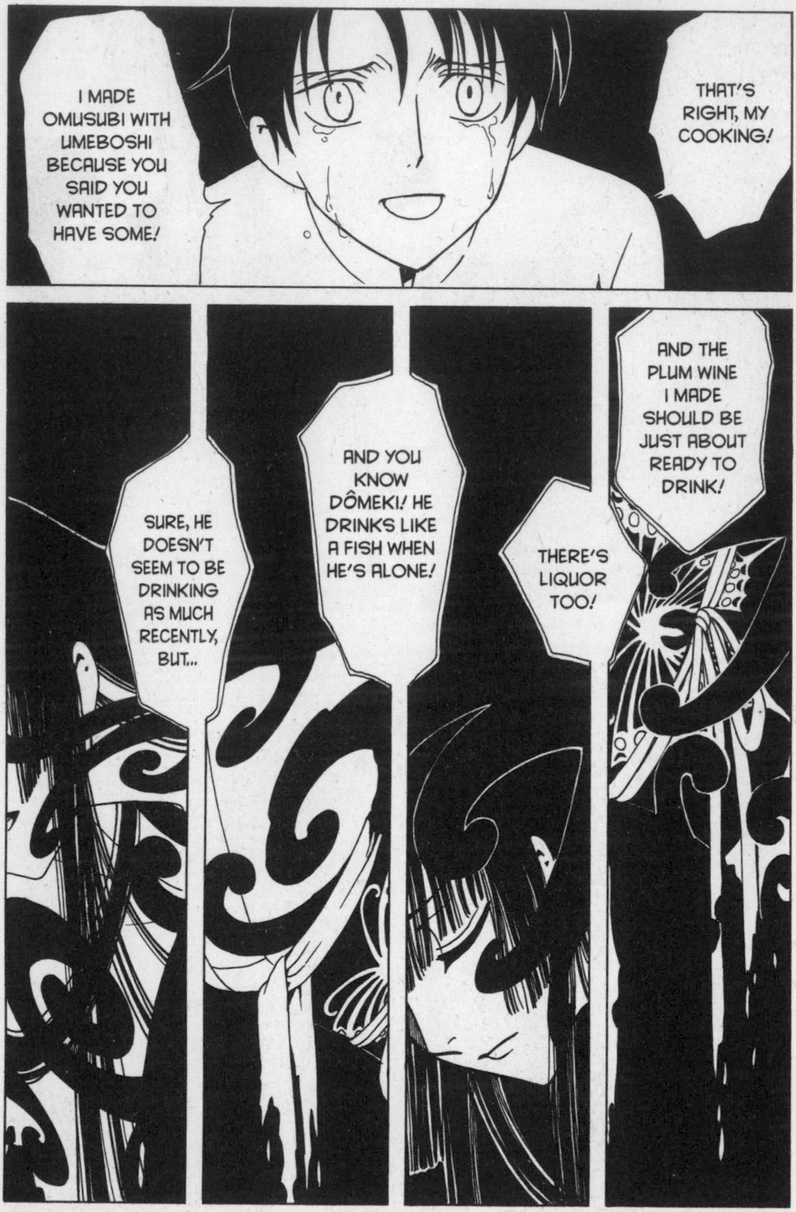
THAT'S RIGHT, MY COOKING!
I MADE OMUSUBI WITH UMEBOSHI BECAUSE YOU SAID YOU WANTED TO HAVE SOME!
AND THE PLUM WINE I MADE SHOULD BE JUST ABOUT READY TO DRINK!
THERE'S LIQUOR TOO!
AND YOU KNOW DÔMEKI! HE DRINKS LIKE A FISH WHEN HE'S ALONE!
SURE, HE DOESN'T SEEM TO BE DRINKING AS MUCH RECENTLY, BUT...

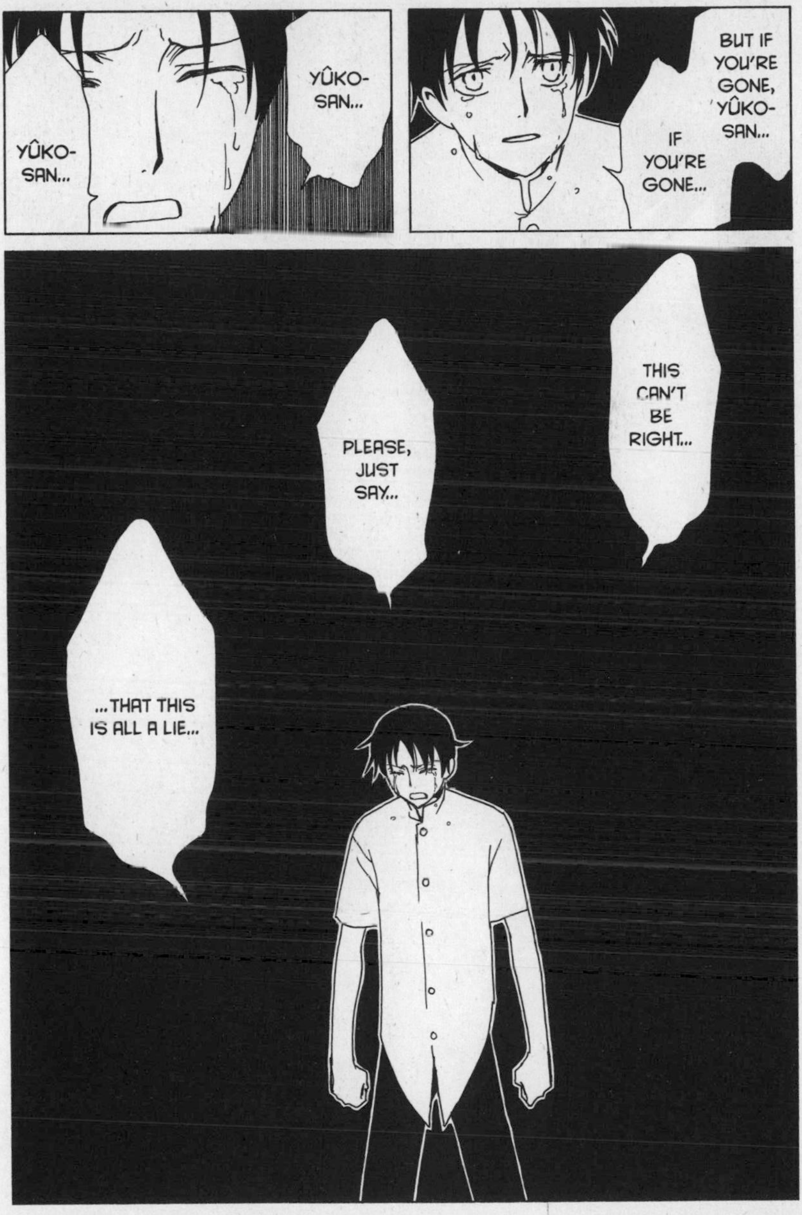
BUT IF YOU'RE GONE, YÛKO-SAN...
IF YOU'RE GONE...
YÛKO-SAN...
YÛKO-SAN...
THIS CAN'T BE RIGHT...
PLEASE, JUST SAY...
...THAT THIS IS ALL A LIE...

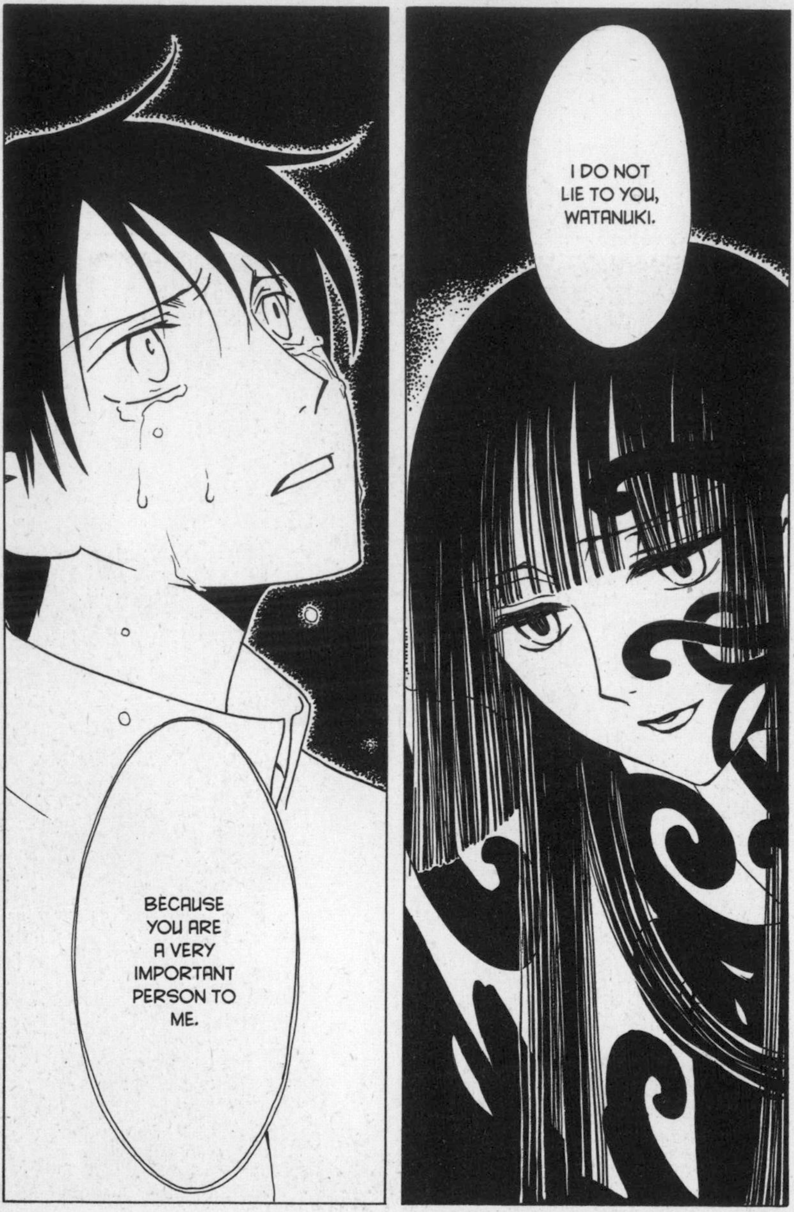
I DO NOT LIE TO YOU, WATANUKI.
BECAUSE YOU ARE A VERY IMPORTANT PERSON TO ME.

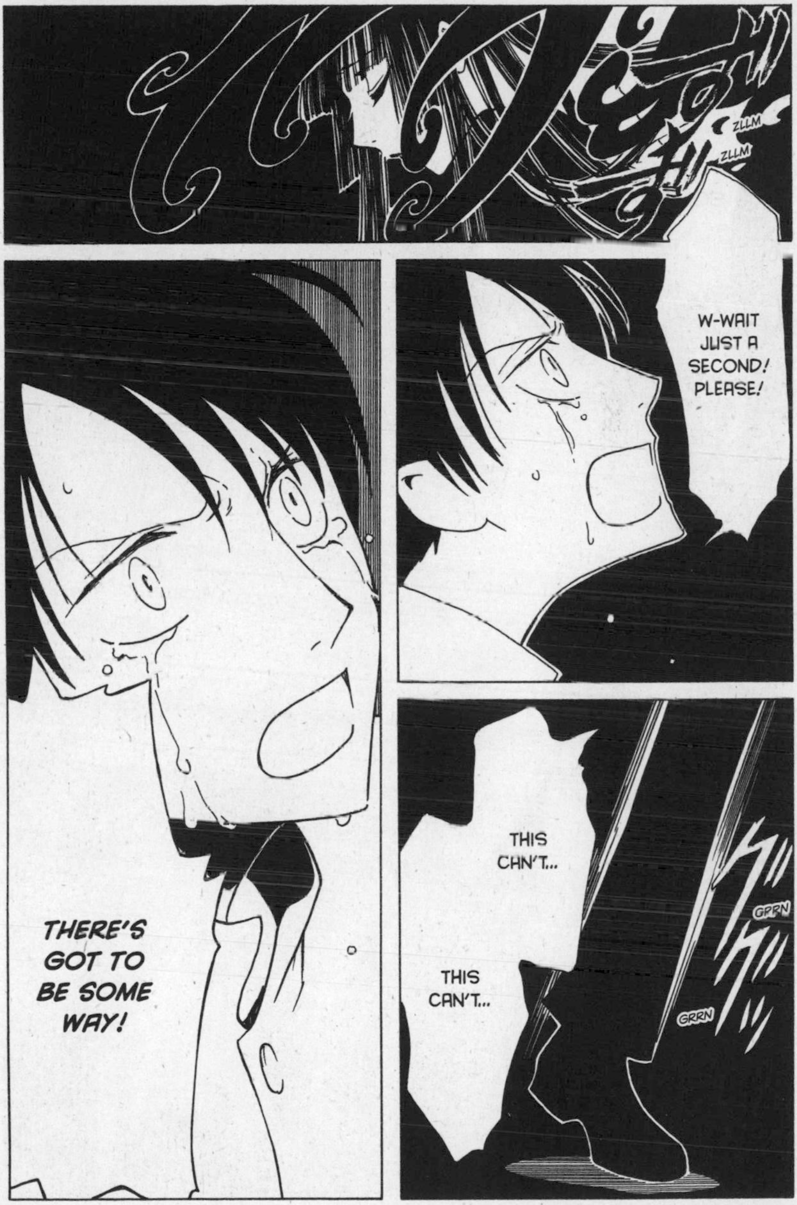
ZLLM
ZLLM
W-WAIT JUST A SECOND! PLEASE!
THIS CAN'T...
THIS CAN'T...
GRRN
GRRN
THERE'S GOT TO BE SOME WAY!

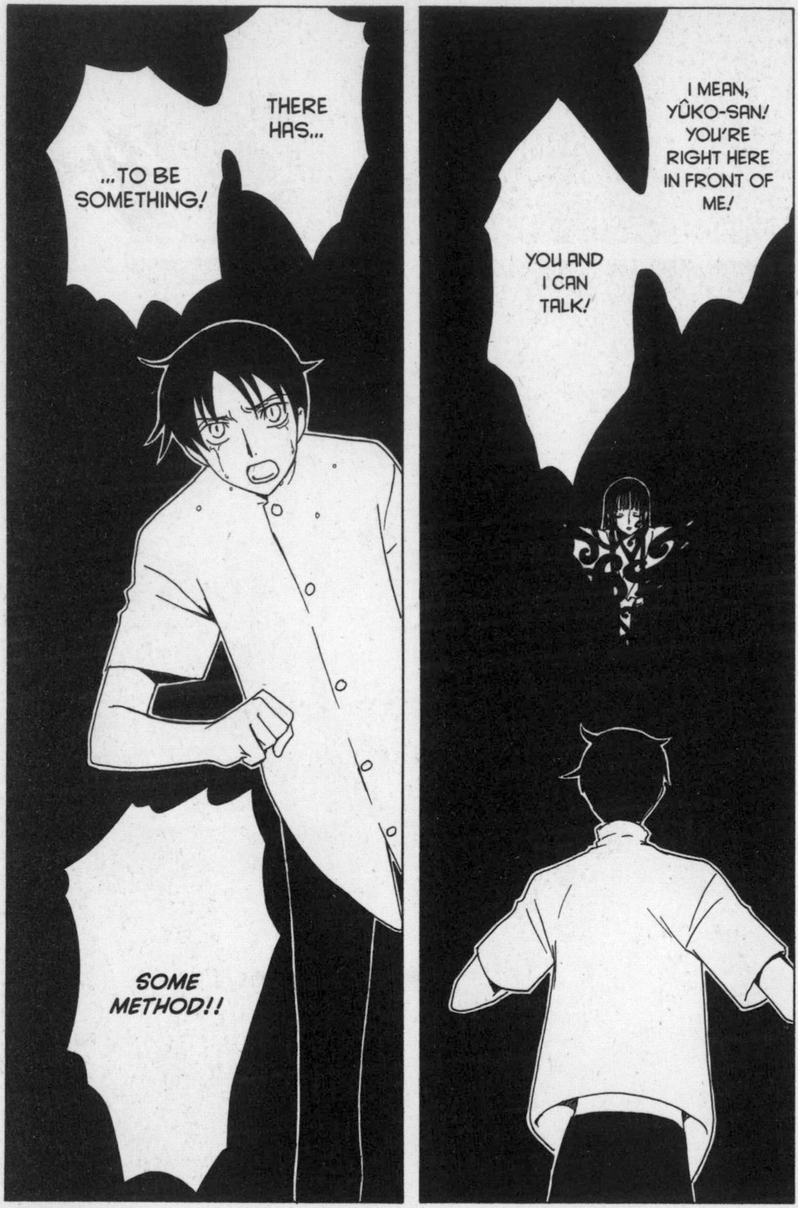
I MEAN, YÛKO-SAN! YOU'RE RIGHT HERE IN FRONT OF ME!
YOU AND I CAN TALK!
THERE HAS...
...TO BE SOMETHING!
SOME METHOD!!

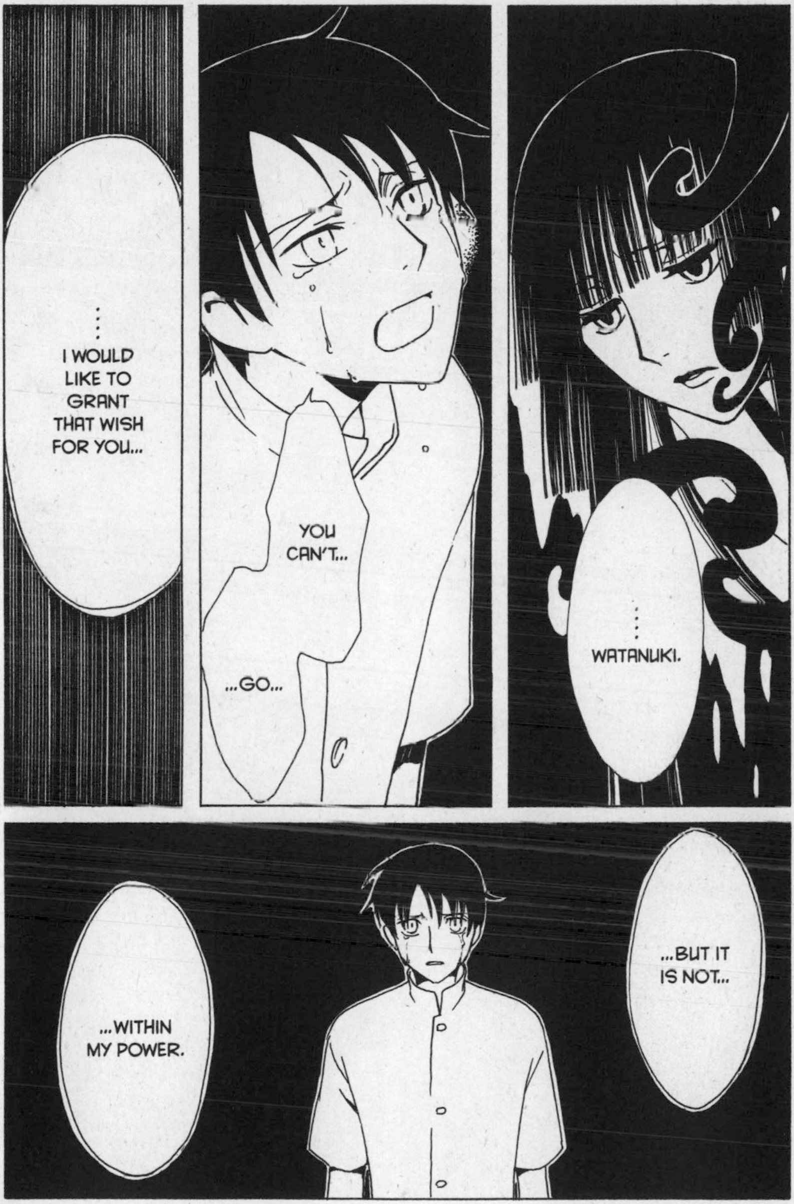

......
WATANUKI.
YOU CAN'T...
...GO...
......
I WOULD LIKE TO GRANT THAT WISH FOR YOU...
...BUT IT IS NOT...
...WITHIN MY POWER.

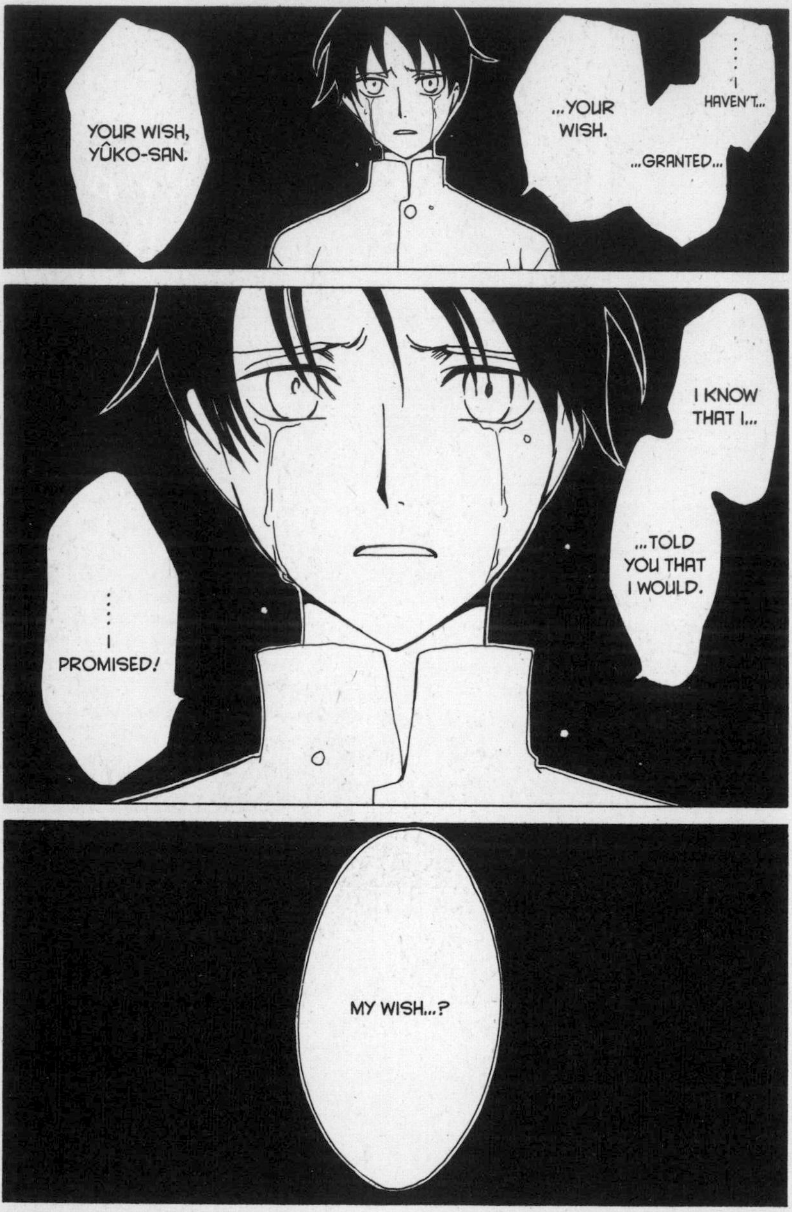
....I HAVEN'T...
...GRANTED...
...YOUR WISH.
YOUR WISH, YÛKO-SAN.
I KNOW THAT I...
...TOLD YOU THAT I WOULD.
....I PROMISED!
MY WISH...?

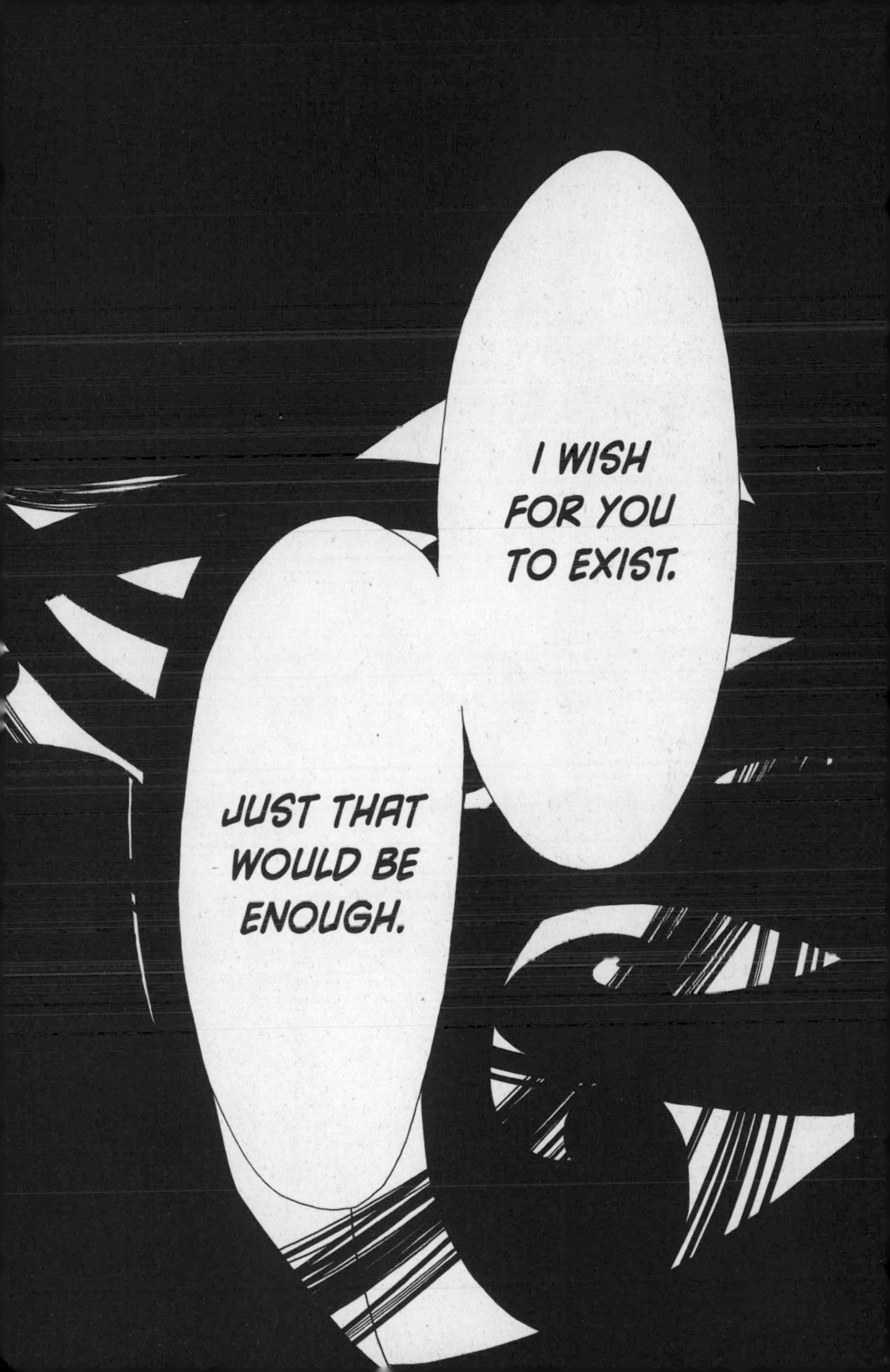
I WISH FOR YOU TO EXIST.
JUST THAT WOULD BE ENOUGH.

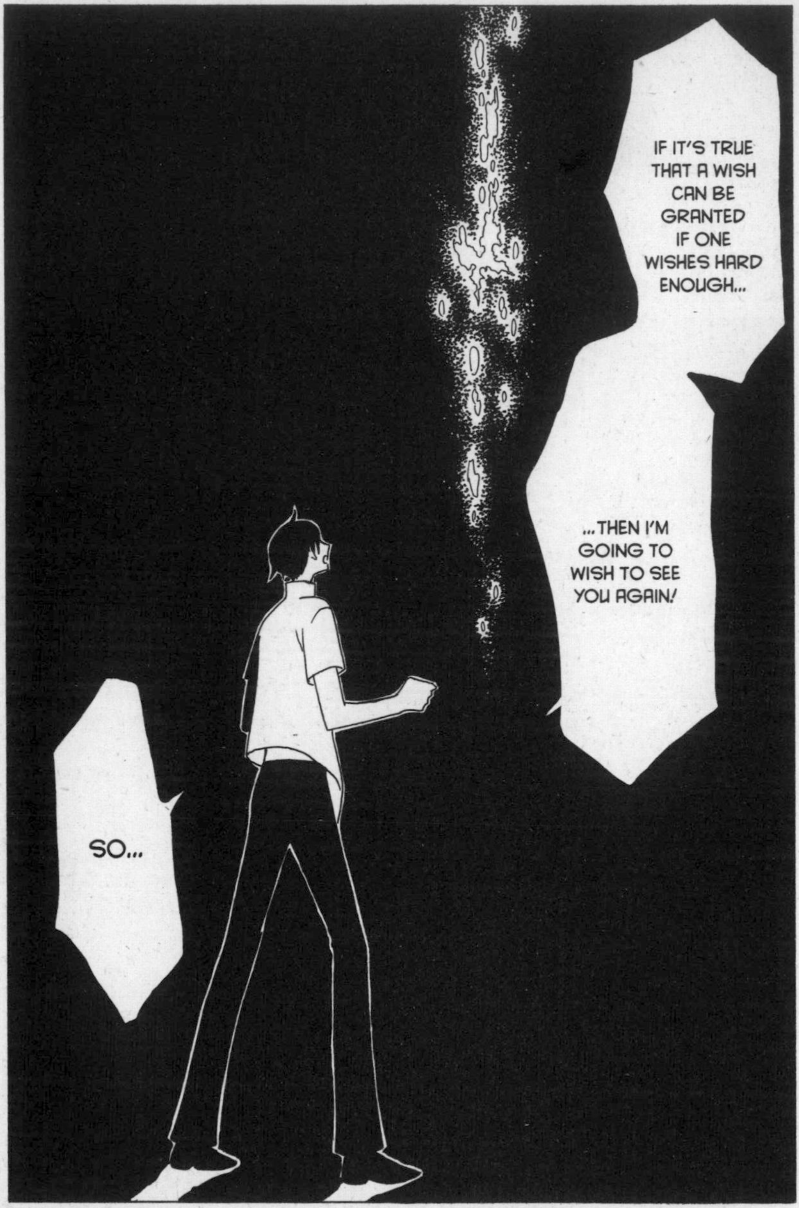
IF IT'S TRUE THAT A WISH CAN BE GRANTED IF ONE WISHES HARD ENOUGH...
...THEN I'M GOING TO WISH TO SEE YOU AGAIN!
SO...

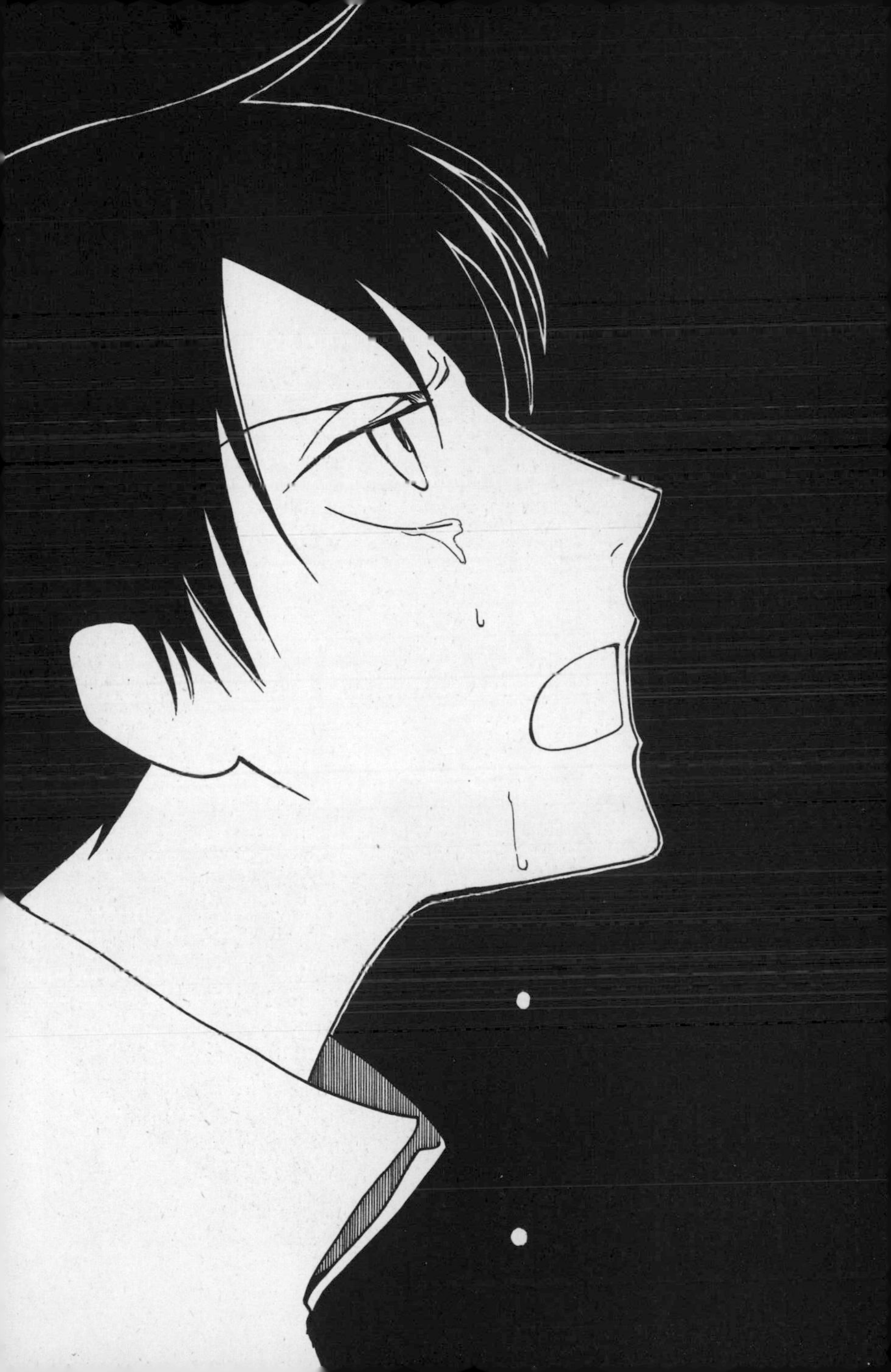

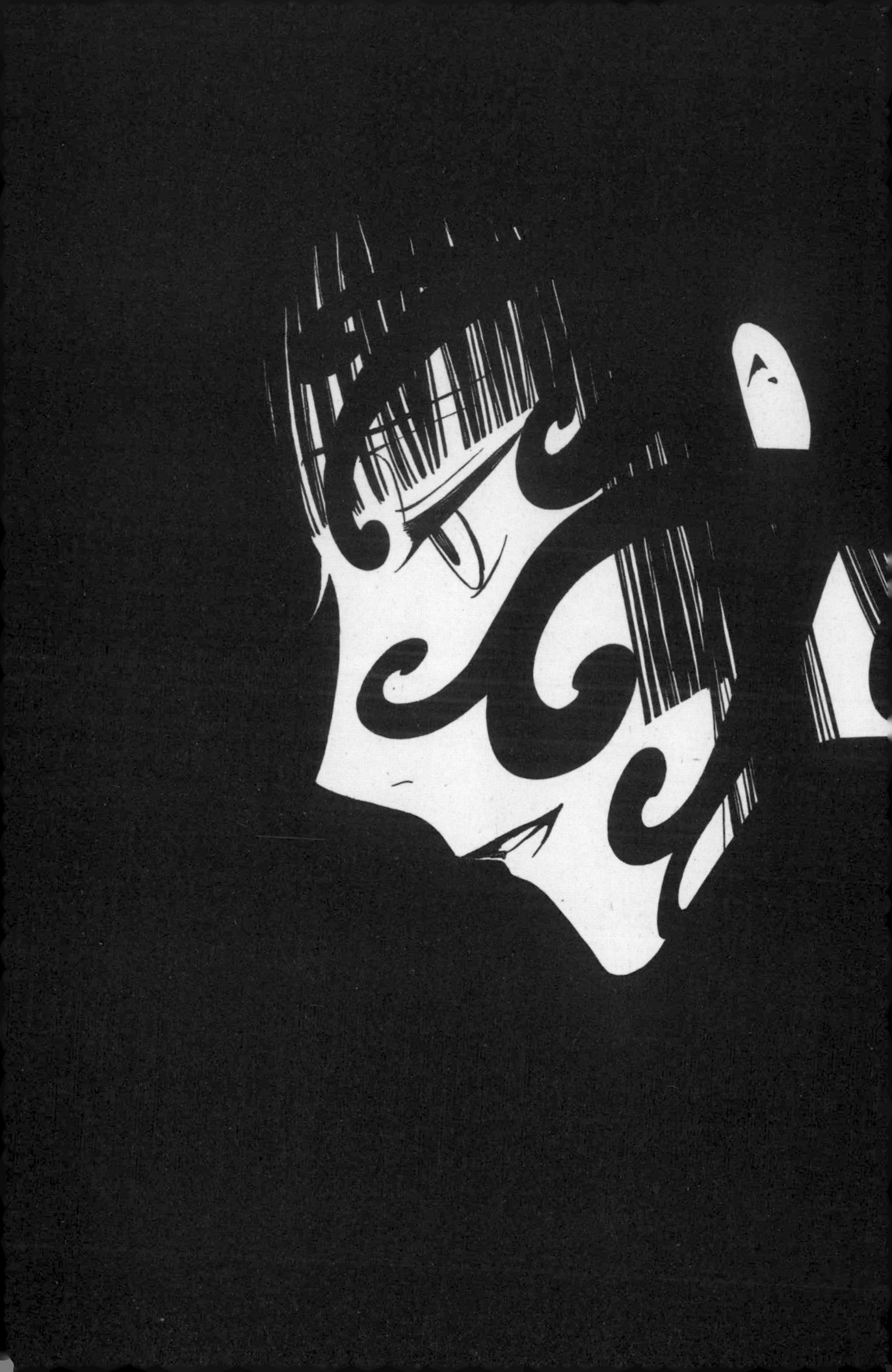

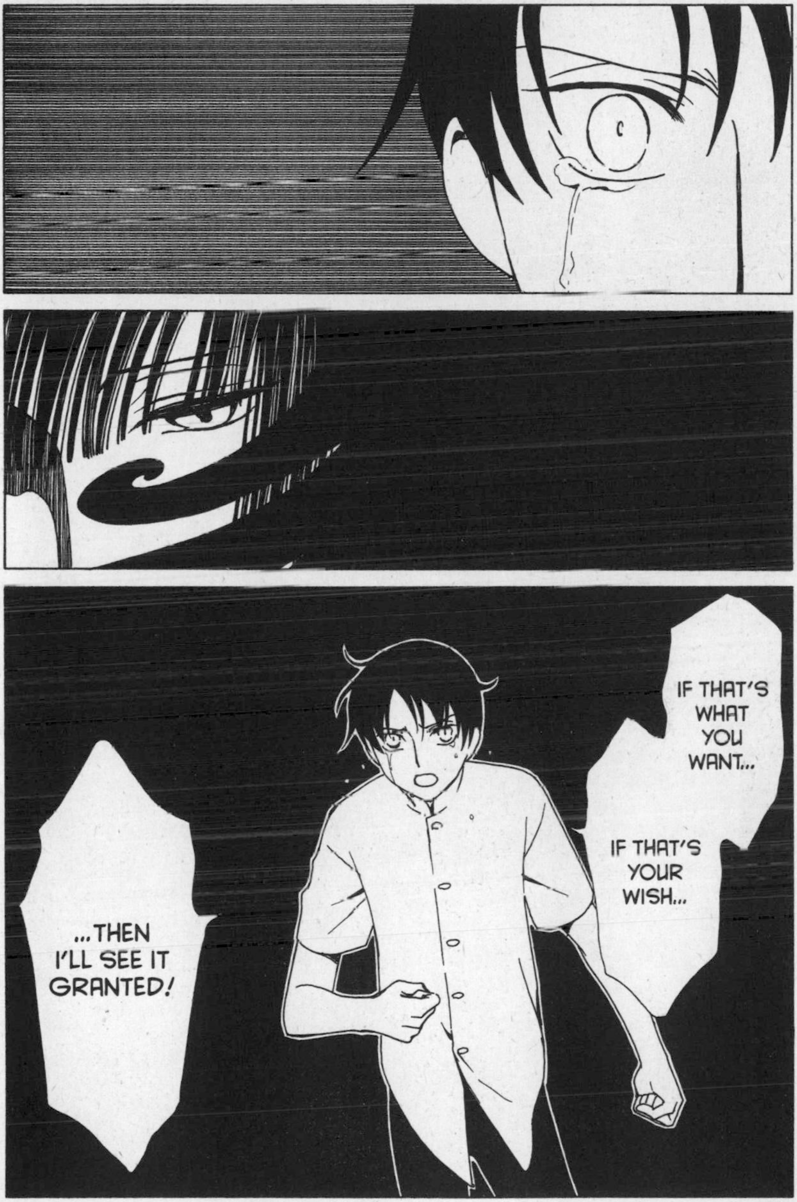
IF THAT'S WHAT YOU WANT...
IF THAT'S YOUR WISH...
...THEN I'LL SEE IT GRANTED!

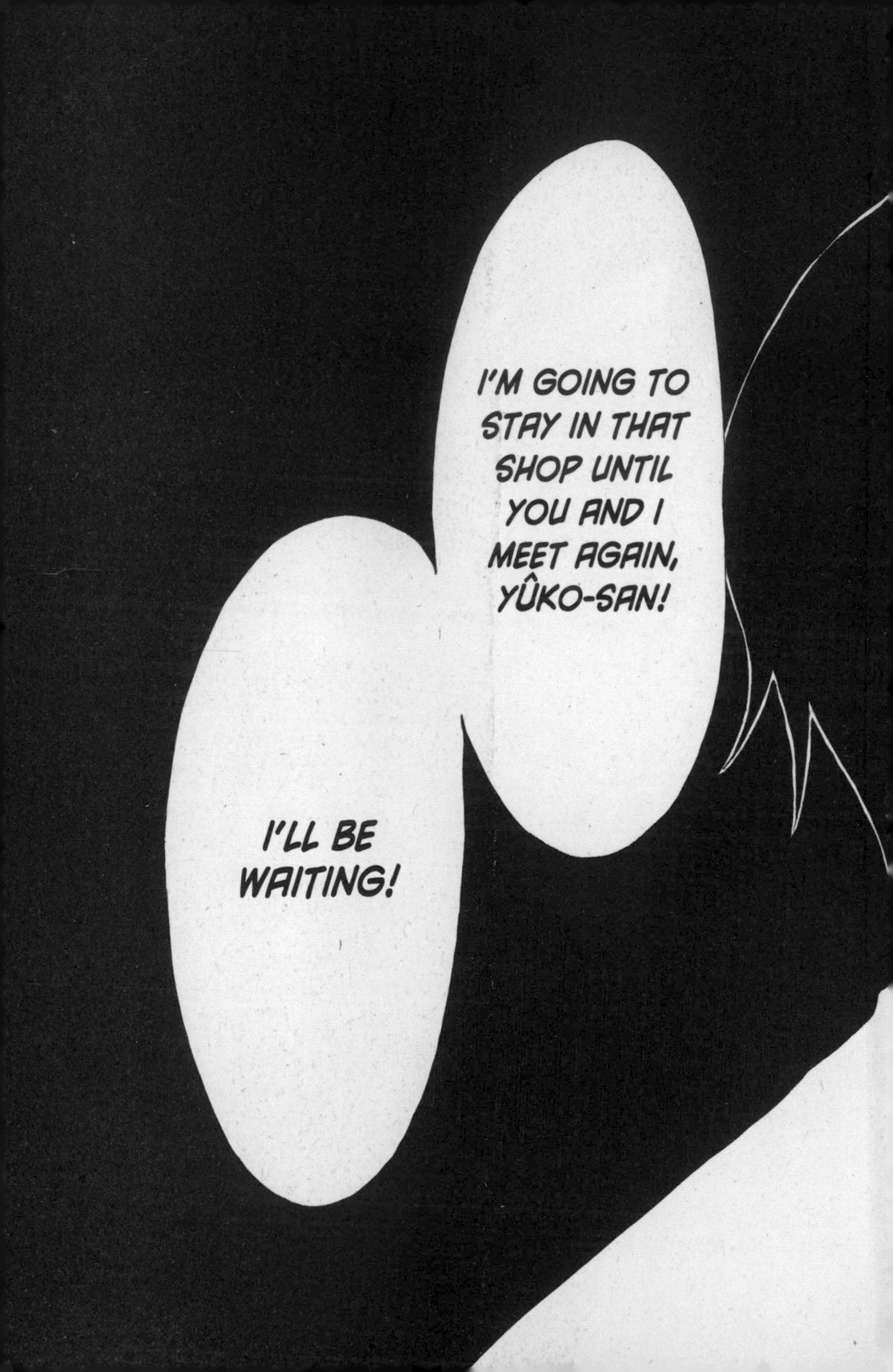
I'M GOING TO STAY IN THAT SHOP UNTIL YOU AND I MEET AGAIN, YÛKO-SAN!
I'LL BE WAITING!

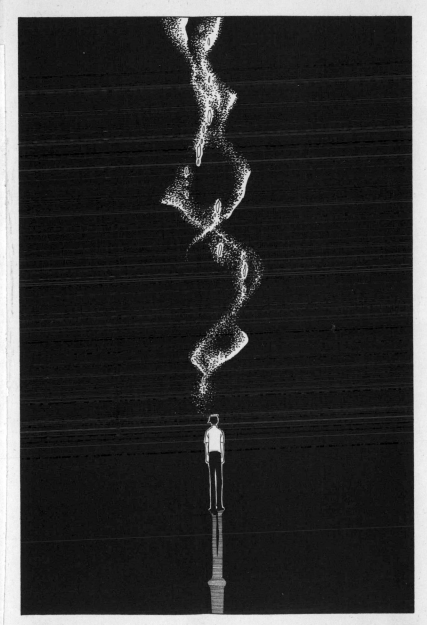

# ❧ Continued ❧

in *xxxHOLiC*, volume 16

YES. THE DREAM WILL SOON END.

# About the Creators

CLAMP is a group of four women who have become the most popular manga artists in America—Nanase Ohkawa, Mokona, Satsuki Igarashi, and Tsubaki Nekoi. They started out as *doujinshi* (fan comics) creators, but their skill and craft brought them to the attention of publishers very quickly. Their first work from a major publisher was *RG Veda*, but their first mass success was with *Magic Knight Rayearth*. From there, they went on to write many series, including Cardcaptor Sakura and Chobits, two of the most popular manga in the United States. Like many Japanese manga artists, they prefer to avoid the spotlight, and little is known about them personally.

CLAMP is currently publishing three series in Japan: Tsubasa and xxxHOLiC with Kodansha, and Kobato with Kadokawa.

# Translation Notes

Japanese is a tricky language for most Westerners, and translation is often more art than science. For your edification and reading pleasure, here are notes on some of the places where we could have gone in a different direction or where a Japanese cultural reference is used.

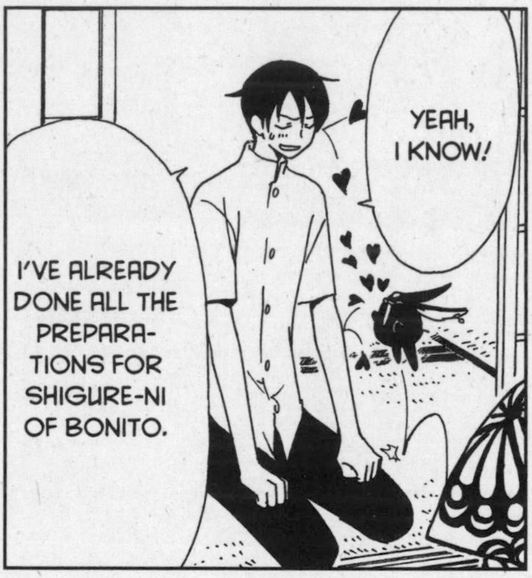
YEAH, I KNOW!
I'VE ALREADY DONE ALL THE PREPARA-TIONS FOR SHIGURE-NI OF BONITO.

### Page 5, *Shigure-ni* of Bonito

*Shigure-ni* is a cooking process in which one boils the item (usually shellfish, but this time it's bonito) in a mixture of soy sauce, mirin (sweet saké), and ginger.

## Page 6, *Omusubi*

*Omusubi* are normally called *o-nigiri*, rice balls with some food inside them, added for flavor. You can read more about rice balls in the notes for Volume 13. One of the reasons that CLAMP might have used the alternative naming may be because the base verb for the word, *musubu*, means "to tie." This may be a direct reference to the concept of *en-musubi*, the ties that bind a relationship.

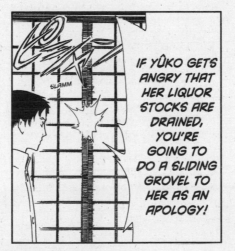

IF YÛKO GETS ANGRY THAT HER LIQUOR STOCKS ARE DRAINED, YOU'RE GOING TO DO A SLIDING GROVEL TO HER AS AN APOLOGY!

SLAMM

## Page 67, Sliding Grovel

When one bows down before a very high lord, one doesn't simply bow at the waist—one goes down on all fours into an almost fetal position, groveling on the ground. This is called *dogeza*, and although the practice is hardly ever used today, it is commonly seen in Japanese period dramas on television and in movies, so the average modern Japanese reader is familiar with it. This translator can only guess what a "sliding *dogeza*" is (Watanuki used the English word "sliding"), but I have two guesses: One would be rushing forward and sliding into the groveling position. The other would be going into the groveling position first and sliding yourself backward in supplication, away from Yûko's dominant presence. Either would make an impressive display; neither of which I can imagine Dômeki actually doing.

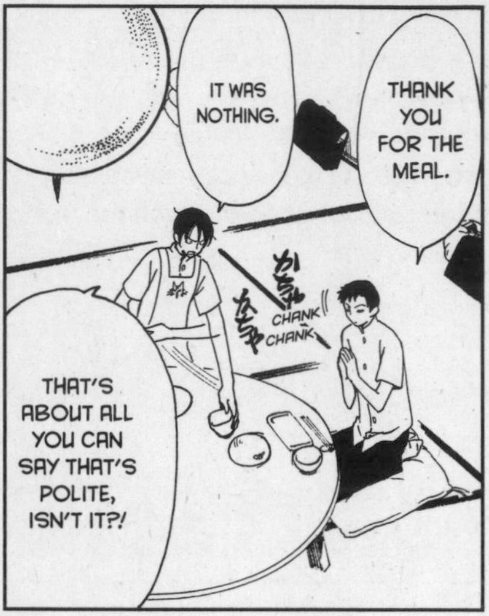
THANK YOU FOR THE MEAL.
IT WAS NOTHING.
CHANK CHANK
THAT'S ABOUT ALL YOU CAN SAY THAT'S POLITE, ISN'T IT?!

## Page 72, Thank you for the meal/It was nothing

As noted in the notes for Volume 11, this is a standard phrase and response at the end of a meal. *Gochisô-sama deshita* ("thank you for the meal") is said at the end of nearly every meal in Japan. Watanuki's response of *Osomatsu-sama deshita* ("It was a poor performance") is used less often.

## Page 72, Growing up in a temple

Unlike certain members of the clergy (such as the Roman Catholic priesthood), Buddhist priests in Japan are allowed to marry and have children. However, since Buddhism places value on austerity and discipline, it is a common conception that one growing up in a temple would receive a harsh and disciplined upbringing.

## Page 80, *Nozawana* and *umeboshi*

*Nozawana* is a large, dark green leaf that originates from a turniplike vegetable. It is often used for pickling or in stir-fry dishes. In this case, it is probably the pickled version that Watanuki put in the center of the rice balls. *Umeboshi* are a pickled fruit that is the most common flavoring of Japanese rice balls. They are so often called "pickled plums" in English that even this translator thought they were actually plums, but it turns out that *ume* are more closely related to apricots. A chemical inside the pit, amygdalin, combines with an enzyme to become benzaldehyde, which then oxidizes to become benzoic acid. Benzoic acid is a food preservative, so not only is the *umeboshi* preserved (some say it's good for one hundred years), but the pickled *ume* also preserves the rice around it.

## Page 87, Nighttime baths

Although there is a section of the Japanese population who enjoy morning showers, the majority of Japanese enjoy taking a bath in the evening, either before or after dinnertime. The hot water of the bath is said to relax and refresh a person after a stressful day.

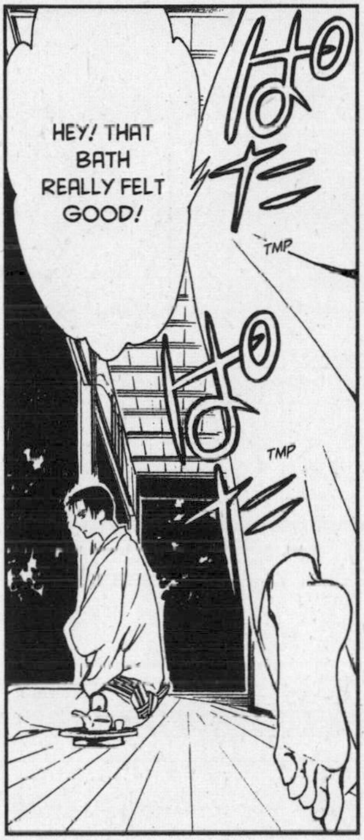
HEY! THAT BATH REALLY FELT GOOD!
TMP
TMP

## Page 87, *Isshôbin*

One can sometimes see the *isshôbin*, a huge 1.8-liter bottle of saké, in Japanese dramas and anime when one wants to show that a character is a hard drinker or a hard partier.

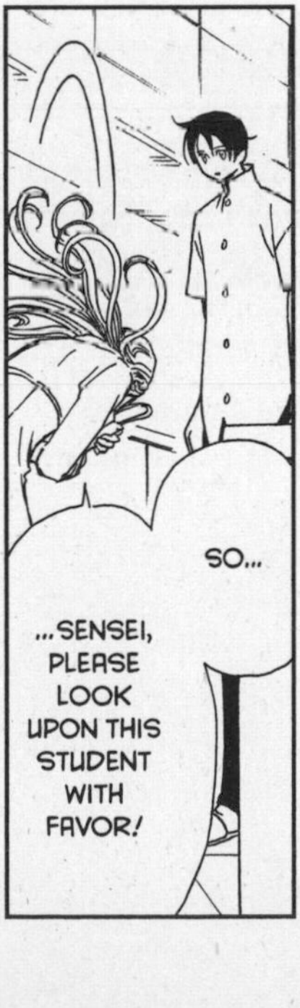
SO...
...SENSEI, PLEASE LOOK UPON THIS STUDENT WITH FAVOR!

## Page 122, Please look upon this student

This is another hard-to-translate standard Japanese phrase. In many cases *yoroshiku onegaishimasu* ("please think well of me"), can be translated through context into such phrases as "nice to meet you" or even "thank you." But in this case, none of the standard substitutes would serve, and I had to fall back on an awkward but literally close translation of the words. Please note that similar to the Japanese phrase *sumimasen, yoroshiku onegaishimasu* has many meanings in many different contexts, and a literal translation of the words usually does not give the best or even the most accurate sense of the phrase. In this rare case, it did.

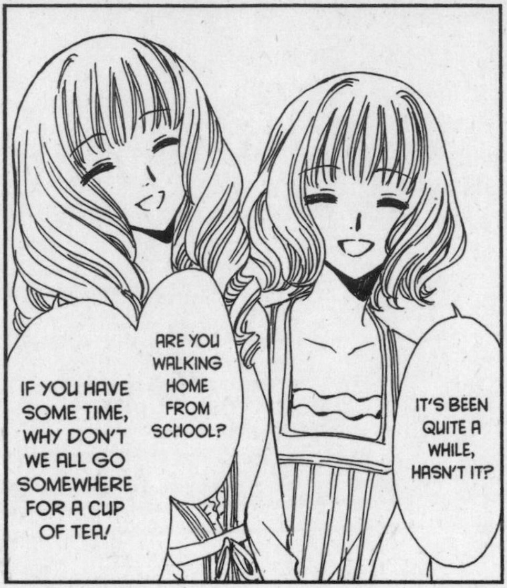
IT'S BEEN QUITE A WHILE, HASN'T IT?
ARE YOU WALKING HOME FROM SCHOOL?
IF YOU HAVE SOME TIME, WHY DON'T WE ALL GO SOMEWHERE FOR A CUP OF TEA!

## Page 131, A cup of tea

They say "tea," but they don't necessarily mean tea. "Let's go have a cup of tea" is another standard phrase in Japanese. It normally indicates going somewhere for a drink, but the main purpose is an invitation to go somewhere quiet where they can talk. Since in most Japanese urban centers the most convenient place to find a seat and talk are *kissaten* (tea shops or coffee shops), the literal meaning of the phrase and its idiomatic meaning ("find a place to talk") tend to coincide. By the way, other versions of "Let's go have a cup of tea" can be used as pick-up lines to get dates. However, in this instance, the twins are not trying to pick up Watanuki and Dômeki, but simply hoping to catch up on news.

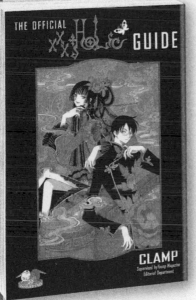
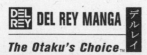
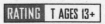

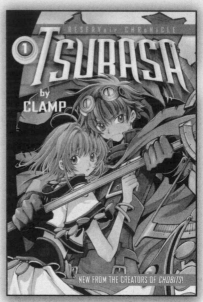

# MUSHISHI

## YUKI URUSHIBARA

### THEY HAVE EXISTED SINCE THE DAWN OF TIME.

Some live in the deep darkness behind your eyelids. Some eat silence. Some thoughtlessly kill. Some simply drive men mad. Shortly after life emerged from the primordial ooze, these deadly creatures, mushi, came into terrifying being. And they still exist and wreak havoc in the world today. Ginko, a young man with a sardonic smile, has the knowledge and skill to save those plagued by mushi . . . perhaps.

**WINNER OF THE KODANSHA MANGA OF THE YEAR AWARD!**

Now a live-action movie from legendary director Katsuhiro Otomo (*Akira, Steamboy*)!

MU
SHI
SHI
1
YUKI URUSHIBARA

***Special extras in each volume! Read them all!***

**VISIT WWW.DELREYMANGA.COM TO:**

- Read sample pages
- View release date calendars for upcoming volumes
- Sign up for Del Rey's free manga e-newsletter
- Find out the latest about new Del Rey Manga series

RATING OT AGES 16+

DEL REY DEL REY MANGA デルレイ

*The Otaku's Choice*

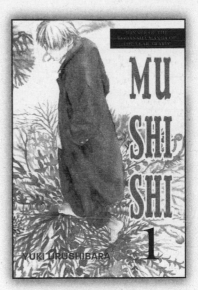

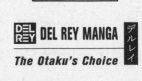

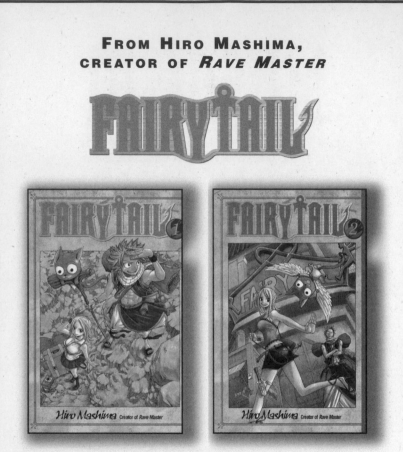
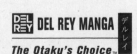

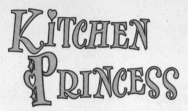

## STORY BY MIYUKI KOBAYASHI
## MANGA BY NATSUMI ANDO
## CREATOR OF ZODIAC P.I.

### HUNGRY HEART

**N**ajika is a great cook and likes to make meals for the people she loves. But something is missing from her life. When she was a child, she met a boy who touched her heart—and now Najika is determined to find him. The only clue she has is a silver spoon that leads her to the prestigious Seika Academy.

Attending Seika will be a challenge. Every kid at the school has a special talent, and the girls in Najika's class think she doesn't deserve to be there. But Sora and Daichi, two popular brothers who barely speak to each other, recognize Najika's cooking for what it is—magical. Could one of the boys be Najika's mysterious prince?

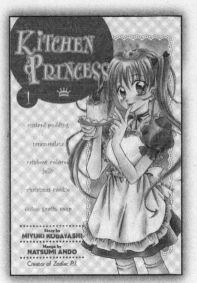

### *Special extras in each volume! Read them all!*

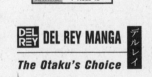

**DEL REY MANGA** デルレイ

### *The Otaku's Choice*

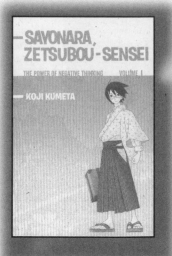
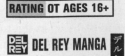

# TOMARE!

## [STOP!]

You're going the wrong way!

Mang... ... different type of reading experience.

To ...

That's right!
way—from ri
books are re
book, and rea
side, starting
was meant to